CLINICAL HEALTH PSYCHOLOGY IN MEDICAL SETTINGS

CLINICAL HEALTH PSYCHOLOGY IN MEDICAL SETTINGS

A PRACTITIONER'S GUIDEBOOK

SECOND EDITION

Cynthia D. Belar and William W. Deardorff

American Psychological Association • Washington, DC

Published by
American Psychological Association
750 First Street, NE
Washington, DC 20002
www.apa.org

To order
APA Order Department
P.O. Box 92984
Washington, DC 20090-2984
Tel: (800) 374-2721; Direct: (202) 336-5510
Fax: (202) 336-5502; TDD/TTY: (202) 336-6123
Online: www.apa.org/books/
E-mail: order@apa.org

In the U.K., Europe, Africa, and the Middle East, copies may be ordered from
American Psychological Association
3 Henrietta Street
Covent Garden, London
WC2E 8LU England

Typeset in Minion by Circle Graphics, Inc., Columbia, MD

Printer: Maple-Vail, Binghamton, NY
Cover Designer: Mercury, Rockville, MD
Technical/Production Editor: Tiffany L. Klaff

The opinions and statements published are the responsibility of the authors, and such opinions and statements do not necessarily represent the policies of the American Psychological Association.

Library of Congress Cataloging-in-Publication Data

Belar, Cynthia D.
  Clinical health psychology in medical settings : a practitioner's guidebook / Cynthia D. Belar and William W. Deardorff. — 2nd ed.
    p. ; cm.
  Includes bibliographical references and index.
  ISBN-13: 978-1-4338-0378-9 (alk. paper)
  ISBN-10: 1-4338-0378-X (alk. paper)
  1. Clinical health psychology. I. Deardorff, William W. II. American Psychological Association. III. Title.
  [DNLM: 1. Psychology, Clinical. WM 105 B426pb 2009]
  R726.7.B445 2009
  616.89—dc22

                                                                    2008005489

British Library Cataloguing-in-Publication Data
A CIP record is available from the British Library.

Printed in the United States of America
Second Edition

To my parents,
Herbert and Glennie Belar,
the wisest people I have ever known.
To my husband,
Jean-Louis Monfraix,
for his loving support.
—*Cynthia D. Belar*

To my wife,
Janine,
for her enduring love,
patience, and support.
To my sons,
James and Paul.
—*William W. Deardorff*

Contents

Preface

Since the writing of our book *The Practice of Clinical Health Psychology* over 20 years ago (Belar, Deardorff, & Kelly, 1987), the scientific knowledge base of professional practice has continued to expand. In addition, board certification is now available for clinical health psychologists through the American Board of Professional Psychology, and clinical health psychology has received formal recognition as a specialty by the American Psychological Association (APA). Clinical health psychology has the potential to be a major player in the health care system of the future given the now well-established linkage between health and behavior (Institute of Medicine, 2001b) and the increased demand for evidence based practice (Institute of Medicine, 2001a). Psychology needs practitioners who are appropriately trained to fulfill these roles. Thus, we believe it is timely to update our second edition, taking into account new knowledge, current issues in practice, and trends for the future.

The most extensive update is the discussion of ethical issues, which reflects the new version of the "Ethical Principles of Psychologists and Code of Conduct" (APA, 2002). The chapter on assessment includes an expanded discussion of specific psychometric instruments, many of which are new since our previous edition. We also include an in-depth evaluation of the pros and cons of each instrument. The chapter on malpractice risks now includes a focus on the high-risk areas pertinent to clinical health psychology and incorporates strategies to reduce practitioners' liability. This second edition is an effort to combine an overview of the constantly expanding roles and functions of clinical health psychologists with updated literature and contemporary case studies as well as the various social and policy changes that affect the field.

Acknowledgments

Special acknowledgment is given to Karen E. Kelly, who was a coauthor in the earliest version of this book.

I acknowledge Joe Matarazzo for his sustaining influence on the field and on my own thinking; Nathan Perry and Philip Shulman for supporting my development of education, training, research, and practice programs in clinical health psychology; and all of my students, whose intellectual curiosity, need for guidance, and enthusiasm for learning have enhanced my learning and commitment to the field.

—*Cynthia D. Belar*

I acknowledge my mentors, Wilbert Fordyce, Judy Turner, Joan Romano, Saul Spiro, Harold Dengerink, Herbert Cross, and Cynthia Belar, for introducing me to the complex and challenging field of clinical health psychology as well as Theodore Goldstein, a spine surgeon, who understands and values my contribution as a clinical health psychologist to the treatment of spinal disorders on a day-to-day basis.

—*William W. Deardorff*

CLINICAL HEALTH PSYCHOLOGY IN MEDICAL SETTINGS

1

Introduction to Clinical Health Psychology

Health psychology, to which all areas of psychological science contribute, has become mainstream in psychology in the United States since the 1970s; its application in the practice of health care has thrived as well. When we wrote the first edition of this book in the early 1980s, it was based on a practicum developed by Cynthia D. Belar to train professional psychology students at doctoral, internship, and postdoctoral levels to work with medical–surgical populations and in medical–surgical settings. Our intent was to provide a more "nuts and bolts" approach to the topic than could be found in the clinical training literature. Over the years, our work has evolved to reflect more than 3 decades of firsthand experience of each author in clinical health psychology practice, education, training, and research. The issues we deal with (e.g., core content, professional roles, assessment, intervention, ethics, malpractice) represent those areas we have found to be of special importance in practice. Each case example, unless otherwise noted, is one with which one of us has had personal experience, although identifying data have been changed. It is also important to note that although one of us is now a professional staff member of the American Psychological Association (APA), the views expressed herein are not those of APA as an organization.

This book is not designed for the novice clinician but is intended for the professional psychology student or practicing psychologist who wishes to develop special expertise in clinical health psychology. It might also be useful to other mental health professionals who want to retool for practice with medical–surgical populations and environments, although sections related to psychometric assessment might be less useful. This work is best considered as an overview, and we have written it with the underlying assumption that the reader has already developed competence in basic clinical skills.

Subsequent chapters address education and training, as well as professional and personal issues involved in becoming a clinical health psychologist (chap. 2); they also articulate a model for assessment and intervention in clinical practice (chaps. 3 and 4). We raise issues frequently encountered (e.g., learning the sociopolitical context of health care, learning how to deal with reluctant patients) and provide numerous resources for further study with respect to specific assessment methods, intervention strategies, and problems addressed. Throughout the book, we note common pitfalls in practice, and we attempt to provide ideas for their effective management in chapter 5. Anticipation of such pitfalls may be the best preparation. Chapters 6 and 7 address the distinctive ethical issues encountered in clinical health psychology as well as what we believe are increased liability risks. We end this work with viewpoints on the future of the field and the challenges to be met (chap. 8). For each major topic, suggested readings and resources for further study are provided. The appendixes are designed as concise resources of pertinent information (e.g., medical abbreviations, professional organizations). As with other areas of practice, being a practitioner of clinical health psychology involves a commitment to lifelong learning.

We begin with an examination of relevant definitions, and a brief overview of historical perspectives in clinical health psychology. Because health psychology and its applications is such a broad area of practice, we cannot provide an exhaustive treatment for this primer, but we focus in subsequent chapters on those settings and experiences with which we have had the most experience.

DEFINITIONS

Clinical Health Psychology applies scientific knowledge of the interrelationships among behavioral, emotional, cognitive, social and biological components in health and disease to the promotion and maintenance of health; the prevention, treatment and rehabilitation of illness and disability; and the improvement of the health care system. The distinct focus of Clinical Health Psychology is on physical health problems. The specialty is dedicated to the development of knowledge regarding the interface between behavior and health, and to the delivery of high quality services based on that knowledge to individuals, families and health care systems. (APA, n.d., ¶ 1)

When the APA formally recognized *clinical health psychology* as a specialty in 1997, this definition was archived from the petition for recognition on which one of us worked. The definition reflects an adaptation of that for *health psychology* as defined by Matarazzo (1980) and adopted by the APA Division of Health Psychology:

the aggregate of the specific educational, scientific, and professional contributions of the discipline of psychology to the promotion and maintenance of health, the prevention and treatment of illness, and the identification of etiologic and diagnostic correlates of health, illness, and related dysfunctions. (p. 815)

Millon (1982) actually offered the first definition of *clinical health psychology,* merging concepts from clinical psychology, with its focus on the assessment and treatment of individuals in distress, and the content field of health psychology. The first primer for practice in clinical health psychology was published in 1987 (Belar, Deardorff, & Kelly, 1987). See Belar, McIntyre, and Matarazzo (2003) for a more detailed history of health psychology.

Although professional activity in clinical health psychology has long preceded the usage of this term, we believe this designation best describes this area of practice and that related labels are inappropriate, confusing, or too narrow. Examples of these terms include *behavioral medicine, medical psychology,* and *psychosomatic medicine.*

Behavioral medicine is an interdisciplinary field. A psychologist cannot "practice" behavioral medicine; psychologists can only practice psychology. The most commonly accepted definition of *behavioral medicine* is,

the interdisciplinary field concerned with the development and integration of behavioral and biomedical science, knowledge and technique

relevant to health and illness and the application of this knowledge and
these techniques to prevention, diagnosis, treatment and rehabilitation.
(G. E. Schwartz & Weiss, 1978, p. 250)

Stemming from a landmark conference at Yale University in February
1977 and further refined at a meeting of the National Academy of Sciences
in April 1978, this definition was specifically intended to not represent either
a single theoretical orientation (behavioral) or a single discipline (medicine). However, it is often misinterpreted, and the more chauvinistic assert
it as the province of medicine. All health psychologists and all clinical health
psychologists are contributors to the field of behavioral medicine, as are
social workers, nurses, epidemiologists, physicians, nutritionists, and members of other disciplines who choose to practice, to teach, to develop policy,
or to conduct research related to the integration of behavioral and biomedical sciences relevant to health and illness.

Another term, *medical psychology,* can be confusing in that it has at
least three well accepted definitions. Medical psychology has been defined as
(a) the practice of psychology in the medical school establishment (Gentry
& Matarazzo, 1981, p. 12); (b) the study of psychological factors related to
any and all aspects of physical health, illness, and its treatment at the individual, group, and system levels (Asken, 1979, p. 67); and (c) traditional
psychiatry in Great Britain. More recently there has been a resurgence in
medical psychology's usage, in this case referring to psychologists trained
to prescribe medication. No matter what, the term conveys a narrowness
of focus (e.g., it excludes psychologists practicing primarily with dental
populations).

The term *psychosomatic medicine* has historically been the most
prominent label for work in the field. Although originally intended to refer
to the unity of mind–body relationships, this term usually conveys to most
health professionals and to the public the notion of psychological causation of physiological disorders. As such, it carries with it some pejorative
overtones. Again, the use of the term *medicine* would be inappropriate for
the practitioner of the discipline of psychology. Other labels found in the
field, such as *pediatric psychology, rehabilitation psychology,* and *neuropsychology,* are pertinent to more narrow content and practice areas.

In summary, we believe that the term *clinical health psychology* best conveys the breadth of the field (health) while designating a focus on applied practice (clinical). The practice is discipline specific (psychology); however, the recognition that many other disciplines practice in the field of health makes much of the following information relevant to those practitioners as well.

HISTORICAL PERSPECTIVES IN CLINICAL HEALTH PSYCHOLOGY

In Western culture, the roots of clinical health psychology date back to the 5th century BC and the Hippocratic school of medicine. Health was viewed as a natural balance of both physical and emotional aspects, mediated by a harmonious mixture of the humors (phlegm, choler, blood, and melancholy). Centuries later in 1747, Gaub, a professor of medicine, wrote "the reason why a sound body becomes ill, or an ailing body recovers, very often lies in the mind" (cited in Lipowski, 1977, p. 234). However, it was from 1920 through 1950 that the more formalized field of psychosomatic medicine emerged. Two major frameworks dominated: psychodynamic and psychophysiologic. One of the best representatives of the psychodynamic viewpoint was Franz Alexander (1950), who, inspired by psychoanalytic theory, developed a specificity theory of illness. Specific unresolved unconscious conflicts were thought to produce specific somatic disorders in this *nuclear conflict theory* (e.g., frustrated oral and dependency needs result in duodenal ulcer).

In the area of psychophysiology, Harold G. Wolff (1953) used highly innovative experimental designs to study the effects of psychological stimuli on physiological processes. By means of these methods, Wolff developed a theory of psychological stress, which he applied to a wide range of somatic diseases. For example, he noted that during subjects' discussion of relationship problems (stress), resentment was associated with increased blood pressure, whereas despair and depression were associated with lowered blood pressure (Wolff & Wolf, 1951). These results were particularly true of subjects with hypertension. In general, the first half of the 20th century was marked by the passage of mind–body processes from the province of philosophy and religion to the domain of respectable scientific inquiry. Shorter (1992) provided an interesting historical account of cultural and scientific influences on theories of mind–body interactions.

The past 5 decades have been marked by a decrease in the influence of psychodynamic theories and an increased focus on psychophysiological processes in attempts to explain mind–body processes. There has also been the addition of social, cultural, and ecological dimensions to these models and the development of psychological interventions to prevent or ameliorate disease and improve the health care system. Psychology as a discipline has made significant contributions in these endeavors.

From the experimental psychology laboratory has come information about learning and bodily processes, with subsequent successful efforts at physiological self-regulation through biofeedback. Studies of cognitive processes have revealed the importance of meaning, belief systems, and information processing and have underscored the need for attention to issues such as help seeking, adherence to medical regimens, and pain tolerance in the delivery of health care services. Research in psychoendocrinology has helped us to understand relationships between physiological processes and emotions, and behavior-change technology has been applied in attempts to reduce behavioral health risks. Some of the most exciting developments have occurred in the field of psychoneuroimmunology, which is shedding more light on the mediating mechanisms between psychological processes and health (Ader, 2007). Psychology, as the science of behavior, will continue to be an integral part of the now widely accepted biopsychosocial model of health. The 2001 report on health and behavior from the Institute of Medicine clearly documents the interplay of health and behavior and the importance of this understanding to our health care system (Institute of Medicine, 2001b).

THE GROWTH OF CLINICAL HEALTH PSYCHOLOGY

Clinical health psychology has mushroomed since the mid 1970s. Gentry's (1984) summary of reasons for this explosion are still pertinent: (a) The biomedical model has failed to adequately explain health and illness; (b) concern with quality of life and prevention of illness has increased;

(c) the focus has shifted from infectious disease to chronic disease as the major challenge in medicine, with a concomitant recognition of the influence of lifestyle factors; (d) behavioral science research has matured, including the application of learning theories to disease etiology and illness behavior; and (e) the increased cost of health care has led to the search for alternatives to the traditional health care system.

Those health psychologists involved in this rapid growth remember the fervor with which we worked to establish new professional and scientific groups to foster our communication and help build our identity. The year 1978 was a real high point in this developmental process. The Academy of Behavioral Medicine Research was established in April, with Neal E. Miller as its first president. And, at the 86th Annual Convention of the American Psychological Association, we celebrated the recognition of the new Division of Health Psychology under the leadership of Joseph D. Matarazzo. Soon after, on November 16, 1978, we held the charter meeting of the interdisciplinary Society of Behavioral Medicine in Chicago. Also that year, the *Journal of Behavioral Medicine* began under the editorship of W. Doyle Gentry. Four years later, the journal *Health Psychology* began publication— a journal that has now become one of the most subscribed APA journals. The European Health Psychology Society was formed in 1986, and the *International Journal of Behavioral Medicine* began publication in 1994.

As health psychology developed, our concern for quality led to the Arden House National Working Conference on Education and Training in Health Psychology. This conference developed recommendations for education and training at the doctoral, apprenticeship, and postdoctoral levels for research and professional career paths in psychology. A full report of this conference can be found in G. C. Stone (1983). These recommendations remain well accepted in the field, having been reaffirmed and extended by a summit of leaders in health psychology in Tempe, Arizona, in 2007 (France et al., in press).

Anticipating the need for board certification of individual practitioners, Matarazzo incorporated the American Board of Health Psychology in 1984 (Belar & Jeffrey, 1995). In 1993, this board gained full affiliation status with the American Board of Professional Psychology (ABPP), the oldest national credentialing body for professional psychologists. As such, practitioners wishing board certification have access to well-established and respected mechanisms within the profession. When APA recognized the specialty as clinical health psychology, the name of the ABPP board was also changed. At present the American Board of Clinical Health Psychology seeks to promote excellence in professional practice and provides board certification to those practitioners who demonstrate advanced competence in the science and practice of psychology related to health, including the prevention, treatment, and rehabilitation of illness. According to the Web site of the ABPP, 106 psychologists are currently board certified in clinical health psychology (http://www.abpp.org) and 123 psychologists are board certified in rehabilitation psychology, with which there is considerable overlap.

Although a focus on health is now mainstream in American psychology, the 1970s and 1980s were a time in which many of us felt that we had a mission to accomplish in spreading the word about health psychology and the potential for practice in this area. Yet we knew that we were certainly not the first to recognize the importance of psychological factors in health and health care, and vice versa.

PSYCHOLOGY'S ROLE IN HEALTH CARE

The role of the psychologist in the health care system began early this century. Psychologists first assumed the role as teachers of medical students (see A. A. Stone, 1979); the area most frequently represented was physiological psychology as related research flourished. However, there was little application of psychology to the problems of the health care system itself. As the field of clinical psychology developed after World War II, the focus was primarily on mental disorders. There were some studies on overusers of the health care system, some pathology-oriented treatment reports on classic psychosomatic disorders, and an important body of work by Janis (1958) on psychological preparation for surgery. Yet the role of clinical psychology continued to be somewhat limited. It was Schofield's (1969) report on psychology in the delivery of health services that marked the beginning of an explosion in the psychological literature.

Indeed, Belar remembers well the times in the early 1970s when she was required, while attempting to establish herself in academic clinical psychology, to justify to skeptical senior professors her clinical interest in medical–surgical patients and the treatment of chronic pain problems. The usual challenge ("Is this real clinical psychology?") reflected the mind–body dualism extant in the field. Actually, that process proved helpful in that it facilitated critical thinking about the field. It also increased sensitivity to many professional and political issues involved in extending the boundaries of professional practice.

The authors' subsequent experiences have confirmed that mind–body dualism is as alive and well in psychology, psychiatry, and psychiatric social work as it is in general medicine. Remarkable numbers of mental health practitioners feel no need to review a patient's medical chart before undertaking psychotherapy. Many such clinicians actually dislike dealing with medical–surgical patients because these patients have "real" (meaning possibly insoluble) problems. When these practitioners conduct consultations, findings are often expressed in either–or and functional versus organic terminology.

Mind–body dualism also continues to be deeply ingrained in health policies. Although we continue to advocate for mental health parity, there is a division and disparity in coverage between mental health and medical–surgical insurance benefits, with mental health coverage being less extensive. Although the Mental Health Parity Act (MHPA) of 1996 requires plans that offer mental health benefits to set lifetime dollar limits equivalent to limits for medical–surgical benefits, it does not require all plans to offer mental health benefits. Even with mental health coverage of some type, the "allowables" are often significantly less for mental health treatment (e.g., 50% coverage up to an allowable of $50 per hour) relative to medical benefits. Limits for substance abuse or chemical dependency benefits are not included in the determination of parity. Therefore, the term *parity* relative to mental health coverage is somewhat of a misnomer (see http://mentalhealth.samhsa.gov/publications/allpubs/insurance/#parity for more information on this issue). Conceptually, this poses difficult problems when attempting to determine which coverage is responsible for such things as psychological management of a hypertensive medication adherence problem, biofeedback treatment of surgically induced fecal incontinence, or cognitive–behavioral management of headache. A major advance in addressing this dilemma was the addition of new health and behavior codes to the current procedural terminology

(CPT). Prior to their establishment, psychological services were covered only under mental health benefits, a health policy that perpetuated rigid mind–body dualism. For instance, under the old system, a clinical health psychologist would essentially be required to render some type of psychiatric diagnosis (most often Psychological Factors Affecting Physical Condition) even when it was truly not necessary and was not the focus of treatment. An example of this dilemma is psychological preparation for surgery of a patient who did not have any type of diagnosable psychiatric condition. The Interdivisional Healthcare Committee (IHC), a coalition of APA health-oriented divisions, and APA's Practice Directorate were successful in gaining approval for CPT codes that reflect psychological assessment and interventions services for the prevention, treatment, or management of physical health problems—the Health and Behavior Codes (APA, 2002a). In addition, reimbursement for these codes comes from medical rather than psychiatric funding dollars.

Mind–body dualism is also found in administrative and architectural arrangements. Many mental health clinics are actually located at some distance from the medical center, the mainstream of health care. However, there has been a consistent movement toward integrated services in primary care settings, especially in large health care systems such as Veterans Affairs, the Department of Defense, and staff model HMOs such as Kaiser Permanente. Advocacy for the inclusion of psychologists in this nation's "safety net"—the federal community health centers—has been a significant focus for APA's Education Directorate, as is advocacy for training for psychologists as health service providers and not just as mental health professionals. The 2002 establishment of the APA-initiated Graduate Psychology Education Program in the Department of Health and Human Services' Bureau of Health Professions provided formal federal recognition of this role of psychology as a more comprehensive health profession, and granted it a place in the organizational chart of the Bureau. In addition, APA Education Directorate advocacy was successful in getting psychologists listed as primary care providers along with physicians, nurses, and dentists in the 2002 Safety Net bill while also obtaining eligibility for psychologists in the National Health Service Corps Scholarship and Loan Repayment Program.

The attitudinal set of mind–body dualism and related administrative issues have significant implications for the professional functioning and practice of clinical health psychologists. Indeed, readers are advised to be alert to the instances in which mind–body dualism seeps into our own writing—a product of our language system; our cultural heritage; and our own struggle to integrate psychological, physiological, and sociocultural concepts.

In summary, our model of clinical health psychology actually incorporates mental health psychology as a complete subset in the domain of clinical health psychology. For some years we have predicted a figure–ground reversal in this regard. However, for the purposes of this book, we have chosen to deal primarily with practice in medical–surgical settings. In general, we shall assume existing expertise on the parts of readers in more traditional areas of professional clinical, counseling, or school psychology.

ROLES AND FUNCTIONS
OF CLINICAL HEALTH PSYCHOLOGISTS

Clinical health psychologists have a diversity of roles and functions. They teach, conduct research, become involved in policy development, and provide direct services. With respect to health care services, the focus of this book, the heterogeneity in assessment, intervention, and consultation is enormous. Exhibit 1.1 contains samples of these activities. Clinical health psychology practitioners use the range of diagnostic and therapeutic techniques available to professional psychology: diagnostic interviewing; behavioral assessments; psychometric testing; insight-oriented psychotherapies; behavioral therapies; psychophysiological self-regulation and biofeedback; family, marital, and group therapies; psychoeducational counseling groups; and staff-level interventions. Their theoretical orientations include, but are not limited to, psychodynamic, behavioral, systems, existential, and social learning theory approaches. They deal with the problems of coping with illness, medical regimen adherence, psychophysiologic disorders, the doctor–patient relationship, health care systems design, differential diagnoses, rehabilitation, occupational health, and

Exhibit 1.1

Examples of Health Care Activities
Provided by Clinical Health Psychologists

1. Assessment of candidates for back surgery, organ transplantation, in vitro fertilization, or oocyte donation.
2. Desensitization of fears of medical and dental treatments including fear of needles, anesthesia, or magnetic resonance imaging procedures.
3. Treatment to enhance coping with or control over pain including chronic back pain, headache, or severe burns.
4. Interventions to control symptoms such as vomiting with chemotherapy, scratching with neurodermatitis, vasospasms with Raynaud's phenomenon, or diarrhea with irritable bowel syndrome.
5. Support groups for patients with chronic illness, patients in cardiac rehabilitation, patients who are HIV positive, or families of terminally ill patients.
6. Training to overcome disabilities after trauma, cognitive retraining after stroke, or training to use prosthetic devices effectively.
7. Behavior-change programs for behavioral risk factors such as smoking, obesity, stress, and sedentary lifestyle.
8. Consultations and workshops to deal with issues of staff burnout, health care communications, and role conflict.
9. Consultations and program development regarding medical regimen adherence (e.g., inpatient units for insulin-dependent diabetic children).
10. Consultations with industry to develop worksite health-promotion programs and management of occupational stress.
11. Development of psychosocial services for oncology patients.
12. Neuropsychological assessments for baseline, diagnostic, and treatment-planning purposes.

prevention of disease. They serve populations throughout the entire life span and address health problems in every category of the International Classification of Diseases (World Health Organization, 1992). Figure 1.1 illustrates a three-dimensional model portraying the breadth of the specialty. A fourth dimension reflecting the timing of service, whether for

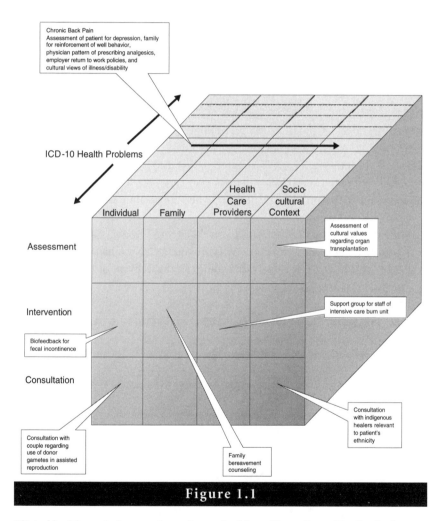

Figure 1.1

Clinical health psychology services × focus × health problems. From *Handbook of Clinical Health Psychology* (p. 15), by S. Llewelyn and P. Kennedy (Eds.), 2003, New York: Wiley. Copyright 2003 by Wiley. Reprinted with permission.

primary prevention, secondary prevention, or tertiary prevention, could also be added.

It is important to note that no one clinical health psychologist is an expert in all possible areas of practice. And because of the diversity and volume of information in clinical health psychology, it is not possible within the context of this book to provide an educational background in each potential area of practice. Thus, we focus our comments on more generic issues of preparation and clinical practice for the health psychologist, emphasizing process issues and pitfalls in medical–surgical settings in which we have had the most experience.

SUGGESTED READINGS

Belar, C. D. (1997). Clinical health psychology: A specialty for the 21st Century. *Health Psychology, 16,* 411–416.

Belar, C. D., McIntyre, T. M., & Matarazzo, J. D. (2003). Health psychology. In D. K. Freedheim (Ed.), *History of psychology* (pp. 451–464). New York: Wiley.

Engel, G. L. (1977, April 8). The need for a new medical model: A challenge for biomedicine. *Science, 196,* 129–136.

Institute of Medicine. (2001). *Health and behavior: The interplay of biological, behavioral, and societal influences.* Washington, DC: National Academy Press.

Schofield, W. (1969). The role of psychology in the delivery of health services. *American Psychologist, 24,* 565–584.

Stone, G. C., Weiss, S. M., Matarazzo, J. D., Miller, N. E., Rodin, J., Belar, C. D., et al. (Eds.). (1987). *Health psychology: A discipline and a profession.* Chicago: University of Chicago Press.

2

Becoming a Clinical Health Psychologist

In this chapter we address issues in becoming a clinical health psychologist. We review core knowledge content areas and issues in clinical supervision, and we provide numerous resources for further study. A specific focus is placed on the personal and professional issues raised in practice because we believe that knowledge and clinical competencies are necessary, but insufficient, ingredients for success.

EDUCATION AND TRAINING

Surveys of education and training in health psychology have attempted to delineate programmatic offerings at the doctoral, internship, and postdoctoral levels. In their initial survey of graduate departments of psychology, Belar, Wilson, and Hughes (1982) identified 42 programs that offered doctoral training in health psychology. Although six of these described a specialized program, the predominant model (almost 70%) was that of a specialized track within another area of psychology, usually clinical, counseling, social, or school psychology. With respect to postdoctoral training, Belar and Siegel (1983) identified 43 programs offering postdoctoral training in health psychology, 90% of which emphasized applied research.

In comparison with these earliest data, *Graduate Study in Psychology 2005* (American Psychological Association [APA], 2005) lists 68 doctoral programs across clinical, counseling, and school psychology, with opportunities in health psychology. The online listing from the APA

Division of Health Psychology (n.d.) lists 44 programs with a significant focus in the area. In addition, the 2006 directory of the Association of Psychology Postdoctoral and Internship Centers (APPIC) lists 381 internships with minor rotations, 201 with major rotations, and 51 postdoctoral programs with training in clinical health psychology. By 2008, six postdoctoral residencies had attained APA accreditation in the specialty of clinical health psychology.

Of great interest are the findings of Sayette and Mayne (1990) in their survey of APA-accredited clinical psychology programs. Health psychology was the most popular area of clinical research and the second most frequent specialty clinic for clinical training, with 75% of programs offering some opportunity for work in the area. It is clear that health psychology is now part of mainstream clinical psychology and is actively represented in counseling and school psychology programs as well.

APPIC publishes an annual directory, which facilitates the identification of relevant professional psychology postdoctoral and internship programs (http://www.appic.org). Other major sources of current information on health psychology education and training are the Division of Health Psychology of the APA (http://www.health-psych.org), the Society of Behavioral Medicine (http://www.sbm.org), and, soon, the newly invigorated Council of Clinical Health Psychology Training Programs.

Recommendations for Education and Training

As indicated in chapter 1, the Arden House Conference detailed a set of recommendations for the education and training of health psychologists (G. C. Stone, 1983). Although a summary of these recommendations is beyond the scope of this book, certain recommendations deserve highlighting. For example, given that clinical health psychology grew out of the interplay between science and practice, the scientist–practitioner model was endorsed at every level of training to ensure the future development of the field. As a later national conference affirmed, the scientist–practitioner model is essential for the ever-changing discipline of psychology and "ideal for psychologists who utilize scientific methods in the conduct of professional practice" (Belar & Perry, 1992, p. 72). Arden House Conference delegates also agreed that professional education and training in health psychology should include a broad set of experiences leading to knowledge and skills in the following core areas: (a) biological bases of health and disease; (b) social bases of health and disease; (c) psychological bases of health and disease; (d) health assessment, consultation, intervention, and evaluation; (e) health policy and organization; (f) interdisciplinary collaboration; (g) ethical, legal, and professional issues; and (h) statistics and experimental design in health research. In addition, exposure to health care settings, a multidisciplinary faculty, and experienced professional health psychology mentors were considered crucial.

Early in its development Belar (1980) described what can be adopted from traditional clinical psychology training and what needs to be added to better train graduate students to function effectively in this growing field. A basic assumption is that the understanding of the fundamentals of human behavior and the critical-thinking, hypothesis-testing approach to research and clinical problems are transportable to any area in which the psychologist chooses to work. Research skills are necessary to the critical evaluation of research reports in this burgeoning area. They are also necessary for the conduct of program evaluations so often required as an aspect of accountability, as well as for the design of research capable of making contributions to the science base of this expanding field. However, in this book, we focus on practitioner activities, and our discussions assume that the reader is either a fully trained professional clinician or a student in an organized professional training program.

Core Content Areas

With respect to specific content, a psychologist can develop one's own course of study through readings or enrollment in basic courses. The core areas of education and training in clinical health psychology include anatomy, physiology, pathophysiology, applied pharmacology, genetics, social and psychological bases of health and disease, health policy and health care organizations, and health assessment and intervention. One needs to understand not only disease—its treatment, its course, and its emotional and behavioral correlates—but also the context within which the health care system operates. Changes are so dramatic in this area that references over a year old on health policy and the health care system should be considered outdated. However, there are resources that continue to provide context for the changes we are witnessing, such as *Jonas and Kovner's Health Care Delivery System in the United States,* which is updated every few years (Kovner & Knickman, 2008), and the classic book by Paul Starr, *The Social Transformation of American Medicine* (1982).

Courses basic to other health professions are often useful (e.g., nursing, physical therapy, occupational therapy, respiratory therapy, health education); thus, the reader is encouraged to investigate local university or community college offerings. For the general clinical health psychologist, we have found that the courses offered in medical schools are frequently too detailed, although some prefer the anatomy and physiology classes offered there. We are aware that our neuropsychologist colleagues report that the neuroanatomy courses obtained in academic medical centers are fundamental to their areas of practice. However, in general, these courses are probably less accessible to the practicing clinician than to the graduate student.

The reader might also investigate the availability of courses in medical terminology that are frequently found in hospital administration and secretarial programs. The resources provided by Gylys and Wedding (2004) are most useful in this respect. Familiarity with the language of the health care system and understanding the most commonly used medical abbreviations are essential if one is to be able to read medical charts. (See Appendix A of this volume for some common medical abbreviations and their definitions.) We have witnessed scores of students and fellow professionals struggle with these language and code issues. There is considerable potential for negative outcomes in terms of efficiency, communication, and rapport with medical colleagues, as well as in terms of misunderstandings of the nature of referral questions.

If the clinician is planning to work in a general hospital setting, it would also be wise to obtain cardiopulmonary resuscitation training, if one is not already certified in this skill. Certification and renewals are often required for hospital staff privileges. Courses are available through community service agencies such as the Red Cross.

It is important to remember that the goal of these didactic experiences is not to become a "junior physician." In our experience, such an attitudinal approach meets with disdain on the part of physicians, who sometimes criticize their psychiatrist colleagues for not being "real physicians" when it comes to up-to-date medical knowledge and practice. Rather, one might make an analogy to learning enough of a foreign language to be able to get around in another country but also being willing and able to ask for help from the inhabitants. We find physicians much more open to and respectful of this approach.

Reference Materials

The neophyte clinical health psychologist should obtain a familiarity with core readings in the field. The suggested readings at the end of this chapter can provide a general background. Appendix B lists relevant scientific journals that publish research as well as theoretical articles in health psychology. It is noteworthy, however, that in recent years articles relevant to health psychology can be found in many of the traditional medical and psychological journals as well. In addition, at the end of each chapter, we provide suggested readings that offer more in-depth review and analysis of the scientific literature related to chapter topics. Of course, the use of the Internet provides rapid access to an almost unlimited amount of information.

Appendix A contains a list of common medical abbreviations. Note, in reviewing this list, that small differences might indicate significant changes in meaning. For example, *BS* means breath sounds, whereas *bs* means bowel sounds; *Gr* indicates gravida, whereas *gr* is the abbreviation for grain. Although the context of the abbreviation can sometimes prevent errors in interpretation, this might not always be so: Note the small difference between *NC* (no change) and *N/C* (no complaints). Because different institutions have different approved medical abbreviations, it is imperative that the clinician obtain the appropriate list for his or her site of practice. For example, at the University of Florida's Shands Teaching Hospital, *AS* meant aortic stenosis, whereas at the Los Angeles Kaiser

Foundation Hospital, the same abbreviation meant arteriosclerosis. In fact, the Institute for Safe Medication Practices (ISMP) and the U.S. Food and Drug Administration (FDA) have recently launched a campaign to help eliminate the ambiguity in medical abbreviations that can lead to mistakes (see the ISMP and FDA campaign to eliminate use of error-prone abbreviations at http://www.ismp.org/tools/abbreviations/).

Worthwhile purchases include a good medical dictionary such as *Stedman's Medical Dictionary* (2006) and an up-to-date *Physicians' Desk Reference* (2007, see also http://www.pdr.net), which provides information about medications (e.g., indications, contraindications, side effects). One might also subscribe to a free online drug formulary and drug-interaction service such as that available through Epocrates (http://www.eprocrates.com). The Epocrates service will send updated drug information to your computer, which can then be linked to a personal digital assistant, for easy access. The service can also send automatic updates directly to a smartphone. *Harrison's Principles of Internal Medicine* (Kasper et al., 2005) contains a thorough review of medicine. However, many clinicians find the less expensive *Merck Manual* (Beers, 2006) to be useful in that it provides brief descriptions of symptoms, course, laboratory findings, and prognosis of various diseases. Internet sites such as WebMD (http://www.webmd.com) and Medscape (http://www.medscape.com/home) are also invaluable. Taken together, these references provide a comprehensive resource list for basic study in clinical health psychology.

Additional Resources

One can also obtain information through continuing education workshops and courses. The Society of Behavioral Medicine, the Association for Applied Psychophysiology and Biofeedback, the American Psychosomatic Society, and the APA (especially its Division of Health Psychology), among other professional groups, organize workshops at their annual meetings. Other specialized groups (e.g., the American Pain Society, the Arthritis Foundation) have educational programs designed specifically for health professionals, in addition to those targeted at the general public. For example, the Association of Rheumatology Health Professionals regularly offers foundation courses in the rheumatic diseases, appropriate for the clinical health psychologist interested in gaining further expertise in this area.

Nearly every major disease has a related organization whose goals include public and professional education (e.g., American Cancer Society, American Lung Association, American Tinnitus Association). Many of these groups provide substantial information at no cost. A list of names and Web sites of relevant scientific societies and special-interest groups can be found in Appendix C.

Hospital libraries are repositories of audiovisual aids provided by pharmaceutical houses. These are often used by physicians to obtain continuing education (CE) credits and are at a level that psychologists can usually understand. Finally, online courses have become common; most states allow a significant number of required CE credits to be earned through distance learning methods. Keeping current in any area of clinical health psychology can be done efficiently through these online courses. APA launched its own APA Online Academy (http://www.apa.org/ce/) a few years ago with a number of courses relevant to clinical health psychology developed in collaboration with the APA Division of Health Psychology.

Supervised Training

Note that didactic experiences, although necessary, are not sufficient for the practice of clinical health psychology. As is true of all professional training, the availability of appropriate role models, supervisors, and mentors is crucial. The implementation committee appointed at the Arden House Conference delineated a number of techniques and skills that should be acquired through supervised training (Sheridan et al., 1988). Exhibit 2.1 lists those areas—it was recommended that clinical health psychologists develop competence in at least six.

More recent work at the APA Division of Health Psychology Tempe Summit in 2007 built on previous work on foundational and functional competencies in professional psychology to articulate suggestions for specific competencies in clinical health psychology at the entry level of practice (France et al., in press). As educational systems increasingly focus on

---

Exhibit 2.1

Competence Areas for Clinical Health Psychologists

1. Relaxation therapies
2. Short-term individual psychotherapy
3. Group therapy
4. Family therapy
5. Consultation skills
6. Liaison skills
7. Assessment of specific patient population (e.g., pain patients or spinal cord injury patients)
8. Neuropsychological assessment
9. Behavior modification techniques
10. Biofeedback
11. Hypnosis
12. Health promotion and public education skills
13. Major treatment programs (e.g., eating disorders, stroke rehabilitation, pain programs)
14. Compliance motivation

---

student learning outcomes, the specification of such competencies is critical to measures of accountability and student success.

Obtaining appropriate training in service delivery requires a careful assessment of the program faculty, or if one is already in practice, the pursuit of an ongoing formal consultation relationship. Exhibit 2.2 displays areas in which to assess a potential supervisor.

The need for clinical supervision cannot be overemphasized. First, psychologists are bound by their ethical code to practice only in areas of competence. Second, the wisdom acquired from clinical practice will never be totally communicable in a purely didactic framework. This would be analogous to expecting that one could learn psychotherapy through a set of readings, or how to conduct research by reading reports. As all trained clinicians are aware, one of the hallmarks of professional training is a

---

Exhibit 2.2

Competence Areas for Clinical Health Psychology Supervisors

1. Special competencies in clinical health psychology—do they match the desired areas of practice?
2. Sensitivity to ethical issues in supervision.
3. Model of supervision to be used (including goals and methods).
4. Availability to the supervisee.
5. Perspective and knowledge of the field of clinical health psychology.
6. Knowledge about the health care system.
7. Affiliation with appropriate professional groups.

---

developmental process under the tutelage of masters. Third, with increasing malpractice litigation, there is an increased risk of successful suits without proper training and supervision in this area of practice. (Ethical and malpractice issues are fully discussed in chaps. 6 and 7.)

Fourth, naive or incompetent practitioners do a disservice to the rest of the profession. We have, on numerous occasions, heard stories about health care units being "spoiled" for entry by new psychologists because of previous experiences with traditionally trained (and, in our view, insufficiently trained) professional psychologists, or health psychologists who lack training in applied professional practice. Sometimes these difficulties arise from lack of specific knowledge or technique (e.g., gross misinterpretation of medical abbreviations, what physicians call "stupid questions" and "irrelevant reports," inappropriate charting, misapplication of psychodiagnostic instruments). However, they often occur because of a failure to comprehend the sociopolitical features of health care, as medical settings have their own cultures, which require understanding if the clinician is to be an effective participant. This culture has significant implications for professional role behavior because the personal conduct and attitude of the psychologist could determine the difference between the success of a service and its death because of disuse.

Expansion of Practice

Clinical health psychologists need a commitment to lifelong learning, which is, for the most part, a self-directed process in psychology. Being able to accurately assess one's knowledge and skills is essential. To promote the ethical expansion of practice, Belar and colleagues proposed a model for self-assessment in clinical health psychology by articulating a series of questions that psychologists can use to gauge their expertise in core domains of requisite knowledge and skills (Belar et al., 2001; see Exhibit 2.3). A self-study program involving both knowledge acquisition and professional consultation might then be more easily designed.

PERSONAL AND PROFESSIONAL ISSUES

Knowledge of specific facts and expertise in technical clinical skills are not sufficient for the successful practice of clinical health psychology. The health care system itself, along with its various subcultures, must be understood for one to achieve credibility and acceptance as a professional health service provider. In addition, we have found that professional behaviors, attitudes, and personal characteristics of the clinician are related to performance as a clinical health psychologist.

Clinical health psychologists frequently practice in one or more of three settings: medical–surgical hospitals, outpatient clinics, or independent private practices. Given the nature of the work, close collaboration with medical–surgical or dental specialties is required wherever the practice is located. Historically, many psychologists have been unaware of the customs, practices, and sociopolitical issues associated with the practice of medicine or dentistry or in the hospital environment. As discussed previously, in recognition of the need for such understanding, the Arden House Conference (G. C. Stone, 1983) declared that professional health psychology training should occur in multidisciplinary health service settings under the tutelage of experienced psychologist–mentors who themselves were bona fide members of those settings.

As an example, one requirement of a graduate level medical psychology course taught by Belar involved a semester-long observational experience in either an inpatient or outpatient service (e.g., dialysis unit, women's

Exhibit 2.3

Template for Self-Assessment in Clinical Health Psychology

1. Do I have knowledge of the biological bases of health and disease as related to this problem? How is this related to the biological bases of behavior?

2. Do I have knowledge of the cognitive–affective bases of health and disease as related to this problem? How is this related to the cognitive–affective bases of behavior?

3. Do I have knowledge of the social bases of health and disease as related to this problem? How is this related to the social bases of behavior?

4. Do I have knowledge of the developmental and individual bases of health and disease as related to this problem? How is this related to developmental and individual bases of behavior?

5. Do I have knowledge of the interactions among biological, affective, cognitive, social, and developmental components (e.g., psychophysiological aspects)? Do I understand the relationships between this problem and the patient and his or her environment (including family, health care system and sociocultural environment)?

6. Do I have knowledge and skills of the empirically supported clinical assessment methods for this problem and how assessment might be affected by information in areas described by Questions 1 through 5?

7. Do I have knowledge of, and skill in implementing, the empirically supported interventions relevant to this problem? Do I have knowledge of how the proposed psychological intervention might impact physiological processes and vice versa?

8. Do I have knowledge of the roles and functions of other health care professionals relevant to this patient's problem? Do I have skills to communicate and collaborate with them?

(continued)

Exhibit 2.3

**Template for Self-Assessment
in Clinical Health Psychology (*Continued*)**

9. Do I understand the sociopolitical features of the health care delivery system that can impact this problem?
10. Am I aware of the health policy issues relevant to this problem?
11. Am I aware of the distinctive ethical issues related to practice with this problem?
12. Am I aware of the distinctive legal issues related to practice with this problem?
13. Am I aware of the special professional issues associated with practice with this problem?

Note. From "Self-Assessment in Clinical Health Psychology," by C. D. Belar et al., 2001, *Professional Psychology: Research and Practice, 32*, p. 137. Copyright 2001 by the American Psychological Association.

health clinic, oncology service, coronary care unit, primary care clinic, genetic counseling clinic). The purpose of this assignment was to provide an opportunity for experiential learning about the medical setting, its language, its culture, and the nature of interdisciplinary functioning. It also provided in vivo exposure to the patient's experience and to the stressors the health care staff endured. Students could then compare notes with respect to such things as differences among settings, types of personnel who tended to work there, and clinical problems that were likely to surface. On course evaluations, every student reported that this experience was crucial to his or her learning. It facilitated the integration of published clinical research findings, provided numerous hypotheses for future investigations, and stimulated ideas about potential professional roles on each service. Perhaps most important, students became much more sophisticated about the sociopolitical aspects of health care. Such observational experiences are relatively simple for students to obtain, but the practicing clinician might have to seek special arrangements with community-based practices or settings. We believe that such experiences are extremely useful.

Formalized Aspects of Health Care Settings

Hospitals are typically organized into three systems of authority and responsibility: the board of directors (with ultimate responsibility for the activities of the hospital), the hospital administrator (responsible for the day-to-day operation of the hospital), and the medical director (responsible for all clinical care within the hospital). The hospital administrator and medical director work jointly to carry out the goals of the board of directors. The hospital professional staff report to the medical director. The board also has a number of committees such as the credentials committee (to review credentials of professional staff), the executive committee (usually consisting of chiefs of service and department heads), the quality assurance committee (to maintain standards of practice), and the medical records committee (to ensure proper documentation).

Hospital bylaws delineate qualifications for practice at the hospital, categories of professional staff, conditions of appointment, issues of quality assurance, and personnel due process procedures. *Hospital rules and regulations* are documents that accompany bylaws and contain specifics regarding practice. Rules and regulations concern documentation, standards of care, admission and discharge procedures, infection-control procedures, and so forth.

Psychologists who wish to develop successful clinical health psychology practices must be aware of these rules and avoid violating them. For example, some hospitals have actual dress codes (in other settings, the code is not explicit but is just as important to understand). Identification badges are required, and their absence is taken seriously. Belar recalls one instance when, in a hurry to deliver a final consultation report to a ward, she left her white coat with badge behind and received an embarrassing lecture from the chief of nursing. Both the traditional white coat and identification badge are important means of quick identification of authorized personnel. Another example of specific rules of the health care setting is the guidelines for making chart entries (e.g., using military time, black ink only, specific procedures for correcting errors). Infractions are actually monitored by special committees. Bylaws and rules and regulations can vary across hospitals. It is imperative that the clinical health psychologist obtain copies of these documents to learn what privileges and responsibilities are relevant to a particular institution before undertaking practice there.

Hospital bylaws define various categories of membership of the hospital staff. Although these categories vary from institution to institution, they are generally organized as follows:

Active Organized Staff

This is the highest level of hospital privilege and responsibility. Members of this group are eligible to vote on hospital policy and may hold office. They have a full range of clinical responsibilities within their area of competence. Sometimes nonmedical personnel are excluded from membership within this category.

Courtesy Organized Staff

Members of this group are limited in the number of patients they may admit to the hospital and may not vote on hospital policy. Usually, these staff members hold active organized staff privileges at another facility.

Consulting Organized Staff

Consulting staff members act only as consultants in their particular fields of expertise. They have no voting privileges and may not hold office. They may attend staff meetings and can be asked to serve on various committees.

Affiliate or Allied Health Staff

Affiliates tend to be allied health professionals and ancillary or paramedical personnel. They are granted privileges to participate in patient care under direct supervision of active or courtesy staff members. They hold no voting privileges and may not serve on committees. Although there is change nationally, psychologists are often relegated to affiliate or consulting categories (without voting or admission privileges). Psychologists have long fought for admission and discharge privileges. However, in the field of clinical health psychology, this professional issue has been relatively less important because, if hospitalization is required, it is usually for reasons of physical health, necessitating that the primary provider be a physician. What we find more important is the psychologist's ability to vote on rules and regulations, to participate in setting standards, to serve on staff committees, and to participate in health policy formation for the hospital. Psychology should not find affiliate categories acceptable for the profession.

Psychologists must apply for *staff privileges* to practice in a hospital. These privileges are specifically delineated in the application materials (e.g., patient admission; the writing of orders, consultation reports, and progress notes; personality and neuropsychological assessment; individual, family, and group psychotherapy; hypnosis; biofeedback; crisis intervention–emergency care; pain management; staff development). The applicant's training, experience, and demonstrated competence in requested practice areas are reviewed by the credentials committee and approved by the executive committee.

The process will generally include the application procedure, including documentation of training, hospital experience, and appropriate malpractice coverage. On approval of the application, the psychologist will go through a proctoring period, which is required for any discipline when applying for staff privileges. During this period, one might be expected to contact the proctor before doing a consultation, or simply send reports for the proctor to review as the consultation and treatment progress. Once the proctoring period is finished, advancement to active staff (or active allied health staff) can be completed. Note that application for privileges in a psychiatric hospital may be quite different than those in an acute-care hospital. Often, in an acute-care hospital, the clinical health psychologist will be a member of the department of medicine, because there may not be a psychiatry department.

Professional behavior and practice are also governed by the standards of the Joint Commission on Accreditation of Healthcare Organizations (JCAHO), by state laws that regulate practice, and by federal policy that affects healthcare, usually through the reimbursement process (e.g., Medicare). For example, JCAHO is a private, nonprofit organization developed to set standards for hospitals to ensure proper health care. Guidelines for JCAHO accreditation affect professional behavior through requirements for charting, quality assurance, staff privileges, and so forth. JCAHO also requires attention to patients' rights; most hospitals have a formal Patients'

Bill of Rights, which specifies rights to privacy, dignity, knowledge about treatment and the treating professionals, interpreter services, and so forth.

State statutes affect practice with respect to limits on confidentiality in cases of child abuse and dangerousness, as well as through licensing requirements. Federal policy has a profound effect on health care practices through the reimbursement system, proposals for health care reform, and legislation such as the Health Insurance Portability and Accountability Act (enacted by Congress as Public Law 104–191 in 1996; full text available at http://www.cms.hhs.gov/HIPAAGenInfo/Downloads/HIPAALaw.pdf).

Informal Aspects of Health Care Settings

In addition to formal structures, there are the informal rules that govern behavior in a medical setting and affect professional roles and effective functioning.

Professional Role Issues

It is valuable for the clinician to understand both the implicit and the explicit power hierarchy. An important point to consider is who has credibility in the system. It is sad but true that some physicians who see themselves as holistic have the least credibility with their colleagues, although in some cases this might be justified. These physicians can be very eager to collaborate and to affiliate with the beginning clinical health psychologist and can make the newcomer feel most welcomed. However, these alliances could prove disastrous if the reputation of the psychologist suffers as a result.

It is important to observe and learn about the hospital environment and "the players" before establishing solid alliances. As an example, we are aware of a clinical health psychologist who was attempting to establish a pain management service within an acute-care hospital. In doing so, he developed close relationships with the hospital administration and a few orthopedic surgeons in the hospital to the exclusion of the Anesthesia Department and other orthopedists who also operated out of the hospital. The establishment of the service, over the objections of the anesthesia department, resulted in intense turf wars between orthopedics, anesthesiology, and psychology. The service was ultimately closed because the disciplines were unwilling to cross-refer or cooperate. Yet, another pain service was opened a short time later within the anesthesia department. This service did not include the expertise of a clinical health psychologist.

Stories abound of professional mistreatment of psychologists by physicians (e.g., as "one down," second-class citizen, technician). Although we have a few scars in this regard, in general, we have been viewed with respect as professional experts in our own areas. When dealing with more aversive situations, we have found it helpful to stay task oriented and to look for areas of mutual agreement. This usually means that we must appreciate that we all have the same goal: good patient care. Focusing interactions over this mutual goal, and not engaging in unnecessary power struggles, is not only more effective for the patient but can also be a major professional coping strategy.

Being a psychologist, and thus somewhat outside of the normal medical hierarchy, has also been beneficial. As a profession, we have sufficient status to warrant attention from other health care professions, but we are not so intimidating as to thwart communication at various levels. It is often necessary for us to seek medical information from the referral source, which can make it easier for the physician to learn from us about psychosocial material. We become mutual students in the biopsychosocial understanding of the patient. We never have to prove ourselves as "real physicians," as do our psychiatric colleagues.

Referral Customs

Understanding referral customs in both inpatient and outpatient settings is very important. For instance, a hospital consultant does not provide feedback to a patient about results unless given permission to do so by the attending physician (which is usually easily obtained). This can present special ethical issues regarding psychological testing feedback; these are addressed in chapter 6. In most hospitals, a psychologist should never see a patient unless it is requested by the attending physician, even if nursing staff have requested help. However, good relationships with nursing staff are important for a number of reasons: (a) these staff members are frequently responsible for initiating consultations, (b) they have valuable information to offer about the patient, and (c) they are often critical to the intervention process.

It can also be important to understand the roles of all the physicians involved in the patient's care. William W. Deardorff once experienced a situation in which a chronic-pain consultation was ordered by the physiatrist (a physical medicine and rehabilitation doctor) for a patient on the acute-rehabilitation unit. According to accepted standards, this consultation included a Minnesota Multiphasic Personality Inventory assessment. The physiatrist was familiar with the instrument and expected it would be used. In addition, the patient was openly willing to complete the test. Even so, when the attending internist came into the room and observed the patient completing this "ludicrous" questionnaire, he became agitated and took the test away from her, telling her she should not complete it. This was followed by what would be considered an inappropriate note in the chart regarding psychological assessment along with an order canceling any further consultation or psychological treatment.

In these rehabilitation situations, patients are commonly followed by both an internist (who addresses any general medical problems) and a physiatrist (who dictates the rehabilitation treatment). The latter is usually much more involved in the treatment of these patients. Deardorff, in addition to suspending patient contact immediately, discussed the issue with the physiatrist rather than going directly to the internist. The physiatrist was able to educate the internist as to the necessity of the evaluation (including the testing) and elicit his cooperation. The consultation was reordered and completed. Deardorff then followed up by presenting the results to the internist (in a nondefensive manner), providing concrete and usable information. In addition, the internist was sent an article on the use of psychological evaluation and assessment in treating chronic-pain problems. This feedback further educated him as to the validity and usefulness of such procedures.

In outpatient consultation work, it is important to remember that one should never refer a patient to a medical or dental colleague for consultation without going back to the original referral source to tactfully obtain his or her permission—something we have never been denied. This is especially important in clinical health psychology, because the psychologist clinician constantly has to assess whether previous medical workups have been adequate, without having competence in that area. It is best to have established relationships with specialty physicians in whom the clinician has confidence. The clinical health psychologist will often obtain "curbside consultations" from these specialists, as well as refer patients to them and thus contribute to their practices.

An important aspect to keep in mind is that when physicians request services from psychologists, they might actually feel somewhat threatened to admit that they do not understand a patient or that they cannot handle a particular situation. In fact, this might be more of an issue when it comes to behavioral and emotional problems than when consultations are required of other specialists in medicine. In today's culture, many people consider themselves to be experts in human relations. Breakdowns in interpersonal relationships are frequently blamed on the "other person," but not without significant personal fears concerning one's own failure. So it is with health care providers and their patients, and this can result in defensiveness or increased emotional reactivity on the part of the consultee.

These kinds of problems need to be handled with tact. Any type of arrogance or condescending behavior will only exacerbate the problem. Indeed, it is hypothesized that professional arrogance in psychologists is relatively more damaging to collaborative relationships with physicians, in part because of the nature of problems being addressed, than would be arrogance displayed by another medical specialist (e.g., cardiologist to family practitioner). In general, we believe that a number of professional behaviors and personal attributes can facilitate or hinder successful clinical health psychology practice.

Special Issues in Professional Behavior

Another discipline often cannot judge the quality of psychological services, but physicians can judge whether such services are delivered in good professional style. Unfortunately, *quality of care* is often confused with *quality of service* (how the care is delivered), although the latter is certainly also important. However, style is frequently the only frame of reference from which physicians can judge, and the standards used are those of their own profession. Given this understanding, we suggest that the clinical health psychologist should do the following: (a) avoid overidentification with medicine, (b) fine-tune communication skills, (c) be prompt and follow through, (d) accept limits of understanding, (e) be prepared for patient advocacy, and (f) advocate for quality of care and services.

Avoid Overidentification With Medicine

Although clinical health psychologists need to understand the health care system and to behave in a fashion that can gain them credibility, it is also important to be aware of the potential for the inappropriate medical socialization of clinical health psychologists. Elfant (1985) described the traditional medical model with its authoritarian stance and action orientation and expressed his concerns that health psychology practitioners would overidentify with it and, in so doing, forgo the psychological treatment model that insists on autonomy and freedom of choice for both patient and therapist.

Elfant (1985) also stated, "The fact that psychological assessment raises a multiplicity of hypotheses, issues and clinical guesses is disturbing news in the hospital environment where quick action is the norm" (p. 61). There are strong pressures in health care to reach bottom-line decisions to "fix" people. This is especially relevant to psychologists in the area of compliance with medical regimens, wherein the clinician must carefully evaluate who the actual client is: the health care system or the patient. We agree with Elfant that clinical health psychology must avoid the mistakes of the traditional medical model that portrays the patient as sick and dependent and the professional as imperialistic and heroic.

Fine-Tune Communication Skills

Suffice it to say that competence in the eyes of physicians will not be demonstrated through the use of psychological jargon, be it psychoanalytic or behavioral in orientation. We have witnessed physicians' reactions range from sarcasm to bemusement at terms such as *oral fixation, cognitive restructuring, projective identification,* and *contingency management.* The rule of thumb is to be *concrete, practical, brief,* and *succinct.* Recommendations should be relevant to the consultee's behavior. It is often said that the longer the report, the less likely it is to be read.

Be Prompt and Follow Up

In hospitals, consultations usually must be initiated within 24 hours or less, with full reports available immediately. Many consultations require more than one contact. A frequent complaint about psychological consultants is that they do not inform the referring source about the course of the consultation process, or "drop the ball" by rendering an opinion and then leaving the case to the attending physician to manage without either specific directions or proper follow-up support.

Outpatient services are sometimes described as "rabbit holes" for patients, who are thought to disappear after the referral is made. Often this is not the result of inattention to the patient's needs, but a lack of following through in communication back to referral sources.

Accept Limits of Understanding

Every discipline has its limits in understanding. Clinical health psychologists must not overestimate or overstate the boundaries of knowledge. As psychologists attempt to prove themselves in medical settings, this might be tempting, but it is ill-fated. One needs to know and to accept the limits inherent in the state of psychological knowledge and therapeutic efficacies and to be able to ask for help or information when appropriate. The psychologist should not project the image of a general "fixer" of human behavior; rather, she or he should convey a more limited range of expertise. Lipowski (1967) described the physician's view of the psychiatrist as "a scientifically unsophisticated, medically ignorant, and impractical man, given to sweeping statements about other people's motives based on abstruse theories of questionable validity" (p. 158). For over 20 years, he called on psychiatrists to contradict this image, a message never completely heeded by either psychiatrists or psychologists, as has been demonstrated by some of the consultation reports we have seen.

Be Prepared for Patient Advocacy

A final issue has to do with patient advocacy. Often the clinical health psychologist will find him- or herself in a mediating role between the health care system and the patient, sometimes having to actively advocate for patient needs. For example, a previous psychiatric diagnosis can affect physicians' willingness to pursue medical evaluations. We remember well the case of a 45-year-old former alcoholic who complained of back pain and was considered a "crock." It was ultimately determined that the woman was actually experiencing a recurrence of bowel cancer. Thorough documentation of the nature of the complaints, the lack of evidence for psychological mechanisms to explain the symptoms, and several phone calls to the attending physician persuaded him to do a more extensive workup. As a result, the patient felt more authenticated, and throughout her remaining therapy, worked through her anger at caregivers as she became increasingly dependent on them until her death.

Setting-related issues can also be extremely important in patient advocacy. For example, it has been said that in an HMO in which the patient has less autonomy and control than in fee-for-service health care, health care professionals have special obligations to advocate for the patient and to act as internal critics of unfair HMO policies and colleagues' practices.

Advocate for Quality Care and Services

If the psychologist witnesses a violation of patient rights or an inappropriate standard of care, he or she must take appropriate action. Psychologists must know the local professional mechanisms, chains of authority, and structures available to deal with such problems.

According to Koocher and Keith-Spiegel (1998), psychologists' ethical principles implicitly encourage whistle-blowing if other mechanisms fail to resolve the problem. However, such activity is not without personal and professional self-sacrifice and risk. Koocher and Keith-Spiegel have encouraged the use of questions developed by Nader, Petkas, and Blackwell (1972), which could assist the clinical health psychologist with decision making concerning this issue:

1. Is my knowledge of the matter complete and accurate?
2. What are the objectionable practices and what public interest do they harm?
3. How far should and can I go inside the organization with my concern or objection?
4. Will I be violating any rules by contacting outside parties and, if so, is whistle-blowing nevertheless justified?

5. Will I be violating any laws or ethical duties by not contacting external parties?
6. Once I have decided to act, what is the best way to blow the whistle—anonymously, overtly, by resignation prior to speaking out, or in some other way?
7. What will be the likely responses from various sources—inside and outside the organization—to the whistle-blowing action?
8. What is expected to be achieved by whistle-blowing in this particular situation? (p. 6)

Many of these questions are also useful in determining for oneself how far one wants to go, either within a setting or within a profession, to resolve problems related to professional practice.

Personal Characteristics

Before undertaking work in clinical health psychology, it is important to review some of the personal issues that we have found to be related to one's ability to adjust to practice in this area. Some individuals are just not suited to the work; thus, it is better to examine these issues early in the process of training.

Because clinical health psychology is receiving increased attention, individuals might be drawn to it for inappropriate reasons or with unrealistic expectations. Mismatches between personal characteristics and professional requirements are costly in terms of time spent and emotional well-being. We have seen mismatches result in early burnout and, in the worst cases, pervasive anger, resentment, and nihilistic thinking. These attitudes are not only damaging to the individual practitioner, but also can reflect negatively on the field as a whole. Personal characteristics thought to be related to successful practice include the following:

Understanding One's Own Stimulus Value

It is important for the clinician to assess whether he or she has any striking peculiarities that could interfere with early establishment of rapport, because rapport must often be accomplished quickly in this field. Given the bad press mental health professionals have had in the past, the more prototypically "shrink-like" person might be at quite a disadvantage. When we think of the most successful clinical health psychologists we have known, the descriptors *active, engaging, open, direct, assertive,* and *energetic* come to mind. In a survey of Veterans Affairs physicians, Schenkenberg, Peterson, Wood, and DaBell (1981) found the following adjectives used to describe important qualities for a psychological consultant: *pleasant, personable, friendly, compassionate, empathic, sensitive, interested, available, able to communicate effectively, cooperative, intelligent, open, perceptive,* and *displaying common sense.*

Possession of a High Frustration Tolerance

The clinical health psychologist must be a persevering, patient person who, given the frustrations in the field, can manage on a thin schedule of positive reinforcement. We believe this to be basic to work in the area. One must be able to tolerate the fluctuation of interest by the medical community in behavioral and emotional components of health. Despite the current focus on integrated health care, it can still be merely lip service by the medical community and policy makers. Some physicians care little about the values psychologists hold most dear. Physicians can be ambivalent, hostile (covertly or overtly), or indifferent. An attitude of benevolent skepticism is welcomed. Physicians sometimes fail to carry out recommendations (about 30% of the time, according to Billowitz & Friedson, 1978–1979), discharge patients before evaluation or treatment is completed, refer patients without adequate preparation, or fail to acknowledge the special expertise of the psychologist.

Of special note is the need for clinicians to respond nondefensively to what could be perceived to be an MD versus PhD prejudice. An early supervisor in this area, Derek Shows, pointed out that psychologists' prejudices against the medical model (which they equate with medicine) can lead to a readiness to project conflict into almost any situation (Shows, 1976). When a defensive or aggressive stance is taken, it can make collaborative efforts difficult. As one becomes more sophisticated in the health care system, it becomes evident that some conflict is a natural, ongoing part of the system and that it occurs among medical specialties as well.

In the authors' experience, psychologists with strong needs for external validation and recognition are not likely to do well on a long-term basis; they soon become angry and resentful. Rather, we believe the work is more suitable to one who is primarily motivated by internal belief systems and achievement needs. This is because the system often yields too little external reinforcement.

Avoidance of Professional Fanaticism

Although we indicated the importance of being motivated by internal beliefs, and earlier mentioned the somewhat missionary zeal with which a number of us embraced the field, we believe it important not to be fanatical in our beliefs about the importance of the biopsychosocial model. Nor should we be wedded to any single treatment technique. We have witnessed the suspension of critical thinking by a number of colleagues who threw themselves into the wellness movement or the use of biofeedback, only to suffer a loss of credibility when they could not deliver the results they anticipated.

Tolerance for a Demanding Work Schedule

It is especially necessary to be able to tolerate a demanding work schedule if inpatient work is involved. Much consultation work in the hospital setting is unpredictable, and the psychologist must be available on short notice. Follow-through is essential, and must be completed despite whatever else has already been scheduled. The work is not leisurely. Pressures can mount, especially when there are demands for immediate solutions to complex problems, as is often the case. Of course, settings do vary, and there are some systems in which clinical health psychologists maintain a 9-to-5 schedule, with few deviations even in hospital work. Scheduling in outpatient practices is much more under the control of the clinician.

Ability to Deal With Hostile and Reluctant Patients

Specific suggestions for handling hostile patients are given in chapter 5, but it is noted here that clinical health psychologists frequently see patients who are upset about the referral. They often display indifference, if not outright antagonism, when meeting the clinician. This is sometimes due

reparation by the physician but is most often due to the mind–
~~~, alism that is alive and well in patients as well as physicians. If the clinician has strong needs to see patients who are actively seeking psychological help, this is not the most suitable area of practice.

Ability to Cope With Diverse Sets of Data

The clinical health psychologist needs to be comfortable with diverse sets of data (e.g., biological, psychological, social, cultural) and to attempt to integrate these while recognizing that no single theory of behavior provides an adequate conceptualization. The clinician must remain flexible in operating within a variety of conceptual models, depending on the case. The clinical health psychologist must guard against being too easily intimidated by biological models (which are often presented as being more precise than they actually are) while being overly self-critical of the behavioral sciences.

Ability to Work With Physically Ill Patients

Patients seen by the clinical health psychologist are sometimes gravely ill, deformed, mutilated, disabled, or dying. A period of acclimation is needed as one struggles within oneself with such potential stressors as the sight of blood, the burn unit, the fears of chronic pain, and the acceptance of terminal illness. The clinician's reactions to the patient in these areas are critical. The colostomy or mastectomy patient who is concerned with body image and fears of unacceptability must not be treated with squeamishness. Yet it is easy to be distracted from addressing patient feelings and attitudes in the presence of massive physical changes (e.g., those found on a head and neck surgery service).

Clinicians need to design their own programs to facilitate dealing with these issues. Medical libraries are full of pictures and videos that can provide stimuli for desensitization purposes. Colleagues, supervisors, personal therapists, and families are important resources in dealing with personal issues regarding death, dying, and threats to body integrity.

Empathy for Health Care Providers' Perspectives

It is important to be able to communicate respect for the consultee and his or her problem (e.g., a demanding or noncompliant patient). Collaboration with medicine requires empathy not just in the evaluation of the patient but also in dealing with the referral sources. The clinician needs to understand consultees' thinking styles and perspectives on patient care. This requires an in-depth understanding of the roles, functions, and stressors in various hospital units and outpatient clinics. This is perhaps best obtained through naturalistic observation.

Acceptance of Dependence on Another Profession

Psychology is an independent profession, but the practice of clinical health psychology has aspects of a forced dependency on the expertise and performance of another profession, usually medicine or dentistry. Some psychologists we have known have had special difficulty with this forced dependency, especially when it involved a profession of greater social status.

Appropriateness as a Health Model

Early on, Weiss (1982) highlighted the importance of health psychologists' assessing their personal suitability as role models. The clinical health psychologist should be aware of personal habits such as smoking, overeating, alcohol usage, and physical fitness. Modeling of appropriate personal health behavior is related not only to therapeutic effectiveness, if one adopts a social learning theory model, but also to ethical principles, as discussed in chapter 6.

In summary, beyond acquiring the core body of clinical health psychology knowledge and skills, preparation to become an effective clinical health psychologist requires significant attention to professional and personal issues. This chapter has addressed the general education, training, professional and personal issues that we believe should be considered in preparation for practice. In the next chapter we examine more specific issues associated with the practice of assessment in clinical health psychology.

DESK REFERENCES

Beers, M. H. (2006). *The Merck manual* (18th ed.). Rahway, NJ: Merck Research Laboratories.

Gylys, B. A., & Wedding, M. E. (2004). *Medical terminology systems: A body systems approach* (5th ed.). Philadelphia: F. A. Davis.

Kasper, D. L., Braunwald, E., Fauci, A., Hauser, S., Longo, D., & Jameson, J. L. (2005). *Harrison's principles* of *internal medicine* (16th ed.). New York: McGraw-Hill.

Physicians' desk reference (61st ed.). (2007). Boston: Thomson PDR.

Stedman's medical dictionary (28th ed.). (2006). Baltimore: Lippincott, Williams & Wilkins.

SUGGESTED READINGS

Baum, A., Revenson, T. A., & Singer, J. E. (Eds.). (2001). *Handbook of health psychology.* Mahwah, NJ: Erlbaum.

Belar, C. D., Brown, R. A., Hersch, L. E., Hornyak, L. M., Rozensky, R. H., Sheridan, E. P., et al. (2001). Self-assessment in clinical health psychology: A model for ethical expansion of practice. *Professional Psychology: Research and Practice, 32,* 135–141.

Cohen, L. M., McChargue, D. E., & Collins, F. L. (2003). *The health psychology handbook: Practical issues for the behavioral medicine specialist.* Thousand Oaks, CA: Sage.

Frank, R. G., Baum, A., & Wallander, J. L. (Eds.). (2004). *Handbook of clinical health psychology: Vol. 3. Models and perspectives in health psychology.* Washington, DC: American Psychological Association.

Frank, R. G., McDaniel, S. H., Bray, J. H., & Heldring, M. (2004). *Primary care psychology.* Washington, DC: American Psychological Association.

Gatchel, R. J., & Oordt, M. S. (2003). *Clinical health psychology and primary care: Practical advice and clinical guidance for successful collaboration.* Washington, DC: American Psychological Association.

Haas, L. J. (Ed.). (2004). *Handbook of primary care psychology.* New York: Oxford University Press.

James, L. C., & Folen, R. A. (Eds.). (2005). *The primary care consultant: The next frontier for psychologists in hospitals and clinics.* Washington, DC: American Psychological Association.

Kaplan, R. M. (2000). Two pathways to prevention. *American Psychologist, 55,* 382–396.

Kazarian, S. S., & Evans, D. R. (Eds.). (2001). *Handbook of cultural health psychology.* San Diego, CA: Academic Press.

Kovner, A. R., & Knickman, J. R. (Eds.). (2008). *Jonas and Kovner's health care delivery system in the United States* (9th ed.). New York: Springer Publishing Company.

Llewelyn, S., & Kennedy, P. (Eds.). (2003). *Handbook of clinical health psychology.* New York: Wiley.

MacLachlan, M. (2006). *Culture and health: A critical perspective towards global health* (2nd ed.). New York: Wiley.

McDaniel, S. H., Belar, C. D., Schroeder, C., Hargrove, D. S., & Freeman, E. L. (2002). A training curriculum for professional psychologists in primary care. *Professional Psychology: Research and Practice, 33,* 65–72.

Raczynski, J. M., & Leviton, L. C. (Eds.). (2004). *Handbook of clinical health psychology: Vol. 2. Disorders of behavior and health.* Washington, DC: American Psychological Association.

Sarafino, E. P. (2005). *Health psychology: Biopsychosocial interactions* (5th ed.). New York: Wiley.

Satcher, D., & Pamies, R. J. (Eds.). (2006). *Multicultural medicine and health disparities.* New York: McGraw Hill.

Starr, P. (1982). *The social transformation of American medicine.* New York: Basic Books.

3

Clinical Health Psychology
Assessment

Clinical assessment precedes clinical intervention, although assessment alone can also be an intervention. In this chapter we describe a model for assessment that addresses biological or physical, affective, cognitive, and behavioral components at the level of the patient, the family, the health care system, and in the sociocultural context. We focus on the need for understanding interactions among these components, and we describe some of the most commonly used assessment methods.

As has been previously documented, psychodiagnostic assessment is a frequent activity of clinical health psychologists (Linton, 2004; Morrow & Clayman, 1982; Rozensky, Sweet, & Tovian, 1997; Stabler & Mesibov, 1984). It is also probably one of psychology's most unique contributions to patient care. Although psychologists often use assessment as the first step in developing a treatment program for their own patients, in clinical health psychology it is frequently used to answer questions and thus solve problems regarding patient care for other health professionals. As Sir William Osler, the esteemed physician, so aptly stated, "it is more important to know what kind of man has a disease than to know what kind of disease a man has" (Osler, 1971, p. 14). For clinical health psychologists, the assessment activity is, then, inextricably intertwined with the consultation activity.

The kinds of consultation requests made of clinical health psychologists depend on the type of practice that one has delineated. It is clear that the referral bases that are developed (e.g., pediatric, oncology, neurology) influence the types of assessment questions posed. The diagnostic issues that a professional in a multidisciplinary consultation–liaison team is likely to encounter were described early on by Lipowski (1967) and remain relevant today: (a) psychological presentations of organic disease (e.g., pancreatic cancer presenting as depression), (b) psychological complications of organic disease (e.g., postcardiotomy delirium), (c) psychological reactions to organic disease (e.g., depression subsequent to amputation), (d) somatic effects of psychological distress (e.g., angina), and (e) somatic presentations of psychiatric disorder (e.g., masked depression).

A report by Shevitz, Silberfarb, and Lipowski (1976) on 1,000 referrals for psychiatric consultation in a general hospital noted that approximately 57% of the patients were referred for differential diagnosis, 56% were referred for management problems (disturbing behavior on the ward, psychiatric disorders that complicated a known organic disease, somatic problems with no known organic pathology), and 28% were referred for disposition, especially after a suicide attempt that mandated a psychiatric referral (see also Bouton-Foster, Ferrando, & Charlson, 2003).

From Belar's experience in developing a medical psychology service in an academic health science center, the authors have found that a wide variety of medical–surgical patients are likely to be referred specifically to clinical health psychologists. The psychiatric services at the same center tended to receive the consultations concerning suicidal and combative behavior, psychotropic medication, and mental-status changes. In contrast, the psychologists received relatively more consultation requests concerning such issues as coping with illness, compliance, preparation for surgery, presurgical screenings, diagnostic and treatment issues associated with chronic pain, and, of course, neuropsychological evaluations.

The authors have also had experience initiating and developing a behavioral medicine outpatient team in a staff model health management organization setting that resulted in nearly 600 referrals per year. Over half of those involved requests from neurology, internal medicine, and family practice units to provide services in the areas of headache management and neuropsychological assessment. A significant number of other clinical problems were also addressed for consultation or treatment purposes, and these included such varied disorders as angina, asthma, arthritis, back pain, blepharospasm, bruxism, cancer or cancer phobia, cardiac disease, chronic obstructive pulmonary disease, compliance issues, deafness, diabetes, fibrositis, hyperhidrosis, hypertension, interstitial cystitis, irritable bowel syndrome, multiple sclerosis, neurodermatitis, penile prosthesis surgery, Raynaud's phenomenon, temporomandibular joint pain, tinnitus, and vomiting. Other services were delivered in collaborative care in the family practice primary care clinics.

The growth of knowledge provided by applied research in health psychology has resulted in an increased need for clinical services. This is especially true in areas not always addressed by traditional consultation–liaison psychiatry or clinical psychology models. In general, these include (a) consultations and treatments involving psychophysiologic self-regulation or the application of learning theory, either as the treatment of choice for a medical problem or as an adjunct to standard medical care; (b) consultations involving predictions of response to medical–surgical treatments; and (c) reduction of health-risk behaviors.

Given the possible range of consultation and assessment activities in clinical health psychology, it is not possible to detail problems associated with specific diseases or to address the use of specific assessment measures, which are well described elsewhere (see suggested readings). Instead, we focus on a model for assessment in clinical health psychology and briefly describe the most common procedures used. Chapter 5 focuses on more process-oriented issues, which are common among various settings, roles, and types of illnesses.

A MODEL FOR ASSESSMENT IN CLINICAL HEALTH PSYCHOLOGY

Following the medical model, psychological assessment has traditionally had two primary purposes: identification and treatment of psychological disorders. As such, psychological assessment measures have been developed to focus on a single dimension of the patient—namely, the state of the patient's mind—without complementary consideration of the patient's body. Conversely, medicine has traditionally focused on the treatment of disease to the exclusion of personality or emotional factors.

Each approach has some value, but the field of clinical health psychology requires an integration of these divergent attitudes, often in the absence of adequate conceptual models. Adequate assessment does not exclude one for the other.

The clinical health psychologist's tasks are to assess the interactions among the person, the disease, and the person's environment and to formulate a diagnosis or treatment strategy on the basis of that understanding. Given the necessity of incorporating physiological, psychological, and sociological information, the clinical health psychologist typically works from a biopsychosocial perspective of health and illness (Engel, 1977).

Over 20 years ago, on the basis of Engel's (1977) work and that of Leigh and Reiser (1980), we elaborated a model for assessment that we still find useful in approaching clinical situations because it facilitates organization of information and subsequent decision making about assessment strategies. Unfortunately, this model reduces various aspects of the biopsychosocial perspective in a manner that could encourage thinking in a compartmentalized, reductionistic fashion about complex, interrelated processes. Note that this is not reflective of our overall orientation toward assessment issues but rather is an artifact of inadequacies in current schemata representing the biopsychosocial model.

TARGETS OF ASSESSMENT

Table 3.1 describes the *targets of assessment* by *domain of information* (biologic or physical, affective, cognitive, behavioral) and *unit of assessment* (patient, family, health care system, or sociocultural context). Within each block are listed examples of the kinds of information that need to be gathered in conducting the assessment or of which the clinician should be aware when attempting to understand the patient from a biopsychosocial perspective.

Each block also has an associated developmental or historical perspective that could be critical to a full understanding of the present condition. In each area, the clinician should attempt to understand the patient's (a) current status, (b) changes since onset of illness, and (c) past history. The focus of the assessment should be not solely on identification of problems

Table 3.1

Targets of Assessment

Domain of information	Patient	Family	Environment		Sociocultural context
			Health care system		
Biological or Physical	Age, sex, race Physical appearance Symptoms, health status Physical examination Vital signs, lab data Prescribed medications OTC medications Psychophysiological data Genetic history and risks Constitutional factors, disabilities History of injury, disease surgery, reproduction	Characteristics of the home setting Economic resources Family size Familial patterning (e.g., headache history) Other illness in family Immigration status	Characteristics of the treatment setting Characteristics of medical procedures Availability of prosthetic aids Accessibility of health care Gender and cultural disparities in care		Social services Financial resources Social networks Occupational setting Health hazards Exposure to violence, terrorism, war Global factors (e.g., political, economic)

(continued)

Table 3.1
Targets of Assessment (*Continued*)

Domain of information	Patient	Environment		
		Family	Health care system	Sociocultural context
Affective	Mood Affect Feelings about illness, treatment, health care, providers, self, family, job, social network History of affective disturbance	Members' feelings about patient, illness, and treatment	Providers' feelings about patient, illness, and treatment	Sentiment of culture regarding patient, illness, and treatment
Cognitive	Cognitive style Thought content Intelligence Education Knowledge about disease Health beliefs	Knowledge about illness and treatment Attitudes/expectations about patient, illness	Providers' knowledge Providers' attitudes toward patient, illness, and treatment	Current state of knowledge Cultural/religious attitudes toward patient and illness

Attitudes and expectations regarding illness, treatment, health care, and providers Perceived meaning of illness Philosophy of life Spiritual/religious beliefs			
Behavioral	Activity level/exercise Interactions with family friends, providers, and coworkers Health habits	Participation in patient care/caregiving roles Reinforcement contingencies for health and illness	Providers' skills in education and training patients Reinforcement contingencies for health and illness	Employment policies Laws regulating health care practice, disability, provision of care, health habits, accessibility
	Health care utilization/history of treatments Substance abuse Adherence Ability to control physical symptoms	Family interactions, interpersonal violence Primary language	Providers' linguistic and cultural competence	Customs in symptom reporting and help-seeking

Note: OTC = over the counter. Updated with input from participants at the 2007 Clinical Health Psychology Training Summit (France et al., in press).

53

but also on delineation of assets, resources, and strengths of the patient and his or her environment.

Patient Targets

Biological Targets

The most obvious biological targets are the patient's age, race, sex, and physical appearance. In addition, the clinician needs to gain a thorough understanding of the patient's current physiological symptoms and how they are similar or different from past symptoms. Recent physical changes could be particularly salient to the assessment, because they are often the precipitating events that elicit the referral (e.g., recent hair loss as a result of radiation treatment, incontinence, gross pedal edema after noncompliance with dietary regimen). The clinician should obtain information on the specifics of the particular disease: nature, location, and frequency of symptoms; current treatment regimen; and health status within the disease process (e.g., Stages I–IV in cancer).

Other sources of biological information include the physical exam, current and past vital signs, the results from relevant laboratory tests (e.g., creatinine levels, blood alcohol levels, HIV status), medications, and use of illicit drugs. Furthermore, a history of the patient's constitution and general health—including previous illnesses, relevant genetic information, injuries, and surgeries—should be obtained.

Depending on the problem, biological targets might also include variables associated with the autonomic nervous system or musculoskeletal activity (e.g., electromyographic [EMG] recordings, peripheral temperature readings) obtained in both resting and stress-related conditions. For example, a psychophysiological profile involving frontal EMG activity under relaxed and stressed conditions could be obtained for a patient suffering from tension headache.

Affective Targets

The assessment of affective targets involves understanding the patient's current mood and affect, including his or her contextual elements and historical features. In addition, an assessment would be incomplete without having obtained information about the patient's feelings about his or her illness, treatment, health care providers, future, social support network, and, of course, self.

Again, it is helpful to obtain data that allow for the comparison between current affective states and those of the past, in that it is often the contrast that prompts the referral. For example, a request we once received stated the following: "Patient recently diagnosed with colon cancer. Had been adjusting well to pending surgery, now crying frequently. Please evaluate." It was the change in affective state that led to this referral, a change that turned out to be related to a family problem rather than maladaptive coping with illness. Previous history of an affective disorder must also be obtained.

Cognitive Targets

Assessment of the patient's cognitive functioning involves gathering information about the patient's knowledge, perceptions, and attitudes, as well as the content and pattern of thinking. It is imperative that the clinical health psychologist be aware of the cognitive abilities and limitations of the patient, from both current and developmental perspectives. Cognitive targets include the following: general intelligence; educational level; specific knowledge concerning illness and treatment; attitudes toward health, illness, and health care providers; perceived threat of illness; perceived control over psychological and physical symptoms; perception of costs and benefits of possible treatment regimens; and expectations about the future outcome.

Another important target is the perceived meaning of the illness to the patient. More generally, the clinician should be aware of the patient's general cognitive style and philosophy of life, including religious beliefs.

Behavioral Targets

Behavioral targets include what the patient is doing (the action) and the manner in which he or she does it (the style). Action primarily involves assessment of motor behaviors, such as facial expressions, foot tapping, bruxism, bracing, body posture, and eye contact. Styles are varied but include flamboyant, hesitant, age appropriate, hostile, restless, and passive. The clinical health psychologist should understand the patient's overall level, pattern, and style of activity in areas of self-care and interpersonal, occupational, and recreational functioning, as well as specific behavioral targets related to the reason for referral.

Of special interest is the patterning and nature of the physician–patient relationship, as well as whether the patient can voluntarily control any of his or her physical symptoms. Once again, a historical perspective is important because past behavior is often the best predictor of future behavior.

Extremely important in clinical health psychology is the assessment of current and previous health habits (e.g., smoking, exercise, eating patterns, alcohol usage) and health care use. The clinician should be able to answer the following questions about the patient: (a) What were the nature, frequency, and pattern of past contacts with health service providers? and (b) What have been the antecedent stimuli and consequences of these contacts (i.e., history of previous help seeking and treatments)?

Finally, an assessment would be incomplete without information concerning the patient's current and past history of compliance with or adherence to treatment regimens, with specific reasons noted for noncompliance whenever it has occurred. Areas of assessment here include medication use as prescribed, history of keeping appointments, and follow through on previous recommendations.

Environmental Targets

The clinical health psychologist also needs to assess aspects of the various environments within which the patient interacts. These include the following: (a) the family unit, (b) the health care system with its various settings and providers, and (c) the sociocultural environment, including social network, occupational setting, and aspects related to ethnicity and cultural background. As with assessment of the individual patient, environmental targets of assessment include physical, affective, cognitive, and behavioral domains, with a focus on relevant demands, limitations, and supports.

Family Environment

In assessing the physical domain of the family environment, it is important to know about available economic resources and perhaps even physical characteristics of the home setting, depending on the problem being assessed (e.g., quadriplegia, blindness). The family's developmental history, size, and experience of recent changes are all important aspects to consider. The clinician should also be aware of other illnesses in family members (e.g., history of hypertension, diabetes) and familial models for various symptoms (e.g., headaches).

In the affective domain, it is important to understand family members' feelings about the patient, the patient's illness, and the treatments rendered. Assessment of past or present affective disorders in the family is essential.

In the cognitive domain, the clinician must assess the family's attitudes, perceptions, and expectations about the patient, the patient's illness and treatment, and the future. Family members' intellectual resources, as well as knowledge that they possess about health and illness, should be understood.

In the behavioral domain, the clinician will want to know whether there have been any changes within the family since the onset of the illness. An example might include a shift in roles and responsibilities of family members. It is also important to find out to what degree family members participate in the patient's care. Assessment of behaviors of family members that could influence the patient's illness or adaptation is crucial. For example, families might model chronic illness, punish patient attempts at self-help, or be secretive in a manner that increases patient anxiety.

Health Care System

The health care system should also be assessed across physical, affective, cognitive, and behavioral domains. For example, in the first domain the clinician needs to know the physical characteristics of the setting in which the patient is being assessed or treated (e.g., coronary care unit, ward, outpatient clinic). Special considerations include degree of sensory stimulation, privacy, and availability of prosthetic aids. In addition, the clinical health psychologist must understand the physical characteristics of the diagnostic procedures and the treatment regimen to which the patient has been, is being, or will be exposed (e.g., pelvic exenteration, colostomy, hemodialysis, chemotherapy).

In the affective domain, one must be aware of how health care providers feel about the patient and about the patient's illness (e.g., requests for sterilization, HIV-positive status). Special problems can occur, for example,

in burn units, in which both perpetrators and victims of severely injurious events can be housed within the same unit. Staff and visitors often feel
split in their feelings and loyalties to these patients. Also, the attitudes of
providers themselves toward the health care system within which they
work can enhance or detract from overall health care. A substantial body
of literature on health disparities needs to be understood as well.

In the cognitive domain, the clinician needs to have some understanding of how knowledgeable health care providers are about the patient's
problems, illness, and treatment. One also needs to assess their attitudes
and expectations about these issues as well as about the patient's future.
Furthermore, it is helpful to be aware of the community standard of care
for the problem.

When assessing the behavior of the overall health care system, the clinician needs to be aware of policies, rules, and regulations that will affect
the patient and his or her treatment (e.g., staffing patterns, single vs. rotat-
ing physicians, appointment schedules, infection control policies). It is also
important to understand which specific behaviors health care providers
might be displaying that could influence patient behavior. Such behaviors
on the part of the health care provider might include transmitting knowledge about disease, providing skill training in self-care, reinforcing verbal complaints, or avoiding affective expression by the patient. Linguistic
impediments to service must also be understood.

Sociocultural Environment

Physical aspects of the patient's sociocultural environment include both
(a) the physical requirements and flexibilities of the patient's occupation
and work setting and (b) the social and financial resources or services available to the patient. In addition, the clinician should be aware of the nature
of the patient's social network (including size, density, and proximity) and
the frequency of the patient's contact with it. Assessment of the natural environment in terms of ecological health hazards (e.g., pollutants, noise levels)
is also sometimes necessary.

In the affective and cognitive domains, the clinician should understand
cultural sentiments, attitudes, and expectations regarding the patient's race,
gender, ethnicity, lifestyle, religion, illness, and treatment (e.g., sentiments

about AIDS, homosexuality, femininity of women who have undergone hysterectomy). What are the cultural attitudes toward prevention? What is the health belief model of the culture itself? Are there prevalent religious beliefs that could affect the patient's willingness to obtain treatment?

In terms of the behavior of large sociocultural systems, the clinician might need to know specific employment policies related to the problem being assessed (e.g., regulations regarding return to work for patients with back problems, hiring guidelines for patients with AIDS). Legislation regulating health care provision and health habits is relevant as well (e.g., disability, smoking in public places). Finally, the clinician should be aware of ethnic customs that could be related to symptom reporting (or underreporting) and health care use.

INTEGRATING ASSESSMENT INFORMATION

It becomes clear from a review of the targets for assessment that these blocks are interrelated and that the nature or relative importance of information obtained in one block is often affected by information found in another. For example, the type and location of physical symptoms can affect the perceived meaning of the illness because of the special psychological significance of certain body parts (e.g., genitalia, heart). Thus, affective reactions might be more pronounced in a patient with cervical carcinoma in situ than those found in a person with an objectively worse health status (e.g., insulin-dependent diabetes). Affective reactions might also be influenced by age. For instance, in the previous example, the loss of ability to bear children could be significantly less traumatic for a 55-year-old woman than for a 17-year-old teenager. Ethnicity might affect this relationship even further if cultural values equated femininity with childbearing potential. For example, in one rural area, we had a number of women past child rearing age who expressed concerns about hysterectomy for such reasons. These women did not want their male partner to know the exact nature of the proposed surgery. Cultural background affects more than just emotional reactions. For example, we have been aware of some instances of more cavalier attitudes about conducting hysterectomies when the potential recipients were unwed women, of low socioeconomic status, with multiple children. These attitudes could affect not only clinical decision making, but also the characteristics of the health care environment and the doctor–patient relationship as well. A growing body of research is exploring the role of ethnicity in treatment seeking, symptom perception, and health care provision (Kazarian & Evans, 2001; Mayberry, Mili, & Ofili, 2000; see also *Agency for Health Care Research and Quality*, 2004).

In conducting an assessment, it is important to understand that the data obtained could be influenced by the type of setting in which the assessment occurs. For example, patients with low-back pain often walk with greater or lesser flexibility depending on who is watching them and in what setting they are being observed. We are reminded of the following example:

> A patient with low-back pain in an inpatient, chronic-pain program was repeatedly observed ambulating with a walker by program personnel. However, on one occasion, when the patient was unaware that he was being observed, he was seen casually carrying his walker over his shoulder while ambulating with appropriate body posture and gait.

Expectations about the purpose of the assessment clearly affect data obtained. As an example, the demand characteristics for patients seeking heart transplant surgery as their only hope of survival versus those seeking disability payments for a cardiac condition are tremendously different and must be considered in the interpretation of data. The presence of other people, their roles, and their behavior can also affect responses during assessment. We have more than once witnessed the emotional breakdown of a patient only a few moments after the patient assured the oncologist that he or she was doing well. The breakdown was not observed until the oncologist left the room, in part because of the need to be a "good patient" for the physician, who is perceived as having so much power over life and death. We have also experienced the reluctance of patients to reveal even significant physical symptoms because they perceive their physician as being too rushed.

Settings also have different base rates of certain phenomena. For example, orthopedic wards tend to have more patients who have had accidents, including more risk takers (e.g., motorcyclists). Also, patients in teaching hospitals report more anxiety than patients in community hospitals (Lucente & Fleck, 1972; see also Bjelland, Dahl, Haug, & Neckelmann, 2002).

We also know that there are physiological effects of various social environments. An example of this is the well-known "white coat hypertension" phenomenon of elevated blood pressure in the presence of health professionals. Another example is the work by Ulrich (1984), who found faster recovery rates and less pain medication use in surgical patients who had a view of a wooded park versus those with a view of a brick wall.

Interrelationships among the targets of assessment are obviously complex. We are reminded of the case of the 75-year-old man who, in a late stage of chronic obstructive pulmonary disease, manifested his anxiety by grumbling at staff. Staff consequently avoided him, thus reinforcing his fear of dying alone and his complaints of poor care.

Exhibit 3.1 displays relationships that influence the interpretation of information obtained during assessment. These represent only a sample of known relationships. In addition, clinical health psychologists must be aware of medical problems that present with psychological symptoms. Appendix D lists what, in our experiences as health psychologists, are the most common of these. To be able to competently interpret the data obtained, the clinician must have a firm grounding in the theoretical and empirical bases of clinical health psychology. In developing a conceptualization of the case, the clinician differentially weights information obtained on the basis of mediating relationships as demonstrated through research and as learned through his or her experience in working with patients. There is no substitute for good clinical judgment.

METHODS OF ASSESSMENT

In performing the clinical health psychology assessment, numerous methods could be used. Many of these provide information about one or more targets in our assessment model. The choice of method depends on the target being assessed, the purpose of the assessment, and the skill of the clinician. We are not wedded to any one particular technique, as each has its strengths and weaknesses. However, we do rely heavily on a good clinical interview as the core clinical method. We also endorse a multiple-measurement model and a convergent/divergent, hypothesis-testing approach to clinical assessment. Detailed descriptions of specific methods will not be provided, but we list

Exhibit 3.1

Relationships That Influence the Interpretation of Information Obtained During Assessment

1. Medication effects on psychophysiological recordings (e.g., diazepam on electromyographic data level).
2. The fund of knowledge of the physician on the accuracy of medical diagnosis. Often specialists need to be consulted to evaluate medical record data, as the referral may come from a general practitioner who had not completely evaluated the presenting problem.
3. Family understanding, emotional support, and involvement on the patient's compliance with the medical regimen.
4. Family members' behavior on the patient's self-care activities (e.g., overprotectiveness often impedes patient self-management and, consequently, hinders the development of a sense of mastery).
5. The effect of legislation on sick-role behavior (e.g., disability payments could reinforce chronic-illness behavior).
6. The effect of religious beliefs on the perceived meaning of symptoms and acceptance of medical regimens (e.g., pain as guilt for past sins or refusal of therapeutic abortion for a life-threatening pregnancy).
7. Providers' attitudes about disease on patient affective responses (e.g., nurses' refusal to minister to patients who have AIDS).
8. The effect of family attitudes toward disease on the patient's affective and behavioral responses (e.g., a wife's negative attitude about colostomy contributing to patient's impotence).
9. Prosthetic characteristics of the environment on patient activity level (e.g., a barrier-free environment facilitates activity level for the patient with a spinal cord injury).
10. Occupational requirements on self-esteem (e.g., loss of bread-winning capacity by an artist who loses functioning in the dominant hand).

(*continued*)

Exhibit 3.1

**Relationships That Influence the Interpretation
of Information Obtained During Assessment (*Continued*)**

11. Providers' attitudes toward treatments on patient suffering
    (e.g., negative attitudes about the use of narcotics resulting in
    the undermedication of cancer pain).
12. Cognitive factors affecting the course of the illness (e.g., the
    maintenance of hope and future orientation facilitating the
    recovery from surgery; unrealistically positive expectations
    about sexual functioning associated with a poor outcome in
    penile prosthesis surgery).
13. Cognitive factors on physical symptoms (e.g., perceived control
    of pain results in increased tolerance for pain).

---

the core techniques used in clinical health psychology. The suggested readings at the end of the chapter provide excellent references for further study in this area. The methods of assessment discussed are interview, questionnaires, diaries, psychometrics, observation, psychophysiological measures, and archival data.

Interview

The clinical interview is perhaps the most common method of gathering information. It has the capacity to elicit current and historical data across all domains (i.e., physical, affective, cognitive, behavioral information regarding the patient and his or her family; health care; sociocultural environments). The interview is also a means of developing a supportive working relationship with the patient. It permits the acquisition of self-report and observational data from the patient, family members, significant others, employers, and health care providers. Understanding one's own stimulus value is crucial to the interpretation of interview data.

The content and style of individual interviews vary depending on the assessment question. The formality of the interview process (unstructured, semistructured, structured) often depends on the personal preference of the clinician as well as the setting and time constraints. Specific intervention programs (e.g., pain management programs) commonly use structured interviews, but we prefer a combination of structured and unstructured approaches. This helps in avoiding interviewer bias and remaining open to exploring areas not immediately recognized as important.

Semistructured and structured interviews have been developed for many purposes including assessment of the Type A behavior pattern (Rosenman, 1978), presurgical screening prior to spine surgery (Block, Gatchel, Deardorff, & Guyer, 2003), psychosocial adjustment to illness (Derogatis, 1986), and primary care evaluation of mental disorders (see Bufka, Crawford, & Levitt, 2002, for a review). However, in many situations, it is most useful to develop one's own structured or semistructured interview for a specific patient population. For instance, we have done this for such areas as chronic pain problems, presurgical screenings, organ transplantation, and craniomandibular disorders. A semistructured interview format allows for flexibility and development of rapport while ensuring that vital information is not neglected.

We believe that every clinical interview should include some elements of the Mental Status Examination (MSE). How extensive an MSE is completed will depend on the presenting symptoms and preliminary findings. Elements of the MSE include the following sections: (a) Appearance, Attitude, and Activity; (b) Mood and Affect; (c) Speech and Language; (d) Thought Process, Thought Content, and Perception; (e) Cognition; (f) Insight and Judgment. We commonly find that the MSE yields information that has not been previously assessed by another health care professional. Many of the areas of assessment (e.g., sexual functioning, drug- and medication-use history, suicidality) are uncomfortable for other providers to explore, but they are of great concern to the patient. For instance, in asking about the effect of a pain problem on sexual functioning, we have often had the response, "I am glad someone finally asked me about that! I've been very concerned." An excellent mental-status exam resource is *The Psychiatric Mental Status Examination* (Trzepacz & Baker, 1993; see suggested readings). The MSE is one component of the initial clinical interview that lends itself well to a structured format. For this purpose, an instrument such as the Mini-Mental State

Examination (MMSE; Folstein, Folstein, & McHugh, 1975) might be considered. The MMSE is an 11-item, clinician-administered examination that assesses the aspects of cognitive functioning listed previously. It is scored against normative data and is most sensitive to moderate to severe impairment. Abnormalities on the MMSE can provide guidance as to the etiology of the mental status changes (e.g., organicity, affective disorders, medications) and guide recommendations (e.g., suggesting a neurology, neuropsychological evaluation).

In some instances, patient interviews are impossible. Occasionally the patient is too agitated or not sufficiently alert to meet the demands of the interview. There are also times in which the patient is uncooperative, in which case the clinician needs to use alternative forms of assessment, delay the consultation, or discontinue the process in the absence of adequate consent.

Questionnaires

Clinician-developed, problem-focused, information-gathering questionnaires are useful in the assessment process. In the outpatient setting, these can be mailed to patients before the first visit and reviewed at the time of interview. We have found this method to be a considerable timesaver in the evaluation of such diverse areas as chronic-pain patients, liver transplant candidates, and potential oocyte donors. The interviewer may review questionnaire data with the patient but can focus more time on areas needing further clarification and on more general psychological issues. Reviewing some questionnaire information with the patient is important in demonstrating the value of the data to the clinician and in establishing rapport, which could affect future patient compliance. Questionnaires are also a mechanism for the systematic recording of data that can facilitate clinical research and subsequent program evaluation.

Our intake questionnaire for use with chronic-pain patients consists of some 80 questions related to the presenting problem, previous treatments, and effects on daily functioning. Of the thousands of patients who have been asked to complete various versions of this questionnaire, virtually none have refused. However, given the initial defensiveness of many patients to seeing a psychologist, we have found it important to limit questionnaire items to variables related to sociodemographic features and the chief complaint, leaving broader psychological exploration to the interview.

Questionnaires can also be developed for significant others and health care providers. The form and content of the questionnaire will depend, of course, on the theoretical orientation of the clinician. Questions can be forced-choice, open ended, simple ratings, checklists, or pictorial in nature (e.g., pain maps). Clarity and ease of response are important features. However, the clinician must take care not to use questionnaire techniques in a fashion that would substitute for the development of a quality professional relationship with either the patient or the referral source.

Diaries

Patient diaries are commonly used to record behaviors, both overt (e.g., vomiting, tics, activity level, frequency of urination, medication use) and covert (e.g., thoughts, feelings, images, blood pressure, body temperature, pain intensity). They are used as baseline measures and as interventions to foster learning about antecedents, consequences, and the relationships among internal and external behaviors (i.e., to promote psychological and physiological insights). Diaries can be an important source of information in helping to assess medical treatment efficacy. For instance, when a patient is being considered for a spinal cord stimulator (SCS) implant to help with pain control, he or she typically undergoes a week-long trial period in which the SCS is used but not fully implanted, as well as psychological screening. As part of our overall screening protocol we have patients keep a pain–mood–medication–activity diary 2 weeks prior to the trial and during the 1-week trial period. The diary data can then be compared (pretrial and during the trial) to help determine whether to go ahead with permanent implantation. This type of data is much more powerful than simply completing the SCS trial and asking the patient whether it worked. Diaries are also used to measure the effectiveness of treatment programs. Although controversies abound about the reliability and validity of diary data, these methods continue to be clinically useful.

Diaries should be easy to use, brief, and nonintrusive. Training the recorder in their use is important. The use of mail-in forms and cues as reminders to record information can increase compliance. Note also that not all diaries are maintained by the patient. Medical charting and psychological-process notes are two examples of diaries that are maintained by staff.

Psychometrics

In general, two kinds of psychometric techniques are used in clinical health psychology: broadband and narrow-focus measures. The following lists include some of the most commonly used broadband and narrow-focus measures. One should be cautious in the application of any of these measures to clinical health psychology and should carefully evaluate their suitability for medical–surgical or dental patient populations and for the specific problems being addressed. For the major broadband measures we include the pros and cons for each measure as well as cautions in use. Information about these tests, with the exception of nonreferenced material in the pro and con sections—the authors' opinions—are from the material provided by the measures' publishers.

Broadband Measures

1. *Minnesota Multiphasic Personality Inventory—2* (MMPI–2; Butcher, Graham, Ben-Porath, Tellegen, & Dahlstrom, 1989, 2001). The original MMPI (Hathaway & McKinley, 1943) had several problems; thus, in 1982, the University of Minnesota Press initiated an extensive revision of the test. The MMPI revision for use with adults (MMPI–2) was published in 1989. Among other changes, the MMPI–2 includes a revision of item content, a restandardization based on contemporary norms, and new validity and clinical scales. To assure that practitioners would have a smooth transition to the new versions of the MMPI, a phase out period was implemented (originally planned to be 5 years). By 1998, over 95% of MMPI users had transitioned to the revised forms. However, a few psychologists held on to the original version or used a mixture of both the original and MMPI–2. The original MMPI was withdrawn from use by the test publisher as of September 1999 and is now considered obso-

lete. For a detailed review of the MMPI–2 development see the MMPI–2 manual (Butcher et al., 2001) and Pope, Butcher, and Seelen (2006). The MMPI–2 contains 567 true–false questions and is designed for individuals 18 years or older with a sixth-grade reading ability. The test publisher estimates that it takes 60 to 90 minutes to complete.

Pros. The MMPI–2 (similar to its predecessor) is the most widely used and researched personality inventory. As such, there is a wealth of research on the MMPI–2, including its use in clinical health psychology. The MMPI–2 contains what are likely the most sophisticated validity scales for detection of response sets. It provides a massive amount of information including 9 validity scales and 127 routinely scored clinical and subscales (according to the test publisher; however, many research scales are not commonly scored).

Cons. Several issues must be addressed when using the MMPI–2 with medical patients, as is commonly the case in clinical health psychology:

- The MMPI–2 was never standardized on a medical patient population and contains items that reflect both psychiatric disturbance and physical illness. Medical patients will often elevate certain scales as a result of endorsement of these physical items, and the test may tend to overpathologize this group. Therefore, the clinician must be acutely aware of appropriate interpretation strategies when using the MMPI–2 with medical patients, and it takes considerable experience to do so properly. Keeping current with research on MMPI–2 interpretation strategies for different medical populations and being aware of the problems with computer-generated MMPI–2 interpretations is essential.

- The MMPI–2 often takes much longer than 60 to 90 minutes to complete when administered to a medical patient. For instance, in our experience, a patient with chronic pain may need up to 4 hours to complete the test, and this is often divided into two testing sessions.

- Medical patients can be particularly sensitive to psychological assessment and may be offended by the MMPI–2 item content. The MMPI–2 was designed to assess psychopathology, and the questions reflect this purpose.

- Medical patients are often taking medications that can affect concentration. This can affect the results of the MMPI–2 testing, especially given its length. The medication issue also applies to all types of psychological testing.

2. *Battery for Health Improvement—2* (BHI–2; Bruns & Disorbio, 2003). The BHI–2 is a 217-item, self-report, multiple-choice instrument that takes 35 to 40 minutes to complete and is designed for the psychological assessment of adult medical patients (18 years or older with a sixth-grade reading ability). The purpose of the test is to provide relevant information and treatment recommendations to professionals who treat injured patients in a variety of settings, including physical rehabilitation, vocational rehabilitation, and general medicine. The BHI–2 has 18 scales organized into five domains: (a) Validity, (b) Physical Symptoms, (c) Affective, (d) Character, and (e) Psychosocial. The BHI–2 was designed for patients who are being evaluated or treated for an injury.

   Pros. Unlike many psychological tests that have been adapted for use with medical patients, the BHI–2 was designed specifically for this clinical population. As discussed in the manual, self-report psychological tests tend to overpathologize what might actually be normal or expected for the average medical or rehabilitation patient. Thus, traditional psychological tests must be used with caution and interpreted accordingly by a qualified individual. The BHI–2 attempts to overcome this problem in several ways: (a) The areas of assessment are those that are particularly useful in the evaluation and treatment of medical patients; (b) the questions have been phrased in a way that is more appropriate to medical patients, as compared with traditional psychological tests; (c) by psychological testing standards, the BHI–2 is relatively brief; and (d) the test was developed and normed using two standardization samples, a community sample and a national sample of physical rehabilitation patient. The test is scored using both normative groups.

   Cons. Unlike the MMPI–2 there is a paucity of research using the BHI–2, outside of that done by the authors during test development. As such, there is a lack of longitudinal research on predictive validity for answering questions related to treatment outcome with medical patient groups (e.g., spine or bariatric surgery outcome, pain rehabilitation programs). In addition, some dimensions of psychopathology are not assessed and its ability to identify psychiatric symptoms in a medical patient population is unknown. Also, the nonrandom sampling procedure used in the test development may have introduced some bias to the norms. The BHI–2 contains only two validity scales and these are not nearly as sophisticated as those on the MMPI–2.

3. *Millon Behavioral Medicine Diagnostic* (MBMD; Millon, Antoni, Millon, Meagher, & Grossman, 2001). The MBMD is an updated version of the Millon Behavioral Health Inventory. The MBMD is a 165-item, true–false, self-report instrument designed for the psychological assessment of adult medical patients (18 years or older, with a sixth-grade reading ability). The scales are grouped into domains: (a) Response Patterns (3 scales that help gauge distorted response tendencies in the patient's self-report), (b) Negative Health Habits (5 scales that help gauge recent or current problematic behaviors affecting health such as alcohol, drugs, eating, caffeine, inactivity, and smoking), (c) Psychiatric Indicators (5 scales that help identify psychiatric comorbidities that may affect health management such as anxiety, depression, cognitive dysfunction, emotional liability, and guardedness), (d) Coping Styles (11 scales that help identify patients' approaches to handling everyday problems, medical conditions, and major life stressors), (e) Stress Moderators (6 scales that help identify attitudes and resources that may affect health care), (f) Treatment Prognostics (5 scales that help predict problems with treatment), and (g) Management Guide (2 scales that help with treatment management).

Pros. The pros of the MBMD are similar to those of the BHI–2 and include (a) The areas of assessment are those that are particularly useful in the evaluation and treatment of medical patients; (b) the questions have been phrased in such a way to be more appropriate to medical patients as compared with traditional psychological tests; (c) compared with the MMPI–2, the MBMD is relatively brief; (d) the test now has a choice of two normative samples: (a) general medical norms include a sample of more than 700 patients with a wide variety of medical conditions and (b) bariatric norms based on 711 prescreened bariatric surgery patients.

Cons. The MBMD was designed for psychological assessment of general medical patients; as such, interpretive strategies for any specific patient population (e.g., chronic back pain, headache, adjustment to trauma, cancer) are unknown. From a psychometric standpoint, the MBMD was standardized on a nonrandom sample, community norms have never been developed, and there is a high level of item overlap on the scales. Similar to the BHI–2, and unlike the MMPI–2, not much research is available to guide the clinician in using the MBMD with a specific patient population.

4. *Symptom Checklist–90–Revised* (SCL-90-R; Derogatis, 1983). The SCL-90-R is a 90-item self-report measure in which each item is rated on a 5-point scale and takes about 12 to 15 minutes to complete. It is appropriate for use on individuals who are at least 13 years old and have a sixth-grade reading ability. The SCL-90-R yields nine primary symptom dimensions (e.g., Somatization, Depression, Anxiety, Psychoticism) and three global indices (Global Severity Index, Positive Symptom Distress Index, and Positive Symptom Total). The test was developed as a rapid screening tool for psychopathology and has been extensively researched. It has been standardized on various populations including adult nonpatients, adult psychiatric outpatients, adult psychiatric inpatients, and adolescent nonpatients.

Pros. The SCL-90-R is a brief measure that allows for rapid screening for psychopathology. Because it is a brief instrument, it is well tolerated by medical patients and is often used as a test–retest measure of response to treatment. It has been used extensively with medical patients in both clinical applications and research. The SCL-90-R contains three scales that provide a rapid measure of global psychological distress. The SCL-90-R yields standardized scores and has shown convergent validity with MMPI scales and cluster analytic findings.

Cons. The SCL-90-R was designed for use with psychiatric patients and was standardized on that patient population. The item content reflects assessment of psychopathology, and this may be objectionable to some medical patients. Medical patients may tend to artificially elevate scales that contain physical items (e.g., Somatization, Depression, Anxiety). Because the test was standardized on a psychiatric patient population it may tend to overpathologize medical patients. The SCL-90-R does not contain validity scales, is face valid, and results can easily manipulated by the patient.

5. *Millon Clinical Multiaxial Inventory—Third Edition* (MCMI–III; Millon, Davis, & Millon, 1997). The MCMI–III is a 175-item, true–false, self-report instrument that takes 25 to 30 minutes to complete and is designed to assess personality and psychopathology. The test is for patients 18 years or older with an eighth-grade reading ability. The MCMI–III conforms to the *Diagnostic and Statistical Manual of Mental Disorders, Fourth Edition* (*DSM–IV*; American Psychiatric Association, 1994) and is designed to assess *DSM–IV* related personality disorders (Axis I, II) and clinical syndromes. The scales are grouped into four domains: (a) Personality Disorder (11 moderate, 3 severe), (b) Clinical Syndrome (7 moderate, 3 severe), (c) Corrections (3 modifying, 1 validity), and (d) the Grossman Personality Facet (42 total). The test was developed and normed on adult psychiatric inpatient and outpatient samples and an inmate correctional sample.

Pros. The MCMI–III has a strong research and theoretical base and the scales are keyed to *DSM–IV* diagnostic criteria. It has demonstrated strength in helping with the differential diagnosis of personality disorders. It yields an extensive amount of information for a relatively brief instrument.

Cons. The cons of the MCMI–III are similar to those of the MMPI–2, including the fact that it was designed as a measure of psychopathology and not specifically for use with medical patients. As such, the items reflect the assessment of psychopathology. Also, the test has never been standardized on medical patients and may overpathologize this group, and there is a high level of item overlap resulting in highly interrelated scales. The ability of the MCMI–III to accurately assess personality disorders and psychopathology in a medical patient population is unknown. Unlike the MMPI–2, little research is available on the use of the MCMI–III with medical patients.

6. *Personality Assessment Inventory* (PAI; Morey, 1991). The PAI is a 344-item, self-report instrument that takes 50 to 60 minutes to complete. It is designed for patients 18 years or older with at least a fourth-

grade reading ability. Each item is rated on a 4-point scale (*false–very true*). It was designed to help with clinical diagnosis, treatment planning and screening for psychopathology. The PAI consists of 22 nonoverlapping full scales covering the constructs most relevant to a broad-based assessment of mental disorders: 4 validity scales, 11 clinical scales, 5 treatment scales, and 2 interpersonal scales. The PAI was developed as an alternative to the MMPI–2 for assessing abnormal personality traits. The PAI was standardized using 3 different samples: a census-matched normative sample of 1,000 community-dwelling adults, a sample of 1,265 patients from 69 clinical sites, and a college sample of 1,051 students.

Pros. The PAI provides a lot of information and is moderate in length compared with the MMPI–2. The PAI has shown decent reliability and validity. Unlike the MMPI–2 and the MCMI–III, the PAI contains nonoverlapping scales that enhance discriminate validity. It is relatively easy to use, score, and interpret.

Cons. The cons are similar to those outlined for other measures not specifically designed to assess medical patients. The PAI was designed as a measure of psychopathology and not specifically for use with medical patients. As such, the items reflect the assessment of psychopathology, and the test has never been standardized on medical patients and may overpathologize this group. The ability of the PAI to accurately assess personality disorders and psychopathology in a medical patient population is unknown. Unlike the MMPI–2, there is little research on the use of the PAI with medical patients.

More Narrowly Focused Measures

A number of more narrowly focused instruments used in the practice of clinical health psychology measure general psychological constructs, experiences, or symptoms.

1. *Beck Depression Inventory—2* (BDI–2; Beck, Steer, & Brown, 1996). The BDI–2 is the revised version of the BDI (Beck, 1972). The BDI–2 contains 21 items and is a measure of severity of self-rated depression. The BDI–2 was designed to resolve weaknesses in the BDI and to be more

consistent with the *DSM–IV*. The BDI–2 includes changes in questions about weight loss, changes in body image, and somatic preoccupation. Also, some of the items were changed because they also occurred frequently in those who were not depressed (sleep, appetite changes). In use with chronic pain patients, the BDI–2 has been found to have a two-factor structure: (a) negative cognitions about self and (b) changes in activity and mood (Poole, Bramwell, & Murphy, 2006). The authors suggest that two-factor scores may be most useful when the BDI–2 is used with chronic pain patients. These findings underscore the need to be aware when using psychiatric measures with medical populations.

2. *Center for Epidemiologic Studies Depression Scale* (Radloff, 1977). A self-report measure of depression designed for research in the general population.

3. *State–Trait Anxiety Inventory* (Spielberger, Gorsuch, & Lushene, 1970). A self-report measure of anxiety.

4. *State–Trait Anger Expression Inventory* (Spielberger, 1988). A self-report measure of both the experience and the expression of anger.

5. *Index of Activities of Daily Living* (Katz, Downs, Cash, & Grotz, 1970). A measure of independent functioning most useful for geriatric and institutionalized populations.

6. Measures of life events such as the *Schedule of Recent Experience* (Holmes & Rahe, 1967) and the *Life Experiences Survey* (Sarason, Johnson, & Siegel, 1978). The latter is a 57-item self-report measure that assesses stressful events in a person's life. Scores have been associated with onset of health problems.

7. *Cognitive Capacity Screening Exam* (J. Jacobs, Bernhard, Delgado, & Strain, 1977). A brief, scorable mental status questionnaire that is easily administered as a screening device.

8. MMS (Folstein et al., 1975). A method of grading the cognitive status of patients.

9. *Family Environment Scale* (Moos & Moos, 1981). An assessment of three domains of family environment: (a) quality of interpersonal relationships, (b) personal-growth goals, and (c) system maintenance factors.

10. *Work Environment Scale* (Moos, 1981). A measure of workplace interpersonal relationships, orientation, and work stress.

11. *Hassles and Uplifts Scale* (Kanner, Coyne, Schaefer, & La
    A life-events scale that focuses on minor hassles and posi

Health-Specific Measures

A number of health-specific measures have been developed that could prove useful, depending on the targets of assessment chosen:

1. *Jenkins Activity Survey* (Jenkins, Zyzanski, & Rosenman, 1979). A self-report measure of the Type A behavior pattern.
2. *Sickness Impact Profile* (Bergner, Bobbitt, Carter, & Gilson, 1981). A self-report measure of functional status and impact of sickness applicable to any disease or disability group.
3. *McGill Pain Questionnaire* (Melzack, 1975). A measure of perceived pain intensity and sensory, affective, and cognitive components of pain.
4. *Multidimensional Health Locus of Control* (Wallston, Wallston, & DeVellis, 1978). A measure of the extent to which patients see their health as attributable to fate, powerful others (e.g., physicians), or their own behavior.
5. *Psychosocial Adjustment to Illness Scale—Self-Report* (Derogatis & Lopez, 1983). A self-report measure of adjustment to illness.
6. *Eating Disorder Inventory—Third Edition* (EDI–3; Garner, 2004). This is a 91-item self-report measure that is the third edition of the EDI (Garner & Olmsted, 1984). The EDI–3 measures the severity of cognitive and behavioral characteristics associated with eating disorders.
7. *Cancer Inventory of Problem Situations* (Schag, Heinrich, Aadland, & Ganz, 1990). An inventory of problems commonly experienced by cancer patients.
8. *Multidimensional Pain Inventory* (Kerns, Turk, & Rudy, 1985). A 52-item self-report measure reflecting pain severity; interference with family, occupational, and recreational activities; appraisals of response from significant others; perceived life control; and affective distress.
9. *Survey of Pain Attitudes* (Jensen, Turner, Romano, & Lawler, 1994). A 52-item self-report measure measuring dimensions of pain beliefs including pain control, solicitude, medical cure, disability, medication, and emotion.

10. *Arthritis Self-Efficacy Scale* (Lorig, Chastain, Ung, Shoor, & Holman, 1989). A 20-item self-report measure assessing three factors of self-efficacy including (a) physical function, (b) controlling other arthritis symptoms, and (c) pain control. This test has been adapted for use in other chronic pain conditions.
11. *Cardiac Anxiety Questionnaire* (Eifert et al., 2000). This 18-item self-report measure assesses heart-focused anxiety in cardiology patients.
12. *Insomnia Severity Index* (Bastien, Vallieres, & Morin, 2001). This is a 7-item questionnaire that assesses sleep impairment.

Obviously these lists are not exhaustive. We cannot overemphasize the need for the clinical health psychologist to be aware of the reliability and validity issues specific to each measure and for each use. Failure to recognize limits of interpretation of test results is contrary not only to good clinical practice but also to ethical standards.

Observation

Observation of the patient is one of the most fundamental methods of assessment and can provide the clinician with information applicable to many of the target areas described in our model. Observation can be unstructured or highly structured. For example, it can occur as part of a general clinical interview or in a more naturalistic setting (e.g., a treatment setting involving interactions with nursing staff or response to medical procedures such as burn debridement). Structured observations can include tasks such as role-playing interactions with family, employer, or physician, as well as in vivo experiences such as observing cold stress challenges for patients with Raynaud's disease and self-administration of insulin by the patient with diabetes. Observations can be made directly by the clinician, by family members, or by health care providers. Furthermore, these observations can be recorded by audiotape or videotape. Because this is an obviously reactive measure, the influence of the measurement process on data obtained must be considered in the interpretation.

Observations can be quantified through rating methods (e.g., Clinician-Administered Posttraumatic Stress Disorder Scale [CAPS], Blake et al.,

1995; Hamilton Anxiety Scale, Hamilton, 1959), content analyses (e.g., somatic focus), or frequency scores (e.g., pill counts to determine compliance), among other methods. The clinician can also collect impressions in an effort to generate hypotheses for more precise testing. It is especially useful to compare direct observation of behavior with others' perceptions of the behavior or to the patient's own perception of his or her behavior (e.g., the demanding patient). Reasons for the lack of correlation could be clinically meaningful and thus help target areas for intervention.

Psychophysiological Measures

Psychophysiology refers to the "scientific study by nonsurgical means of the interrelationships between psychological processes and physiological systems in humans" (Cacioppo, Petty, & Marshall-Goodell, 1985, p. 264). Psychophysiological measures are designed to provide information about biologic events (e.g., heart rate) or the consequences of biologic events (e.g., skin temperature). They can also be used to provide feedback to the person and thus serve as psychological interventions (e.g., biofeedback). Generally, the biological events of most interest to the clinical health psychologist include muscle tension, skin temperature, blood pressure, heart rate, and respiratory activity. Parameters of interest include average resting levels, within-subject variability, and response of the measure to differing conditions (e.g., stress, relaxation, resting, imagery, specified activities).

Psychophysiological profiling (also termed *stress profiling*) is often done as part of the initial evaluation in biofeedback treatment (see Arena & Schwartz, 2005, for a review). Stress profiling starts with baseline measures, during which time the patient is at rest. After the baseline evaluation, the patient is then subjected to different kinds of stressors while a number of psychophysiological measures are monitored. After each stressor is presented, a recovery period is allowed. The goal of the psychophysiological profiling is to identify stressors that produce stronger physical reactions (e.g., increased heart rate, muscle tension, respiration). The pattern of response to the stressors can help to design the biofeedback interventions. Examples of stressors might include presenting aversive imagery related to an injury experience, imagery of situations that aggravate pain, or high-pressure situations in which an athlete performs poorly. Beyond imagery, profiling might include having a patient with back pain assume certain painful positions and assessing the physical response (e.g., muscle tension in the paraspinals with prolonged sittings).

To undertake psychophysiological measurements, the clinician needs to have expertise in, among other things, bioelectric and physiological processes, instrumentation and recording techniques, signal-processing methods, as well as potential artifacts and confounds. We believe that advances in telemetric and ambulatory monitoring will increase the ecological validity of these kinds of measures, with a subsequent increase in clinical usage in the future.

Archival Data

Literature reviews of diseases including cause, symptoms, course, prevention, treatment, and psychological components can provide archival data that are useful in the assessment process. Reviews of previous medical and psychiatric charts are valuable sources of information for the clinical health psychologist. Although these records are not always easily obtained, the clinician will find the information contained within them most useful in providing a historical perspective of the patient, his or her problem, and aspects of help-seeking behavior.

It might also be necessary to consult archival data when assessing the potential effects of various environmental variables on the problem, such as the health care system and the sociocultural environment. Hospital policies, insurance coverage, legislation relating to disability, laws regulating the practice of health care provision, and employers' policies need to be understood to develop an adequate conceptualization for intervention.

Other Methods

A number of other methods of assessment available to the clinical health psychologist could prove useful under specified conditions. For example, pedometers might provide fruitful information about activity level and thus be especially useful in treating problems such as chronic low-back pain. Spirometric measures of pulmonary functioning can be used as dependent measures in work with asthmatics. Smoking behavior may be measured by thiocyanate levels in blood serum, urine, and saliva. Skin fold thickness, as an indirect measure of body fat, might be useful in dealing with problems of obesity. Sleep electroencephalograms are useful in assessing sleep disorders. Body weight can be a useful measure of compliance to dietary restrictions in hemodialysis patients. Measures of the endocrine system and immunologic assays are also sometimes used. The uniqueness of the problem and the creativity of the professional will aid in identifying other methods of assessment that might be useful.

ACHIEVING THE GOALS OF ASSESSMENT: UNDERSTANDING THE PATIENT

At the end of the assessment process, the clinician will have an understanding of (a) the patient in his or her physical and social environment, (b) the patient's relevant strengths and weaknesses, (c) the evidence for psychopathology, (d) the nature of the disease and treatment regimen, and (e) the coping skills being used.

After integrating relevant information, the clinician should be able to answer the seven questions listed here. These questions were derived from Moos (1977), who delineated these areas as the major adaptive tasks for any patient with a medical illness. The relative importance of answers to each question in determining the overall status of the patient will vary, depending on the understandings developed through assessment of the previously mentioned targets.

1. How is the patient dealing with pain, incapacitation, and other symptoms?
2. How is the patient dealing with the hospital environment and the special treatment procedures?
3. Is the patient developing and maintaining adequate relationships with health care staff?
4. Is the patient preserving a reasonable emotional balance?

5. Is the patient preserving a satisfactory self-image and maintaining a sense of competence and mastery?
6. Is the patient preserving relationships with family and friends?
7. How is the patient preparing for an uncertain future?

In conclusion, the purpose of the clinical health psychology assessment is to understand the patient and his or her problem so as to arrive at a treatment strategy or a management decision. One need not be wedded to a particular theory or assessment strategy; indeed, flexibility in this regard is, in our opinion, an asset. However, we do attempt to adhere to the biopsychosocial conceptual framework. In the next chapter we address issues associated with psychological interventions in clinical health psychology.

SUGGESTED READINGS

Cacioppo, J. T., Tassinary, L. G., & Berntson, G. (Eds.). (2007). *Handbook of psychophysiology* (3rd ed.). New York: Cambridge University Press.

Landrine, H., & Klonoff, E. A. (2001). Cultural diversity and health psychology. In A. Baum, T. A. Revenson, & J. E. Singer (Eds.), *Handbook of health psychology* (pp. 851–891), Mahwah, NJ: Erlbaum.

Linton, J. C. (2004). Psychological assessment in primary care. In L. J. Haas (Ed.), *Handbook of primary care psychology* (pp. 35–45). New York: Oxford University Press.

Rozensky, R. H., Sweet, J. J., & Tovian, S. M. (1997). *Psychological assessment in medical settings.* New York: Plenum Press.

Trzepacz, P. T., & Baker, R. W. (1993). *The psychiatric mental status examination.* New York: Oxford University Press.

Vingerhoets, A. (Ed.). (2001). *Assessment in behavioral medicine.* New York: Taylor & Francis.

4

Intervention Strategies
in Clinical Health Psychology

In chapter 3, we presented our framework for applying the biopsychosocial model to the assessment process in clinical health psychology. At the end of that process, the clinician should be aware of patient problem areas, related environmental contributors, and the variety of resources available. The next step, then, is to translate these findings into some plan of intervention. Clinical health psychology intervention can also be conceptualized by our framework, although the focus changes from a historical and developmental one to a focus on the present and future. This chapter addresses our model for intervention, with a brief description of relevant strategies and a focus on issues in selecting an appropriate method.

Many of the targets of assessment described in Table 3.1 can also become targets for intervention. As we discussed previously, intervention for any one target can affect functioning and interventions in others. We discuss this issue further, after we present a general outline of each domain of intervention.

PATIENT TARGETS

At the level of the individual patient, the clinician can attempt intervention in biological, affective, cognitive, or behavioral domains.

Biological Domain

Treatment strategies in this domain are designed to directly change actual physiological responses involved in the disorder. Examples include biofeedback for fecal incontinence and relaxation for hypertension. One can also intervene in an attempt to control specific symptoms associated with the disease or its treatment (e.g., hypnosis for pain control, desensitization for anticipatory nausea associated with chemotherapy).

Of course, medical interventions have a primary focus in this domain, and their interactive effects with simultaneous psychophysiological treatment must be addressed or monitored (e.g., shifting insulin needs during relaxation training, use of muscle relaxants during biofeedback training).

Affective Domain

In the affective domain, one might focus on such emotional states as anxiety, depression, or hostility. For instance, the clinician could provide such interventions as stress inoculation to decrease anxiety about an upcoming medical procedure, cognitive behavior treatment for depression, and anger management for Type A behavior pattern.

Cognitive Domain

Interventions in this domain involve providing information in a psychoeducational approach or changing the manner in which a patient conceptualizes a problem. As examples, one might maximize placebo effects of medical or psychological treatments, provide sensory and procedural information about upcoming diagnostic procedures, challenge unrealistic expectations about sexual activity after penile prosthesis surgery, and use existential psychotherapy to facilitate the development of a philosophy of life in keeping with adaptive coping.

Behavioral Domain

Treatment in this area includes changing the patient's overt behaviors and involves using principles of operant and social learning theory. Thus, the clinician might design a self-monitoring program to enhance compliance with hypertension medication, to teach assertion skills to facilitate communication with the patient's physician, to develop a behavior-change program to modify behavioral health risk factors (e.g., smoking, weight), as well as train the patient in self-management skills (e.g., insulin injections, stoma care).

ENVIRONMENTAL TARGETS

Targets need not be patient focused, however, because the clinician could decide that an environmental intervention is either necessary for change or easier to accomplish. Once again, the environmental units include (a) the family, (b) the health care system, and (c) the sociocultural context. Intervention within each unit might target physical, affective, cognitive, or behavioral domains, as defined previously.

Family

Interventions aimed at the physical aspects of the family environment include redesign of the living space in accordance with patient limitations (e.g., a specified order of spices in the cabinet for the housekeeper who is visually impaired) and referrals to social agencies for financial resources. In the affective realm, the clinician could use supportive therapy to help family members deal with anxiety about the patient's illness. In the cognitive arena, the clinician could facilitate more realistic expectations through the provision of accurate information or use family therapy to work through potential misattributions of the cause of the patient's illness.

In terms of family members' behavior, it might be necessary to train individuals to give appropriate emotional support or to develop a contingency management program, so that the family behavior does not unwittingly reinforce unnecessary sick-role behavior.

Health Care System

The health care system is a frequent target of intervention. One of the most important aspects is the physical domain within which services are provided. Interventions can be as simple as suggestions to increase the orientation of patients in the intensive care unit through the use of time prompts or the orientation of patients who are chronically ill through the posting of calendars.

Privacy is important to patients but is often neglected in the health care system. We are aware of a radiation therapy waiting room that is situated in a busy hallway, where patients with disfigured appearances often sit uncomfortably, subjected to the stares or grimaces of hospital visitors. Environmental design that is sensitive to, and respectful of, patient needs can produce a more relaxing, less anxiety-provoking atmosphere; thus, music, ceiling art, and bubbling fish tanks are increasingly used in many waiting and treatment rooms.

The clinical health psychologist working within an institutional context often needs to adopt an advocacy role to bring about these kinds of health care system interventions. Many of the physical environment manipulations are not costly or difficult to implement.

In the affective domain of the health care system, the clinician might also need to work with medical and nursing staff concerning their feelings about a specific patient, to facilitate a therapeutic relationship between caregivers and patient. An example of this is reframing demanding patient behavior as an attempt to exert control in the face of enforced, threatening dependency. In our experience, it is not uncommon for staff to express angry feelings toward a patient in a passive–aggressive manner that tends to foster retaliatory acting out in the patient. This, of course, sets up a cyclical behavior pattern that can become severe if it is not interrupted.

In the cognitive domain, clinical health psychologists continually find themselves in the role of teacher, because in most interactions they attempt to increase the knowledge of other health care providers about the psychological aspects of health, illness, and patient care. This education also involves dispelling myths and providing correct information about various psychological disorders that present as part of, or simultaneously with, a medical problem.

We suggest that the majority of communications back to referral sources include explicit recommendations about how the health care provider's own behavior could facilitate the treatment of the patient. Sample interventions aimed at the behavior of health care providers include instructions to (a) increase attention for well behavior; (b) provide medication on a fixed interval rather than on an as-needed basis for patients with chronic pain; (c) unify the source of communications to the patient regarding prognosis and care; (d) check for patient understanding of treatment instructions; and (e) train the patient in self-care when possible, even when hospitalized, to maximize a sense of mastery and self-control. Advocacy for progressive health care policies is often warranted (e.g., development of interdisciplinary teams).

Sociocultural Context

Often, only certain aspects of the sociocultural context are available for immediate intervention because other features require interventions outside the control of any individual clinician. It is possible to intervene in the patient's social network and thus use its resources to his or her benefit. We have counseled friends of patients on ways to facilitate coping in patients and have given them information about the grieving process, which enhanced their understanding and ability to support the patient. We have also worked with employers in designing a gradual return to work and resumption of activity for the patient recovering from a serious illness or learning to live with a chronic pain problem. An interesting aside is that we are aware of one major health care system that does not permit its own employees to return to work gradually. Instead, the employee must be released to return to 100% functioning if he or she is to be reinstated, a frequently doomed approach in terms of the principles of rehabilitation.

Other aspects of the sociocultural environment involve long-term interventions by clinical health psychologists and are perhaps as important when considering the future quality of patient care. Such interventions include the following: (a) contributing to the body of knowledge about effective diagnostic and treatment strategies through clinical research (the foundation for the future of the field), (b) serving as volunteers with public information groups to defuse myths and stereotypes, (c) working toward behavioral health legislation (e.g., controls on smoking in the workplace, mandatory helmet laws), and (d) participating in governmental policy-making regarding health care reform.

CHOOSING INTERVENTIONS

When choosing an intervention, one must take into account the effects of any given intervention on other targets, the appropriateness of the goals for intervention, issues of patient and staff cooperation, and cost–benefit issues.

Interrelationships of Interventions

Just as information obtained about one target of assessment can influence the interpretation of information about another, so can interventions affect targets in other areas. Interventions aimed at one target can have positive or negative effects on other areas of functioning or ongoing treatments. For instance, in the positive realm, a patient who is treated for chronic headaches with relaxation and biofeedback approaches might experience less need for pain medication, less depression, an improvement in family relationships, and an increase in activity level. Thus, a positive adaptive cycle of improvement has been initiated by treatment aimed primarily at the headache problem.

However, one must be particularly concerned about negative effects that any area of intervention might have on other areas. For example, let us assume that the initial decision is made to increase self-management skills (e.g., self-catheterization) to promote more independent functioning. Success in this endeavor is likely to bring with it an increased sense of control over bodily functions, which is usually associated with a reduction in anxiety and a decrease in autonomic nervous system arousal. However, self-catheterization can also be associated with an increase in family members' fears because a professional is no longer performing the technique. Or family members might be repulsed by the nature of the procedure occurring at home and subsequently discourage the patient's attempts. We are aware of one patient in whom self-catheterization training that involved using mirrors triggered old memories of sexual abuse and resulted in subsequent phobic responses and increased emotional distress.

In another example, helping a patient with chronic pain manage his or her pain more successfully and become more active can result in changes that affect the family system. In many cases, the sick role of the patient with chronic pain is actually maintained, in part, by operant influences of the family (e.g., attention to pain behavior, distracting the family from other issues). We have witnessed countless instances in which improvement in a patient with chronic pain has been met with a dramatic increase in family relationship dysfunction. Inattention to these interrelationships and their potential effects when designing an intervention program can result in treatment failures, unexpected negative side effects, or, at best, short-lived success. In our experience, it is extremely rare that the clinician can focus solely on a single target for intervention.

In summary, a primary factor in choosing a target is the understanding of its interrelationships with other blocks in the model. This understanding is obtained through knowledge of the specific problem area, the empirical bases of the various interventions available, and a firm grounding in the clinical process of behavior change.

Appropriateness of Goals

Another aspect to consider when designing interventions is the determination of a realistic and attainable goal for treatment. This involves taking into account the likelihood that the targeted goal is amenable to treatment within the current situation. For example, the care-seeking behavior of patients with Munchausen syndrome and patients undergoing polysurgical procedures is notoriously unresponsive to short-term psychological interventions. These patients also tend to elicit anger on the part of health care providers. Thus, it is sometimes wiser to target interventions toward preventing inappropriate acting out by staff, thereby protecting the patient from unnecessary medical procedures, rather than treating the psychological issues related to the help-seeking behavior itself, with appropriate referrals for subsequent care, of course.

It is important to explicitly specify the target or targets of intervention and to operationalize them to permit evaluation of change (e.g., "take medication three times per day with meals" vs. "improve compliance"). Clear articulation regarding the targets for intervention is also critical to obtaining informed consent for treatment. For example, we once saw a young woman in an orthopedic ward who, subsequent to a bicycle accident, had both legs in traction. She was not eating sufficiently to permit bone mending, and she engaged in constant conflicts with nursing staff about her eating behavior. Psychological evaluation revealed the presence of an eating disorder that the patient denied and for which she refused treatment. However, she did consent to a focused treatment goal of obtaining sufficient nutrients to permit bone growth.

Related to the issue of appropriate goal setting is the importance of understanding whether the goal of intervention is a cure or the facilitation of coping. A cure is not unreasonable to expect in some areas, but much of what we do in clinical practice is done to promote coping. The clinician needs to maintain a delicate balance between hope and positive expectations, which can facilitate treatment, and the reality of the situation, which could suggest a poor prognosis.

Cooperation of the Patient and Staff

The choice of a particular intervention often depends heavily on the cooperation of patient, staff, or both, and its feasibility in ameliorating the current problem. One can spend hours designing a powerful treatment program that depends on the staff executing various components, only to have it fail miserably when an uncooperative (or already over-burdened) staff must execute it. We are reminded of a situation in which a relatively straightforward behavioral program was designed to address the acting-out behavior of a girl with a closed-head injury. Theoretically, the program should have worked, but inconsistent application by the staff, lack of commitment, and communication problems ensured its failure.

When designing an intervention that requires staff involvement, one must take into account such things as their willingness and ability to participate, the simplicity and ease of treatment administration, and the potential for sabotage or misapplication. Educating the staff about the treatment and giving them an understandable rationale for its implementation are especially important.

Cost–Benefit Analysis

As discussed before, in deciding among intervention strategies in clinical health psychology, one must consider not only the information obtained during the assessment process (review Table 3.1) but also aspects of the intervention strategies themselves, specifically their costs and anticipated benefits. The clinician should consider issues of treatment efficacy, efficiency, durability, generality, convenience, cost, side effects, and clinician competence.

First, the clinical health psychologist needs to understand how effective the treatment strategy is, in terms of absolute change in the target of intervention. There is no substitute for having a current knowledge of the empirical bases for psychological interventions. For example, relaxation training has been shown to have effects on immune function, but the sustained nature of these effects and their significance in influencing resistance to disease have not been sufficiently documented. Thus, offering relaxation training as a primary intervention in immune functioning might not be warranted. However, it could be offered as a means of enhancing control over some symptoms, increasing tolerance for others, decreasing anxiety and suffering, and so forth, depending on relevant findings in clinical research.

In general, the clinician should address the following questions in the decision-making process:

1. How efficient is the intervention in terms of time involved and effort expended?
2. For how long are the results expected to last?
3. What percentage of patients with similar problems can be expected to respond using the intervention?
4. How convenient or inconvenient to the patient and to his or her environment (including the therapist) is the treatment?
5. What is the cost of the intervention?
6. What are the side effects of the particular strategies or the program to be used?
7. How competent am I in using the particular intervention strategy?
8. How does this intervention interface with the patient's values?

This type of self-questioning can help in the process of deciding among several alternative intervention possibilities, and help to promote evidence-based practice in psychology (EBPP). It is important to note that the American Psychological Association's (APA's) policy that EBPP "is the integration of the best available research with clinical expertise in the context of patient characteristics, culture, and preferences" (APA, 2006, p. 273) is consistent with the definition adapted from earlier work by Sackett, Straus, Richardson, Rosenberg, and Haynes (2000) and promulgated in Institute of Medicine reports such as *Crossing the Quality Chasm* (Institute of Medicine, 2001b). The current emphasis on evidence-based practice in health care is not likely to dissipate and is already finding expression in legislative language and private health care policies. When Cynthia D. Belar conducted a workshop with Frank Collins on training in evidence-based behavioral medicine at the Society of Behavioral Medicine in 2003 (Belar & Collins, 2003), we became more aware of the myths surrounding this approach and addressed them in Collins, Leffingwell, and Belar (2007). To help practitioners, Davidson, Trudeau, Ockene, Orleans, and Kaplan (2004) examined the currently available review systems and their implications for behavioral medicine. In general, there has been increased attention to the need to facilitate the translation from science to practice. At a minimum, the practitioner should be aware of the following resources: Agency for Health Care Policy and Research (http://www.ahrq.gov), Cochrane Collaboration (http://www.cochrane.org), Centre for Evidence-Based Medicine (http://www.cebm.utoronto.ca), and Society of Behavioral Medicine Committee on Evidence-Based Behavioral Medicine (http://www.sbm.org).

INTERVENTION STRATEGIES

In selecting a particular intervention strategy, we encourage flexibility, without rigid adherence to any one or two individual strategies. Historically, the development of psychological interventions for medical–surgical patients has moved from general, broadband techniques to those methods designed to address more narrowly and specifically defined targets. We follow this format in describing the more commonly used therapeutic intervention strategies in the practice of clinical health psychology, giving examples of use and providing references for further study of the method.

Although the following techniques are discussed in a unitary fashion, we recognize that in actual practice many of these procedures are used in combination. In fact, the empirical support for some procedures has been established only within the context of a multistrategy treatment program. For this reason, rather than provide evidence of the empirical basis for each strategy in the brief description that follows, we provide suggested readings for further study of the research relevant to common problem areas in clinical health psychology (see the end of this chapter).

Placebo

The *placebo effect* might be the simplest behavioral change procedure in common use (Guess, Kleinman, Kusek, & Engel, 2002). It refers to changes in behavior that occur because of the patient's expectations and faith that a particular treatment will produce the desired change, and is thus described as "nonspecific." It can influence all patient and family target domains and is undoubtedly a part of all health care interventions. The placebo effect has been found in response to such varied things as inert tablets, the physician's costume (i.e., white coat, stethoscope), physician manner, (e.g., enthusiastic, not enthusiastic), professional style (e.g., therapeutic, experimental), language, and sham surgery (see Moerman & Jonas, 2002, for a review). In many cases, the placebo effect actually causes physical changes. For instance, Beneditti and Amanzio (1997) found that placebo analgesia results in the production of endogenous opiates and that the placebo analgesic response can be reversed with naloxone (an opiate antagonist) and enhanced with proglumide (an opiate agonist). Moerman and Jonas (2002) presented an interesting alternative perspective that conceptualizes the placebo effect as better understood as a *meaning response* (the power of the response lies in the meaning that the patient applies to the situation). There has been a renewed interest in the placebo effect, and there are several excellent reviews of the literature (Evans, 2004; Guess et al., 2002; Harrington, 1999).

Supportive Counseling

Physicians have historically attempted to support patients by reassuring them regarding illness and treatment procedures. Prokop and Bradley (1981) used the term *psychological support* to define this rather vague form of psychotherapeutic intervention directed toward amelioration of the patient's psychological distress. This type of treatment can involve individual or family meetings or consist of organized support groups (Frank, McDaniel, Bray, & Heldring, 2004). Furthermore, supportive psychotherapy can be clinician based or network based, depending on the nature of the problem and the availability of community resources. Other health care providers, paraprofessionals, and family members can be trained to provide supportive counseling and thus become valuable resources to the practicing psychologist.

Individual and Family Approaches

These types of interventions are generally based on a short-term treatment model and focus on helping the patient and family cope successfully with psychologically threatening information or procedures (McDaniel & Hepworth, 2004). This can be done by encouraging active participation in medical decisions, establishing a good patient–therapist relationship, and assuring the patient that feelings of anxiety or depression are normal. The clinician should never underestimate the power of a pat on the back or a squeeze of the hand, procedures unlikely to be practiced in traditional clinical psychology. Note, however, that these behaviors might be construed as offensive by patients in some ethnic groups.

Support Groups

Group discussion typically allows an opportunity for patients with similar illnesses or problems to meet with one another to discuss their concerns, anxieties, and coping strategies, as well as to obtain information. Examples include preparation-for-childbirth groups, postmastectomy groups, arthritis self-help groups, and groups for patients with AIDS and their families. Such groups can have a designated leader or be leaderless, and they typically meet on a hospital ward or in an outpatient clinic. A wide range of local and national associations relevant to specific disease populations can provide information about such groups in the community (see Appendix C). Local newspapers often publish listings of available support groups.

Because the clinical health psychologist frequently uses active approaches to treatment, the clinician might feel that supportive therapy is not "real therapy." However, it is important to remember that insufficient support has been related to increased risk of morbidity and mortality in general (House, Landis, & Umberson, 1988; Pilisuk, Boylan, & Acredolo, 1987) as well as to specific medical conditions such as cardiac events (Kop, 2005; Mookadam & Arthur, 2004) and cancer (Tibbs & Tarr, 2004). There are many patients with significant deficits in social support systems, and this can be a critical area of clinical health psychology treatment.

Education and Information

In clinical health psychology treatment, education about the biopsychosocial model and its specific application to the patient and his or her problem is an essential ingredient. In addition, provision of information is necessary to obtain informed consent for any treatment and to ensure compliance with medical regimens. Information is fundamental to the entire field of health education with which clinical health psychologists often interact.

Information has also been used as a specific intervention to promote coping with stressful medical procedures. There are two types of information: procedural and sensory. *Procedural* refers to information about aspects of the medical procedure itself, and *sensory* refers to information regarding sensations the patient might feel during or after the procedure. Although sensory information appears to be a more important aspect of preparation, interactions among kind of information, individual coping styles, and level of initial anxiety have been found. The belief that more is better is naive. For instance, it has been found that patients can be classified as *information seekers* or *information avoiders* (Deardorff & Reeves, 1997; S. M. Miller, 1992). If information avoiders are overwhelmed with detailed information about a medical procedure, they are likely to do worse. Furthermore, Shelley and Pakenham (2007) found that if patients' levels of health locus of control and self-efficacy will affect their response to preparations for a medical procedures intervention. To practice effectively, the clinician must have a strong knowledge of this literature. (For reviews see Contrada, Leventhal, & Anderson, 1994; Deardorff & Reeves, 1997; Johnston & Vogele, 1993.)

Verbal Psychotherapy

There are a variety of approaches to verbal psychotherapy (e.g., analytic, cognitive behavior, rational–emotive, directive, systems-oriented), some of which are discussed in this chapter. Psychotherapy can be symptom specific, general in focus, or a combination of both. It has been shown to reduce medical utilization (Chiles, Lambert, & Hatch, 2002), enhance overall outcome to surgery (Deardorff & Reeves, 1997), enhance coping after myocardial infarction (Mookadam & Arthur, 2004), and to have a number of other positive influences on medical care (Wedding & Mengel, 2004). Psychotherapy can occur in individual or group formats. Belar (1991) and Gentry and Owens (1986) described several types of behavioral medicine groups.

Issues of patient resources and current trends in health reform require that clinical health psychologists be familiar with the practice of brief psychotherapies. There are several excellent references for this work, such as Antony and Barlow (2002); Austad and Berman (1991); Budman and Gurman (1988); Budman, Hoyt, and Friedman (1992); Garfield (1998); Hersen and Biaggio (2000); and Nathan and Gorman (2002). Many of the cognitive behavior therapies for specific disorders (e.g., pain management, eating disorders, posttraumatic stress disorder) are by nature brief and highly structured interventions.

Crisis Intervention

Life events that overwhelm the patient's ability to cope or those that reinstate earlier conflicts are apt to create crisis situations. In the practice of clinical health psychology, the psychologist is likely to face a sizable percentage of patients whose lives are in crisis. Often these crises are centered on personal or professional losses from illness or death of a family member. However, the actual crisis is not necessarily related to health issues and could be caused by any number of developmental or accidental events. Whatever the precipitating event, the psychologist needs to understand crisis intervention as a therapeutic technique and be aware of the immediate goals of crisis counseling.

Korchin (1976, p. 507) listed three primary goals of crisis intervention: (a) to relieve the patient's present psychological distress (e.g., anxiety, hopelessness, confusion), (b) to restore the patient to his or her previous level of functioning, and (c) to help the patient and significant others learn what personal actions and community resources are available. In practice, these goals are accomplished by acknowledging the patient's thoughts, feelings, and behaviors; helping the patient to stay focused on the problem by exploring alternative explanations and solutions; emphasizing the patient's strengths in coping with previous life events; mobilizing additional resources; and providing information and advice, as appropriate. In working with problems of grief, it is important not to build the patient's defenses too quickly because doing so might result in a longer term maladaptive grief reaction.

Crisis intervention for the clinical health psychologist often involves working with family members, significant others, and health care providers as well as the patient. Medically related crises are addressed in Datilio and Freeman (2007).

Relaxation-Training Procedures

Perhaps the most well-researched clinical health psychology intervention strategy is relaxation training. The literature is replete with studies documenting its usefulness in the treatment of hypertension, tension and migraine headache, insomnia, irritable bowel syndrome, Raynaud's disease, pain tolerance, preparation for stressful medical procedures, and nausea (see Boll, Johnson, Perry, & Rozensky, 2002; L. M. Cohen, McChargue, & Collins, 2003, for reviews.). For many years this training has been considered the aspirin of behavioral medicine (Russo, Bird, & Masek, 1980),

ard pressed to conceive of a practicing clinical health psy-
o does not have expertise in several of the techniques we
aiscuss, all of which have as their goal the reduction of physiological
arousal. Although relaxation strategies were originally proposed as interventions in the physiological state of the patient, their effects in affective
and cognitive domains are well documented, as they decrease subjective
anxiety and enhance a sense of mastery and competence in the patient.
Relaxation strategies have in common that they are all easily learned
and administered by the clinician. The procedures we discuss are diaphragmatic breathing, progressive muscle relaxation, and autogenic relaxation
training

When considering the relaxation therapies, it is important to note
that, similar to aspirin, they have sometimes been used indiscriminately
with the naive notion that they are good for everyone and everything.
Any technique that has such potential benefit must also be assumed to
have the potential for harm. Although there is insufficient attention in
the psychological literature to negative side effects, relaxation training
and related procedures have been noted to produce increased anxiety,
shifting insulin needs, diabetic instability, hypotension in the elderly, and
flooding of intrusive thoughts and impulses (see Heide & Borkovec,
1984; Sakairi, 2004; Seeburg & DeBoer, 1980). Careful pretreatment
evaluation, proper monitoring, and appropriate modification of procedures
are critical to good practice. The reader is referred to the following references for training instructions, transcripts of various relaxation techniques,
and related discussions: D. A. Bernstein, Borkovec, and Hazlett-Stevens
(2000); Davis, McKay, and Eshelman (2000); Linden (1991); Poppen (1998);
J. C. Smith (1999); and Turk, Meichenbaum, and Genest (1983). Poppen
provides an especially good discussion, with guidelines for assessment of
relaxation in the patient.

Diaphragmatic Breathing

Diaphragmatic breathing is perhaps the simplest form of relaxation exercise. Although frequently used before beginning a more in-depth relaxation exercise, this technique is also commonly used by itself to extinguish
a conditioned response to a stressor. Fried (1993) provided a systematic

review of respiratory psychophysiology, with a focus on the role o in health and illness.

Progressive Muscle Relaxation

Progressive muscle relaxation (PMR) is based on the principle that relaxation (i.e., having relaxed muscles) has physiological accompaniments opposite those of anxiety (i.e., physiological tension). Jacobson (1939) developed his technique by teaching patients to intentionally tense, and then relax, various muscle groups. Patients could thereby familiarize themselves with the sometimes subtle distinction between relaxed and tense states—a form of discrimination learning. Variations use different muscle groupings in the training process. This particular procedure is widely used in the practice of clinical health psychology and is particularly useful for those patients who are unaware of their levels of body tension (see D. A. Bernstein et al., 2000, for recent applications). The following example demonstrates the usefulness of PMR in training a patient to relax her neck muscles during conversation.

> Mrs. N. was a 39-year-old woman who experienced muscle tension in her neck with accompanying strained, raspy speech. She entered psychological treatment to learn to decrease the neck cramps she experienced at the end of each workday and to improve the quality of her speech. Mrs. N. was initially trained in basic PMR exercises. After several sessions of total-body relaxation training, she was instructed to specifically focus her attention on the muscles in her neck and throat. After several additional relaxation-training sessions, Mrs. N. developed awareness of tension cues that signaled to her the need to relax before the tension became problematic. Through increased sensitivity to physiological processes, she became better able to control her levels of throat and neck tension, and subsequent neck cramping. The quality of her speech also improved.

Although most patients are capable of tensing and relaxing various muscle groups, it might be necessary for the clinician to slightly modify standard procedures to accommodate certain types of patients: those with chronic low-back pain or spinal fusions, with paraplegia or quadriplegia, or with arthritis or limited mobility.

Autogenic Relaxation Training

Autogenic training (Schultz & Luthe, 1969) can create a deep state of relaxation through the use of positive self-statements suggesting such sensations as warmth, heaviness, and calmness in various body parts. Stetter and Kupper (2002) provided a meta-analysis of clinical outcome studies. We have used autogenic training with many patients, especially those with musculoskeletal problems in which tensing muscles might not be advised.

> Ms. O. was anxious about an impending gynecologic examination designed to determine the cause of her infertility. She had a history of becoming so upset during even routine pelvic examinations that she subsequently missed work, needing a day to recover from her trauma. Ms. O. was trained in autogenic relaxation techniques that she would be able to use while lying quietly during the exam. In addition, a number of preparatory procedures, including guided imagery and coping self-statements, were used. The patient used the autogenic phrases throughout the procedure and coped successfully without incident.

Imagery

Imagery makes use of the private inner world of the patient through created images, imagination, and focused awareness. The use of imagery may be directed at general relaxation and anxiety reduction, symptom treatment, and behavioral change. A review of the use of imagery in psychotherapy is provided by Singer (2006).

Imagery is an ideal relaxation and symptom-reduction treatment for many patients because it does not require active movement or special equipment. However, the successful use of these techniques also requires a moderate ability to concentrate for a sustained period of time and the ability to implement a certain degree of fantasy. Some patients report that they are not good imagers, but this is a skill in which one can be trained. However, patients who are rigidly controlled or who lack adequate reality testing are probably not good candidates for these techniques. Patients taking medications that impair concentration often find these exercises difficult.

In using imagery, it is important to constantly assess the patient's reaction to the image. The standard images of a beach or a mountain scene suggested by the clinician may actually be highly aversive to the patient who has had negative experiences in these settings. Knowledge of the individual patient is important in choosing images, and clinicians must be careful in using mass-produced tapes.

Guided Imagery

Samuels and Samuels (1975) described the positive physiological and psychological effects of visual imagery. Patients are asked to visualize, in minute detail, a scene that they consider to be relaxing. As the scene becomes clearer, the patient begins to relax. Other forms of imagery use all of the body's senses and ask patients to project themselves into the scene being imagined rather than just watching the scene before them. In these exercises, the patient's mind plays an active role through imagined re-creation of certain sights, smells, sounds, tastes, and touch. We use this technique in pain management as a means of recalling a pain-free episode in the patient's life and of re-creating the associated sense of well-being. We also use guided imagery to prepare for stressful medical procedures. Johnson and Kreimer (2005) reviewed its use for chronically ill children.

Covert Sensitization

Covert sensitization is a procedure developed by Cautela (1967) that applies the laws of classical conditioning to imagery. Use of this technique has primarily been directed toward extinguishing previously learned maladaptive behaviors, such as smoking or overeating. This is accomplished by associating a learned habit (e.g., smoking) with detailed and unpleasant, obnoxious, and repulsive stimuli that are imagined (e.g., burning eyes, nausea, sore throat). By pairing the habit with a visualized noxious response, the habit is associated less with pleasure. McKay, Davis, and Fanning (2007) described its use as part of cognitive behavior therapy.

Hypnosis

Hypnosis has been reported to be useful in the treatment of pain, skin diseases, warts, and coping with chronic disease (Heap & Aravind, 2002).

Goals are usually to produce direct physiological changes, to change the perception of a symptom, to foster general relaxation, or to facilitate insight related to a particular symptom. Self-hypnosis, as described by LeCron (1970), is quite similar to therapist-cued procedures but transfers responsibility for trance induction and awakening to the patient. Golden, Dowd, and Friedberg's (1987) clinical guidebook for hypnosis includes cognitive behavior and Ericksonian methods as well as traditional methods, as does a more recent text by T. James (2000). Hilgard and Hilgard (1994) provide a comprehensive examination of the application of hypnosis to pain relief, a topic also addressed by Jensen and Patterson (2006).

Hypnosis has sometimes been useful for uncovering material that has been out of the awareness of the patient and that could have been associated with the onset of a maladaptive symptom. We are aware of one case in which total body palsy in a young adult was cured through the use of both therapist-based hypnosis and subsequent self-hypnosis. Hypnotic procedures helped the therapist to identify the emotional factors related to the onset of the symptom (an urge to hit his father at the beginning of an argument with an effort to hold back, resulting in a trembling in the hand that later spread to the entire body). The patient was then taught self-hypnosis procedures so that he could voluntarily control the symptoms by being able to both produce the palsy and eliminate it.

Biofeedback

The primary goal of biofeedback training is to teach the patient voluntary control over physiological processes. The reader is referred to reviews of the clinical biofeedback literature by Puckhaber (2006) and M. S. Schwartz and Andrasik (2005) for further study in this area.

Although biofeedback was originally thought to be a specific intervention in the physiological realm, analyses suggest that it can also be used as an intervention in the cognitive and affective domains. Successful training facilitates the patient's perceived control over physiological events, a belief that might play a significant role in treatment outcome. Perceived control and lower autonomic nervous system arousal are also associated with decreased affective states, such as anxiety. The technology associated wit biofeedback interventions makes it quite acceptable as a psychological intervention in our technology-oriented society.

The two most commonly used forms of biofeedback include electromyography (EMG) and skin temperature. EMG feedback is useful for educating patients about the level of muscle tension present in selected muscle groups and can thus be useful in musculoskeletal disorders. Fingertip temperature provides an indirect measure of peripheral blood volume and, as such, has been used for disorders associated with vasodilation and vasoconstriction.

In general, biofeedback procedures have been used for a variety of stress-related and psychophysiological disorders, including bruxism, tension headache, anxiety, migraine headache, Raynaud's disease, asthma, chronic pain, and essential hypertension. However, other relaxation-training procedures are often just as successful with these problems. There is little empirical evidence to support a preference for a particular technique such as biofeedback, hypnosis, imagery, or relaxation training, although more sophisticated studies considering individual differences are increasingly common.

Experienced clinicians engage in complex decision making in their choices. As Belar and Kibrick (1986) noted in their discussion of the use of EMG biofeedback in the treatment of chronic back pain, the clinician might choose this technique for one of three reasons: (a) to produce a specific physiological change, such as equalization of muscle tension in the back, or reduction of spasm; (b) to train in general relaxation, which is associated with increased pain tolerance and decreased distress; or (c) to facilitate physiological insight as the patient learns about relationships between psychological and physiological processes.

More specific uses of biofeedback in clinical health psychology include use of feedback about (a) heart rate, to control cardiac arrhythmias; (b) anal sphincter, to control fecal incontinence; (c) airway resistance, for asthma; (d) muscular functioning, for neuromuscular reeducation, dysphagia, and torticollis, among other problems; (e) brain wave patterns, for epilepsy; and (f) blood pressure, for postural hypotension in patients with spinal cord

;ws in Puckhaber, 2006; M. S. Schwartz & Andrasik, 2005).
hniques requires specialized training in bioelectric signal
:hophysiology, and electrical equipment. The Biofeedback
,stitute of America certifies therapists for practice in certain
biofeedback.

Systematic Desensitization

Systematic desensitization, as developed by Wolpe (1958), is designed to teach the patient to emit a behavior that is inconsistent with anxiety. In the practice of clinical health psychology, this procedure is often used to reduce patients' fears and accompanying anxiety concerning certain medical or dental procedures. Systematic desensitization has been found to be as effective as alprazolam in the management of dental injection phobia (Coldwell et al., 2007). As with modeling (discussed later), this procedure can be performed either imaginally or in vivo, and it usually involves a combination of both. Consider the following example:

> Ms. P. was a 13-year-old female diabetic with a needle phobia. She was referred by her endocrinologist for evaluation and treatment regarding her inability to self-inject insulin and the problems encountered with other providers. This patient was treated through the use of systematic desensitization in an effort to help her become less reactive to injections. A hierarchy of progressively anxiety-producing circumstances was first elicited. The patient was then instructed in PMR techniques. While relaxed, Ms. P. practiced imagined scenes of increasing difficulty. Health care professionals and needles were then gradually introduced, allowing the patient to adapt to each set of circumstances before proceeding to the next highest level. After her fears of injection were extinguished, she was trained in self-injection through similar procedures.

Systematic desensitization is also used to decrease fears of childbirth, closed magnetic resonance imaging exams, and self-catheterization; to decrease excessive dependence on nebulizers, ventilators, and cardiac monitoring; and to facilitate reentry into public settings by patients who are burned or surgically deformed. The potential for the use of technology to develop virtual realities has not yet been fully realized in clinical health psychology.

Modeling

On the basis of the theory of observational learning (Bandura, 1969), modeling provides a means of facilitating the learning of adaptive behaviors. This can be accomplished through either in vivo (direct observation) or imaginal (filmed or covert) techniques. Modeling is an important method for teaching patients necessary skills that might be required to meet the demands of their illness (e.g., self-injection of insulin). It also reduces patient anxiety in preparation for stressful medical procedures. Melamed and Siegel (1980) demonstrated that filmed modeling to prepare children for medical and dental procedures, as well as for hospitalization, can be useful in reducing anxiety and behavioral problems. In addition, this technique is useful for interventions directed at patient–staff and staff–staff issues. Finally, the clinician can also model more therapeutic or facilitative interactions.

The clinical health psychologist should be aware of the negative effects of poor models. Consider the following example:

> Mrs. K. was a 59-year-old woman admitted to the hospital for a colostomy. As part of standard procedure, she was interviewed before the surgery and initially appeared to be coping quite well with the information presented to her. On the day of the scheduled surgery (3 days past the planned date, because of a slight elevation in her temperature), Mrs. K. was considerably anxious, fearful of dying, and reluctant to sign the informed consent to the surgery.
>
> On interviewing this patient, the clinical health psychologist learned that the patient sharing Mrs. K's room had recently undergone the same operation and was now coping poorly with the pain and discomfort secondary to a postsurgical infection. Given the similarities in age and diagnosis, the patient had been unwittingly provided with an effective, but negative, role model. In this example, staff had failed to consider the effect of one patient on another. A change in the patient's room helped alleviate some of Mrs. K's concerns.

Skills Training and Behavioral Rehearsal

Skills training can incorporate modeling, role playing, and behavioral rehearsal, as patients learn specific skills that can enhance their psychological and physical adjustment. The importance of self-management in the care of children and older adults was highlighted by Anderson, Svoren, and Laffel (2007) and Qualls and Benight (2007), respectively. The critical role of self-regulation in health promotion was addressed by Bandura (2005).

In our experience, skills in self-assertion are some of the most commonly taught in practice. Whether in a formal or informal manner, we frequently find ourselves helping patients become more assertive, particularly when dealing with medical personnel. Specific tasks that are taught include learning to formulate and to ask direct questions of physicians, requesting special privileges and giving justifications, requesting privacy during physical exams, learning to appropriately inquire as to alternative treatments, and requesting a second medical opinion. We frequently encourage patients to write down questions to ask their physicians and to obtain written answers if necessary. It is well known that patients remember little of the medical information communicated to them by their physician during an office visit. (This issue is reviewed in detail in chap. 6 of this volume.) We also encourage physicians to request that patients repeat back to them an understanding of the problem and the recommended treatment plan. This simple procedure eliminates many miscommunications and unmet expectations.

Other targets of skills training include the learning of specific behaviors necessary for good health care or rehabilitation. Although clinical health psychologists might not directly teach these skills, they frequently interact with other health care providers (e.g., occupational therapists, physical therapists, speech therapists, nurses) to address either the emotional aspects or the learning principles associated with acquiring new, and often unnatural, skills (e.g., proper care of surgical stomas, bowel and bladder care after spinal cord injury, home dialysis, insulin regulation).

Contingency Management

As a treatment strategy, the goal of contingency management is to increase adaptive behaviors and to decrease those that are not adaptive. Positive reinforcement, negative reinforcement, extinction, punishment, response cost, and shaping procedures can all be used to accomplish this goal. Contingency management is often used in the area of pediatric and adolescent clinical health psychology, but is also used in modification of health behaviors (e.g., smoking, diet, exercise).

Examples of positive reinforcement include the awarding of prizes to children for adherence to dietary regimens while on hemodialysis (Magrab & Papadopoulou, 1977), treating children with chronic food refusal (Hoch, Babbitt, Coe, Krell, & Hackbert, 1994), and achieving certain goals in health promotion (Goreczny & Hersen, 1998). Another example of the use of positive reinforcement is providing vouchers to help drug abusers stay in treatment and work toward their recovery (Kellogg et al., 2005).

An example of negative reinforcement is the work by Malament, Dunn, and Davis (1975), who used avoidance of an aversive tone to develop the habit in patients in wheelchairs of doing postural pushups, so as to avoid the formation of decubitus ulcers.

Extinction is commonly used to diminish complaining behavior or behaviors designed to elicit attention for the symptom (e.g., grimaces). It is also used in the context of multidisciplinary pain programs to diminish the frequency of pain behaviors (Sanders, 2002).

Although used much less frequently than in the past, punishment has been effective in a number of areas, including cases of ruminative vomiting in infants. Whereas Lang and Melamed (1969) used electric shock, Sajwaj, Libet, and Agras (1974) were successful with a small amount of lemon juice. In adults, paradigms such as the rapid-smoking technique have been used as another example of aversive conditioning (Grimaldi & Lichtenstein, 1969; see Covino & Bottari, 2001, for a review).

Currently, instead of using punishment, contingency management has focused on such approaches as the differential reinforcement of other behavior (i.e., reinforcing a behavior that is incompatible with the behavior one is trying to decrease). Also, token economies using a response–cost methodology are often preferable to punishment. (See Goreczny & Hersen [1998] for a review of health psychology interventions with pediatrics and adolescents and Sanders [2002] for a review of these techniques for pain rehabilitation.)

A major advantage to contingency management is that it can be administered by persons other than the clinical health psychologist (although careful training is required because contingency management is vulnerable to improper implementation). Frequently, nursing personnel or family members are educated as to how to change contingencies affecting patient behavior. For example, in attempting to cope with a demanding patient, we advised ward nurses to visit the bell-ringing patient on a regular basis rather than continuing to respond (or not respond) to frequent calls for help. As a result, both nursing personnel and the patient were more satisfied and less frustrated by each other's behavior. Family members can be instructed to increase attention and nurturance for well behavior versus sick-role behavior. Contingency management is a fundamental component of comprehensive pain rehabilitation, originally described by Fordyce (1976, 1995), and subsequently by others (Linton, 2005; Sanders, 2002; Turk & Gatchel, 2002).

Although contingency management is effective under well-controlled conditions, its efficacy is diminished by poorly detailed instructions or lack of follow up. Family members often unwittingly abandon recommended treatment suggestions because of a temporary, albeit annoying, exacerbation of symptoms when the patient has been put on an extinction schedule (the *extinction burst*). Additionally, when staff members are implementing a program, it is important to ensure that they are not using contingencies to express their anger at a difficult patient. The failure of a contingency management program is often attributable to the clinician's failure to adequately assess the "ABCs" (i.e., antecedents, behaviors, consequences) of the planned intervention.

Self-Monitoring and the Use of Cues

Because of the reactive nature of self-monitoring, the use of patient diaries can be an effective means of intervention, as well as of assessment and tracking treatment progress. Simply recording eating, smoking, and compliance behaviors often brings about changes in the desired directions.

Other means of self-monitoring include the use of external or internal cues as a signal to institute a behavior. Patients with complicated medication regimens have been directed to categorize and separate pills into daily doses, using a weekly pill box to help them remember when the next dose is due. Another example of external cues for self-monitoring includes using time-of-day or environmental prompts as stimuli to perform relaxation exercises.

In the treatment of obesity, patients are taught to attend to internal rather than external cues for signs of hunger and to self-monitor their food intake. Insulin-dependent diabetics can be taught to recognize early warning symptoms of insulin imbalance and make necessary adjustments. Family members can also participate in cuing strategies (which must be differentiated from nagging). The health care system uses this technique when sending appointment reminders as external cues for preventive care.

Self-monitoring does require a certain degree of self-discipline and commitment to change. Patients who are ambivalent regarding behavioral change are not likely to do well with this procedure unless it is presented in combination with other forms of intervention. Self-monitoring can be a useful method to assess commitment to treatment.

Cognitive Strategies

A variety of interventions use cognitive strategies to effect behavioral change. These include the use of distraction, calming self-statements, and cognitive restructuring. In attention–diversion or distraction procedures, patients are taught to direct their attention away from unpleasant events. Use of pleasant imagery, difficult mental tasks (e.g., counting serial 7s backwards, reciting the States of the Union in alphabetical order), counting aloud, and focusing attention on other neutral stimuli (e.g., counting holes in ceiling tiles) are examples of this process. Patients can also be taught to silently or softly talk to themselves using calming, relaxing, and reassuring statements. These statements could emphasize the temporary nature of a discomfort (e.g., "This pain will not last," "I only have 5 minutes to go"), could be directed at maintaining low physiological arousal (e.g., "stay calm," "stay relaxed," "breathe"), or could be directed toward preservation of self-image (e.g., "I am a strong and worthwhile person," "It's OK to feel uncomfortable," "I can cope with this").

Cognitive restructuring is a generic term that describes a variety of procedures, including stress-inoculation training (Meichenbaum, 1977), rational–emotive therapy (Ellis, 1962), cognitive therapy (Beck, Rush, Shaw, & Emery, 1979), and problem-solving training (Goldfried & Davison, 1976). These procedures educate the patient regarding the relationships among thoughts, feelings, and behaviors and help patients replace self-defeating cognitions with adaptive thoughts. McKay et al. (2007) provided detailed instructions in applying many of these techniques. Cognitive restructuring techniques have been applied to a myriad of health areas including pain management (M. A. Caudill, 1995; Thorn, 2004) and preparation for surgery (Deardorff & Reeves, 1997).

Paradoxical Interventions

Although not well researched in many areas of health, paradoxical interventions have received some support in the treatment of insomnia, urinary retention, and encopresis. Jacob and Moore (1984) suggested that paradoxical procedures may be warranted when symptoms are exacerbated by the patient's attempt to decrease them or when the patient is resistant to direct therapeutic instructions. Weeks (1991) provided an excellent collection of readings detailing the theory and use of paradoxical techniques.

The list of intervention strategies we have provided is not exhaustive, yet skills in those procedures mentioned would prepare the psychologist for practice in clinical health psychology. In general, these intervention strategies are not used in isolation. For example, stress inoculation is an example of a treatment package that incorporates a variety of strategies. Furthermore, these generic strategies need to be adapted for each patient on the basis of the particular disorder and the presentation of the patient's issues.

Note also that a number of these strategies are not necessarily patient focused but can be used either for targets within the family, the health care system, or the social network, or by these environmental agents of change.

Although the clinical health psychologist cannot be expert in all possible interventions and kinds of problems likely to be encountered in this broad field, there are several categories of problems with which the practitioner should have some basic familiarity. These topics are represented in the suggested readings. In the next chapter our attention turns to what we have experienced as pitfalls in the actual practice of delivering assessment, consultation, and intervention services in clinical health psychology.

SUGGESTED READINGS

Ayer, W. A. (2005). *Psychology and dentistry: Mental health aspects of patient care.* Binghamton, NY: Haworth Press.

Baum, A., & Andersen, B. L. (Eds.). (2001). *Psychosocial interventions for cancer.* Washington, DC: American Psychological Association.

Blanchard, E. B. (2000). *Irritable bowel syndrome: Psychosocial assessment and treatment.* Washington, DC: American Psychological Association.

Blanchard, E. B., & Hickling, E. J. (2003). *After the crash: Psychological assessment and treatment of survivors of motor vehicle accidents* (2nd ed.). Washington, DC: American Psychological Association

Blechman, E. A., & Brownell, K. D. (Eds.). (1999). *Behavioral medicine and women: A comprehensive handbook.* New York: Guilford Press.

Block, A. R., Gatchel, R. J., Deardorff, W. W., & Guyer, R. D. (2003). *The psychology of spine surgery.* Washington, DC: American Psychological Association.

Boll, T. J., Johnson, S. B., Perry, N. W., & Rozensky, R. H. (Eds.). (2002). *Handbook of clinical health psychology: Vol. 1. Medical disorders and behavioral applications.* Washington, DC: American Psychological Association.

Camic, P. M., & Knight, S. J. (Eds.). (1998). *Clinical handbook of health psychology: A practical guide to effective interventions.* Toronto, Ontario, Canada: Hogrefe & Huber.

Deardorff, W. W., & Reeves, J. L. (1997). *Preparing for surgery: A mind–body approach to enhance healing and recovery.* Oakland, CA: New Harbinger.

de Ridder, D., & de Wit, J. (Eds.). (2006). *Self-regulation in health behavior.* New York: Wiley.

Dodgen, C. E. (2006). *Nicotine dependence: Understanding and applying the most effective treatment interventions.* Washington, DC: American Psychological Association.

Drotar, D. (2006). *Psychological interventions in childhood chronic illness.* Washington, DC: American Psychological Association.

Friedberg, F., & Jason, L. A. (1998). *Understanding chronic fatigue syndrome: An empirical guide to assessment and treatment.* Washington, DC: American Psychological Association.

Gatchel, R. J. (2005). *Clinical essentials of pain management.* Washington, DC: American Psychological Association.

Jordan, J., Barde, B., & Zeiher, A. M. (2007). *Contributions toward evidence-based psychocardiology: A systematic review of the literature.* Washington, DC: American Psychological Association.

Miller, G. E., & Cohen, S. (2001). Psychological interventions and the immune system: A meta-analytic review and critique. *Health Psychology, 20,* 47–63.

Park, D. C., & Liu, L. L. (Eds.). (2007). *Medical adherence and aging: Social and cognitive perspectives.* Washington, DC: American Psychological Association.

Patenaude, A. F. (2005). *Genetic testing for cancer.* Washington, DC: American Psychological Association.

Phelps, L. (Ed.). (2006). *Chronic health-related disorders in children: Collaborative medical and psychoeducational interventions.* Washington, DC: American Psychological Association.

Pressman, M., & Orr, W. C. (Eds.). (2000). *Understanding sleep: The evaluation and treatment of sleep disorders.* Washington, DC: American Psychological Association.

Raczynski, J. M., & Leviton, L. C. (Eds.). (2004). *Handbook of clinical health psychology: Vol. 2. Disorders of behavior and health.* Washington, DC: American Psychological Association.

Schnurr, P. P., & Green, B. L. (Eds.). (2003). *Trauma and health: Physical health consequences of exposure to extreme stress.* Washington, DC: American Psychological Association.

Schwartz, M. S., & Andrasik, F. (Eds.). (2005). *Biofeedback: A practitioner's guide* (3rd ed.). New York: Guilford Press.

Stroebe, M. S., Hansson, R. O., Stroebe, W., & Schut, H. (Eds.). (2001). *Handbook of bereavement research: Consequences, coping, and care.* Washington, DC: American Psychological Association.

Suinn, R., & VandenBos, G. R. (Eds.). (1999). *Cancer patients and their families: Readings on disease course, coping, and psychological interventions.* Washington, DC: American Psychological Association.

Thorn, B. E. (2004). *Cognitive therapy for chronic pain.* New York: Guilford Press.

Turk, D. C., & Melzack, R. (2001). *Handbook of pain assessment* (2nd ed.). New York: Guilford Press.

Werth, J. L., & Blevins, D. (Eds.). (2006). *Psychosocial issues near the end of life: A resource for professional care providers.* Washington, DC: American Psychological Association.

5

Pitfalls in Practice

In the previous chapters, we presented frameworks with which to conduct a thorough psychological assessment and to develop intervention
strategies. In this chapter, we shift focus from the content and methods of
assessment and intervention to the barriers and problems encountered
while working in the field of clinical health psychology, with suggestions
for solutions when possible. Discussion focuses on practical concerns relevant to both inpatient and outpatient settings. Case examples reflect pertinent practice topics and represent actual experiences that we have either
encountered or witnessed.

PROBLEMS WITH REFERRALS

It is not uncommon to receive vague, poorly defined consultation requests.
In our experience, we have found that many physicians and other referral
sources are still unclear as to what services clinical health psychologists provide and what kinds of information are helpful when making a consultation request. As a result, assessment questions are often ambiguous, unclear,
too specific, untimely, or inappropriate. Listed next are some issues we
have commonly encountered in the referral process.

Determining the Reason for the Referral

"Patient recently diagnosed as having prostate cancer, refuses surgery."
Given the limited amount of information, it is not clear what services are

being requested. One could guess that the referring doctor or nurse is frustrated by the patient's refusal of a surgical procedure and wants the psychologist to convince the patient otherwise. In this type of case, it is essential that the clinical health psychologist attempt to garner additional information from a variety of sources, especially the consultee, before actually speaking with the patient. In addition, the psychologist should be aware that this consultation might reflect conflict between the value systems of the patient and the health care system. Assessment should be directed toward both the patient and the staff.

Handling Predetermined Procedures

"Patient is very tense and has migraine headaches. Please give biofeedback." In this example, the referral source is prescribing a type of treatment that might or might not be appropriate or cost effective for the patient. We have found this to be a frequent problem when a referral source is personally invested in a particular technique.

Problems are created for the consultant when a specific form of treatment (e.g., biofeedback) has already been prescribed for the patient by another professional. First, patients expect the prescribed treatment to be delivered; the fact that such a treatment might be inappropriate must be addressed explicitly at an early stage. In doing this, it is important to remember that patients could feel that they are getting substandard care if they do not receive the promised form of treatment. It is also possible that in an attempt to ally with the psychologist, the patient might lose confidence in or disengage from the referral source. This can enlarge the gulf between professionals and result in fragmented, poor quality care for the patient. Thus, a clear rationale for not providing a prescribed treatment should be given, along with the alternative treatment plan. Referral sources also occasionally order specific tests, such as the Minnesota Multiphasic Personality Inventory, which may not be the appropriate assessment techniques for the domain in question (e.g., ability to comprehend complicated medical regimen). These instances have to be handled in a similar manner.

In addition to dealing with patient issues when inappropriate procedures are ordered, the clinical health psychologist must communicate the inappropriateness of prescription-like consultations to the referral source. In our opinion, the best way to avert further conflict in this regard is to speak cordially, but directly, with the referral source and to clarify what represents an appropriate referral and what does not. Often physicians and medical personnel are so accustomed to ordering specific tests and procedures that they are unaware that the same process does not apply between disciplines. Alternatively, it is important to note that we have found that physicians prescribe treatments such as "biofeedback" or "stress management" as euphemisms for assessment and intervention with perceived emotional problems. Many believe that their patients are more receptive to this language on the referral form.

It is important to train referral sources in methods of discussing the referral with their patients. For example, one can ask the physician to help make the clinician's job easier by preparing the patient for the referral, or one can suggest that careful preparation might avoid having the patient become angry with the physician. We suggest that physicians explicitly state that the referral is not being made because he or she thinks that the problem is "all in the patient's head" but rather that it is being made because of the physician's interest in the whole patient and the awareness that other disciplines have certain skills to offer that have been helpful in similar cases. Physicians need to emphasize that all illnesses have psychological components, because mind and body cannot be separated. Exhibit 5.1 is a handout that is useful for educating physicians.

Phrasing the Referral

Patients may be resistant to the idea of being referred to a psychologist. They may respond by thinking (or saying), "You think the pain (or other symptom) is all in my head," or "I'm being dumped." The following phrases seem to be more palatable to patients:

- a referral for pain or stress management;
- a referral for evaluation for a special symptom-management program;
- a referral to see whether other factors are making the symptoms worse (e.g., stress);

Exhibit 5.1

Sample Handout for Referring Physicians

CONSIDERATIONS FOR
MEDICAL PSYCHOLOGY CONSULTATION

1. Complaints seem out of proportion to organic pathology.
2. Treatment does not yield expected results despite an improved organic status.
3. New symptoms arise as old symptoms resolve.
4. The patient repeatedly raises issues or questions that have already been addressed.
5. The patient seems to require more time and attention than usual.
6. The patient does not adhere to prescribed treatments.
7. The patient takes anxiolytic, sleep, or analgesic medication for a longer period of time than appropriate.
8. The patient resists the idea of attempting to wean from anxiolytic, sleep, or analgesic medications.
9. The patient exhibits a great deal of emotional distress.
10. The patient reports significant family problems in dealing with illness.
11. The patient overuses alcohol or other psychoactive substances.
12. Psychophysiological components could exacerbate the medical condition.

- a referral to help with preparation for surgery, which might improve outcome;
- a referral for symptom management, so that the use of medicines can be reduced to a minimum;
- a referral because of interest in the whole patient, with the recognition that all illnesses have psychological components and that other disciplines have skills to offer that have been helpful in similar cases; or
- a referral with recognition of the stressors that the medical condition has caused the patient (and his or her family).

Identifying the Patient

In some cases, the identified patient might not be the real target for intervention. Consider this referral request: "Patient is a 17-year-old female student undergoing bone marrow transplant. Patient does not seem to appreciate seriousness of condition." After the clinical health psychologist interviewed this patient, it was apparent that the patient had a clear understanding of her medical condition and possible consequences. Her religious beliefs, general optimistic style, and strong social relations were interacting in a manner that produced effective coping techniques and a minimum of psychological distress or depression.

This example demonstrates a case in which health care professionals had projected their own fears and emotions on the patient, who was actually coping with the illness better than the staff. Consequently, when the patient did not behave in the expected manner, a consultation was generated. As a result, the clinical health psychologist needed to refocus attention to acknowledge staff concerns and stressors as the potential targets for intervention. Although it is not always efficacious to attempt to explain psychological defenses (e.g., projection) to staff, recognition of staff concerns and education regarding individual differences in patients can help alleviate some of their anxieties when the patient does not behave in a typical fashion.

Sometimes the referral is made because of family reactions to the patient or illness. One referral we received concerned adjustment issues after a 40-year-old man lost his sight. On further exploration, we found that the patient's wife's reaction to this loss was the real reason for referral; thus, she was the more appropriate target of intervention.

Dealing With the Choice of an Inappropriate Provider

"Patient is a 49-year-old, single male who has had coronary bypass surgery. Unable to care for self at home during recovery. Please arrange for supportive services." Discussion revealed the confusion that sometimes results from the diversity of services available within an inpatient setting. In this case, the referring resident wanted the patient to receive home nursing care during the early stages of recovery. He contacted an inappropriate provider (psychologist) for an appropriate type of service desired (social work). The division of labor often is not clear among the disciplines of psychiatry, psychology, and social work, which are usually housed in separate departments. In fact, these departments often overlap in services provided (e.g., supportive care), so the resulting confusion may be justified. We believe that disciplines should work collaboratively to clarify related issues within any institution, to minimize unnecessary costs and care. However, if the clinician is working within an academic teaching hospital, he or she can expect an especially high incidence of this type of error during times of medical resident rotations and the arrival of new residents.

Patients, as well as referral sources, may also be mistaken about the types of services clinical health psychologists provide. Much of the public remains poorly informed regarding the traditional differences between psychiatry and psychology. When a profession becomes even more specialized within a given discipline, (i.e., clinical health psychology vs. clinical psychology), it is not surprising that people are perplexed when certain services are not offered. This is illustrated in the following example:

> Mrs. M. was a 35-year-old woman with chronic history of severe migraine headaches. Her neurologist referred her to an outpatient headache-management program for evaluation and treatment. On completion of the initial interview, it became obvious that the patient expected the clinical health psychologist to offer some form of medication treatment, and expressed considerable dismay and agitation when this type of headache management was not available.

In the case of outpatients, sending, along with appointment materials, written materials that describe the nature of the services available can minimize these kinds of problems.

Dealing With Poorly Timed Requests

Occasionally, the timing of a consultation request is inappropriate. Referrals can be premature or extensively delayed. We have received more than one consultation request asking for an evaluation of a patient's mental status and ability to cope, within hours of a major trauma (e.g., motor vehicle accident, surgery). In these instances, the patient is often coma-tose and clearly unable to meet the demands of the assessment process. We have found that it is useful to contact ward staff before going to the hospital, and to respond to the physician's concerns, explaining the best timing for such an assessment. Scheduling follow-up times and coordi-nating them with the referral source will provide assurance that the request is not being ignored.

Conversely, we have also discovered that well-meaning health care providers have delayed a consultation request for psychological evaluation or treatment beyond the point of a consultant's ability to provide optimal services. This is particularly true when the referral source has attempted to deal with the patient's problems alone, without seeking a psychologist's opinion. As a result, by the time the clinical health psychologist is con-sulted, he or she often finds a much more severe problem than the initial one. As an example, consider the following case:

> Mr. S. was a 54-year-old man. He was hospitalized for lower extrem-ity edema and phlebitis in his left leg. On admission to the unit, the patient behaved in an arrogant, noncompliant, and demanding man-ner (i.e., he did not stay in bed with leg elevated), which intimidated the newly arrived medical residents. Mr. S. adamantly denied non-compliance with medical regimen; however, laboratory results sug-gested that he had not been taking his medication as prescribed. As Mr. S's hospitalization progressed, he became increasingly disrup-tive. The medical team attempted to independently deal with his behaviors by using increasingly confrontational behavior. As a result, the patient became even more agitated and began acting in a belliger-ent manner toward medical personnel. The medical team then con-sulted the psychology service.
>
> On arriving at bedside, the psychologist conducted an individual interview with the patient that assessed previous general psychologi-cal condition as well as issues associated with compliance. The inter-view revealed that this patient was in the manic phase of a bipolar affective disorder, in addition to having long-standing personality problems that included narcissistic features. Given these psychologi-cal parameters, it became increasingly clear that because this patient

had also been noncompliant with psychotropic medication, he would be unlikely to adhere to any complicated medication regimen, especially when feeling pressured by staff to do so. Had the clinical health psychologist been consulted earlier, staff members could have been provided with information that might have had some preventative value in case management.

Dumping and Turfing

Dumping and *turfing* are two terms with which the clinical health psychologist will unfortunately become familiar. These terms represent assessment and intervention requests for patients for whom other professionals no longer wish to be responsible. Thus, the patients are dumped or turfed to a different department or service. Occasionally, patients are referred for psychological assessment because of the physician's inability to determine a medical diagnosis. Physicians often unfortunately assume that if the patient is not physically ill and still complains, then the patient must be psychologically ill. This is especially true in cases in which patients have a previous history of psychological problems.

Medical personnel are not the only professionals to turf patients. In mental health practices, patients who present with frequent and multiple medical complaints are often viewed as less desirable clients and are referred out as "not amenable to psychotherapy; need stress management." This type of referral implies that the consultee is differentiating *stress management* from *psychotherapy,* reserving the latter term for those treatment approaches that are perceived as more insight oriented in nature (and sometimes more valued). Consequently, outpatients who present with somatization issues and who are not YAVIS (young, attractive, verbal, intelligent, and successful) might be referred to a clinical health psychologist. That is, because the primary therapist has no professional interest in dealing with this kind of patient problem, he or she "turfs" the patient to the clinical health psychologist. The patient might then experience a sense of rejection or diminished self-worth from the initial mental health contact and be less amenable to working with a psychologist. Although we deplore the discrimination against these patients, we believe it to be true that the services of clinical health psychologists often are more useful to them than those of traditional mental health service providers.

ISSUES IN THE CONDUCT OF CONSULTATIONS

Numerous problems arise in the conduct of consultations that require attention and solutions.

Adequacy of Background Information

Throughout this book we have described key resources for background information on the patient and his or her illness. In the actual course of obtaining information, the clinical health psychologist is likely to encounter a number of roadblocks. Ultimately, the amount of time and energy channeled into pursuing background information will be based on the clinician's judgment concerning the necessity and use of the sought-after information. Difficulties in gathering background information include lack of medical expertise, inability to obtain releases of information, unavailability of records, and poor handwriting.

Lack of Medical Expertise

Although the clinical health psychologist will have studied basic medical terminology and will have a general understanding of common medical disorders, many technical reports focus solely on the medical aspects of disease and do not address its behavioral or emotional ramifications. We have found it extremely helpful to ask our medical colleagues to explain various aspects of specific diseases, and their implications, in terms that are understandable to nonmedical professionals. It has been our experience that most physicians are not only willing to provide this information but also respect our judgment and efforts in attempting to understand these issues.

Inability to Obtain Releases of Information

Patients might be unable or unwilling to release information concerning previous psychological or medical treatments. It is common for patients to forget or to be too ill to recall the names of previous health care providers. This is especially true when they have been in treatment with multiple providers over many years. Alternatively, some patients prefer not to disclose information concerning past treatments because they fear it could be perceived in a negative manner or be damaging to them in some way. Over the past 2 decades, we have practiced in a variety of independent, institutional, and managed care settings. The best system for access to history has been at Kaiser Permanente, where medical charts for all of their members, sometimes dating back 40 years, are available to clinicians. Health care is also moving rapidly toward establishing an electronic medical record.

Inability to obtain releases of information also limits with whom the clinician can speak. That is, except under extreme or urgent circumstances, it is unethical to speak with family members, friends, previous treatment providers, or employers regarding the patient without first having the patient's consent to do so. If the patient is not willing to provide releases of information, the clinician needs to consider the ramifications for treatment and to determine whether to proceed given these circumstances.

Unavailability of Records

If a release of information has been provided, the clinician will quickly discover that medical and psychological records are not easily obtainable. Records are occasionally lost or unavailable at time of assessment. The clinical health psychologist might need to be persistent in obtaining previous treatment histories from a variety of sources and to continue the process of gathering information throughout the first few sessions. Note also that when obtained, records can also be surprisingly noninformative. It is often wise to communicate verbally with previous providers to ensure a thorough understanding of previous diagnoses and treatments and the provider's subjective impressions, which might otherwise be unrecorded.

Poor Handwriting

It is a joke that the sine qua non of a good physician is the poor quality of his or her handwriting. In actual practice, poor handwriting is no laughing matter. The inability to read medical personnel's description, diagnosis, or treatment of the patient unavoidably hampers the review of medical records. Not only is poor handwriting frustrating to read, but it can also lead to misdiagnosis or mismanagement of the patient. From our perspective, one is only as effective as one's ability to communicate. The problem is being solved by the use of electronic medical records; clinical health psychologists working in medical centers need to develop competence in working with these. The nonprofit organization Institute for Safe Medication Practices (ISMP; see http://www.ismp.org) has called for the elimination of handwritten prescriptions and orders within the next 3 years. However, electronic medical records still do not prevent errors from being recorded.

Of course, there can be times when gathering background information is not possible. In these cases, we have found it useful to tell the patient of our efforts to do so, because this communicates a high level of professionalism and caring and so elicits cooperation in yet another request for history.

Problems in the Initial Contact

It is crucial that the clinician be knowledgeable about the nature of the medical problem and relevant treatments before seeing the patient. For example, it would be useless to interview a candidate for penile prosthesis surgery (in which it is critical to assess how realistic the patient's expectations are) without being aware of the probable outcomes of this type of surgery. In a similar way, it would be unethical to assess whether a patient could withstand the stressors of heart transplant surgery if the clinician does not know what those stressors are. The clinician also needs to know the potential psychological concomitants of the patient's disease and pharmacological therapies before interviewing the patient.

In addition to considering possible interactions among the person, the disorder, and the treatment, the clinician should have an understanding of the patient's preparedness, if any, for the psychological consultation. Before actually making initial contact with the patient, the clinical health psychologist should consider the following questions to enhance the probability of building adequate rapport with the patient.

1. Does the patient know that a psychologist has been consulted? This question addresses a common problem. Physicians frequently request a psychological evaluation without advising the patient. One study noted that 68% of hospitalized patients had not been informed by their physicians that a psychiatric consultation had been requested (Bagheri, Lane, Kline, & Araujo, 1981). Our current experience, as well as research in this area, confirms that this continues to be a problem (Leigh & Streltzer, 2007). The primary reason given by physicians for not advising the patient was the fear that the patient might view the consultation as an insult. Other common reasons were that the physician did not think of it, the physician was too busy, the physician thought the patient might become belligerent or refuse consultation, or the physician feared that the patient might lose faith in him or her. Note that many of these reasons reflect anxiety responses on the part of physicians. The information in Exhibit 5.1 can be helpful in avoiding this problem.

2. What might a psychological consultation mean to the patient? We find it critical to deal with the reason for referral at the beginning of the interview. A good way to start is to ask the patient about his or her own understanding of the process. A problem frequently uncovered is that the physician has indicated to the patient that he or she has "nothing further to offer medically." This, especially when associated with a referral to a psychologist, is then interpreted by the patient to mean that the problem is thought to be "in my head." On numerous occasions, this is not what the referral source meant (e.g., the patient might have documented medical problems accounting for the symptoms reported, but there is no available treatment other than learning to cope). Because both patients and physicians often subscribe to mind–body dualistic philosophies, there are many opportunities for misinterpretations.

3. Given the background information obtained, what is the best way to approach this person? This question serves as a reminder that each

patient is unique in his or her own idiosyncratic expectations, fears, coping mechanisms, abilities, and medical problems. Patients should not become a "label" or a "diagnosis," a tendency we have seen among some providers in discussing pain patients.

Problems With Settings

With today's soaring costs of medical care, many hospitals have fewer private rooms. As a result, the patient's privacy is often limited; thus, the clinician needs to be acutely aware of confidentiality issues. If the patient is feeling well enough and there are no medical contraindications, it might be possible to meet in the clinician's office. However, this is usually not feasible, particularly for the initial contact. The persistent clinician might be able to locate a family, conference, or waiting room that is not in use. Generally, if such rooms are available, there is usually little objection to allowing the psychologist access to them.

Unfortunately, many patients require bed rest or are housed in specialized units (e.g., burn units, cardiac care units), thereby eliminating the possibility of complete privacy. Under these conditions, the clinician should, at a minimum, close the curtain around the patient's bed and talk in a lowered voice, checking with the patient on occasion as to the extent that limitations on privacy are affecting self-report. Sometimes, roommates can be requested to leave temporarily. In our experience, roommates usually agree to facilitate others' privacy.

Many clinical health psychologists practice in a multidisciplinary office or clinic setting, in conjunction with physicians. These environments offer unique challenges in terms of privacy. For instance, the sign-in sheets for medical clinics are often at the front desk, and patients simply sign their names under the doctor they are coming to see. Of course, the sign-in sheet for the clinical health psychologist would be visible to all other patients. In addition, unlike in a medical practice, psychologists commonly meet their patients in the waiting room and escort them to the office. In a multidisciplinary office, this practice alerts everyone in the waiting room to the fact that the patient is going to see the psychologist. When working in a multidisciplinary setting, it is important to be cognizant of these issues and attempt to address them as effectively as possible. For instance, we have had patients sign in using a first name only, and a nurse commonly escorts the patient from the waiting room.

Problems With Scheduling

Although scheduling the patient for an initial evaluation session seems to be a simple task, it can prove difficult. Working in a hospital poses several problems that the outpatient psychologist might never face. Medical procedures take precedence over all other procedures. As a result, patients are frequently away from the ward for diagnostic work and treatment. Scheduling an appointment with the patient through either the ward clerk or the charge nurse can alleviate this difficulty. However, the clinical health psychologist needs to have sufficient flexibility in his or her schedule to allow for variation in hours.

Scheduling the medical outpatient poses the same difficulties as scheduling any psychological outpatient, with a few additional considerations. Depending on the patient's health status and stamina, it might be better to schedule a shorter appointment than what is customary. Physical limitations of patients often necessitate special considerations in parking arrangements, wheelchair access, and restroom facilities. In addition, many medical patients prefer appointments in the morning or afternoon, because of medication regimens and other treatments (e.g., radiation, occupational therapy, or physical therapy), or because of personal needs (e.g., transportation, sleep habits, availability of significant others, or work schedules). If the clinical health psychologist can remain flexible in scheduling patients, he or she will be more able to capitalize on the optimum performance of the patient. Depending on the nature of the outpatient service, it is often desirable for the clinical health psychologist to schedule patient appointments in the outpatient medical clinic in conjunction with other medical visits to facilitate professional communication.

A common problem in outpatient settings is the lack of follow-through by the patient in scheduling an appointment after referral. One means of overcoming this problem is for the clinical health psychologist to contact the patient initially and not wait for the patient to initiate contact. Alternatively, the clinician can educate the physician in how to make strong referrals and provide the physician with multiple copies of professional brochures. Common referral sources might also be given a specially tailored videotape on relevant issues, which the patient can view in the physician's office. Providing hospitalized patients with business cards and materials describing services and locations is also useful.

The Reluctant or Hostile Patient

Clinical health psychologists, probably more so than those in traditional practice, must often deal with reluctant or hostile patients in the initial visit. The reasons for this can be numerous, but we have found four common ones:

1. The patient was not told about the referral to a psychologist.
2. The patient has negative perceptions about psychological intervention for what the patient has defined as a medical problem (as previously noted, most patients are mind–body dualists).
3. The patient is being asked to shift from a biomedical model of understanding disease, with its passive, external locus of control to a biopsychosocial model of understanding disease, with different responsibilities and a more internal locus of control.
4. Patients are rarely self-referred to a clinical health psychologist and thus tend to be more skeptical about the initial session than those patients who have themselves initiated contact with a psychologist.

Of these, the most typical source of reluctance is patients' focus on the medical aspects of the problem and their ensuing anger about their doctor's implication that it might be psychologically based.

As mentioned earlier, it is imperative to gauge a patient's reaction and emotional state related to the referral for psychological evaluation. If this is not done adequately, with appropriate adjustment in interviewing style, the assessment can yield invalid data and the patient might not commit to any type of treatment, or the patient might sabotage treatment attempts.

We and others (see DeGood, 1983; Weisman, 1978) have observed several early warning signs of patient reluctance or hostility related to psychological assessment, including the following:

- refusal to schedule an appointment or to show up for return visits;
- anger and bewilderment in the initial session as to why the referral was made, or reticence in discussing his or her problem;
- interest in the initial session, then "yes, but-ing" and taking personal exception to what has been discussed; and
- statements implying that the patient wishes to pursue other medical treatments first.

The clinical health psychologist must be alert to these cues, given the challenging task of establishing rapport in a relatively short time. We find helpful DeGood's (1983) and Weisman's (1978) suggestions of ways in which to facilitate reduction of patient reluctance and hostility toward psychological intervention:

Establish Rapport. Self-introduction of name and position is, of course, required. Establish eye contact with the patient. When possible, sit down while talking; if you do not tower over a person who is in bed and who might already feel inferior because of role issues, he or she might feel less threatened. Ask the patient what he or she understands to be the reason for the referral.

Avoid Asking Yes–No Questions. Yes–no questions are usually not questions but statements in disguise. The reluctant patient quickly assumes that the assessing psychologist has already determined a diagnosis without listening to the patient's comments or questions.

Defuse the Organic Versus Functional Myth. Depending on how the primary physician made the referral, this can be more or less of a problem. It can be useful to simply state overtly that many patients have concerns about being referred to a psychologist for medical problems. Further discussion should include the patient's feelings and thoughts about this, and some mention of the interaction between physical illness and psychological state. Allow the patient to present physical symptoms for a short time. Acknowledging the real aspects of the medical condition is crucial, and reduces patient anxiety.

Avoid Psychologizing the Patient's Symptoms. Many patients referred to a clinical health psychologist are not psychologically minded and are not interested in insight. It is important to meet some of the needs of the patient and to provide something concrete in the first interview. This could entail some explanation of psychophysiological aspects of the medical problem, a rationale for treatment, and perhaps some diary forms for self-monitoring of troublesome symptoms.

Shape Adequate Beliefs Rather Than Challenge Misconceptions. The initial contact should involve mostly listening and encouragement. Acknowledging, but not overtly challenging the patient's reluctance to participate, can facilitate the patient's willingness to return. We find it useful to both elicit and negotiate the patient's health belief model. Exhibit 5.2 illustrates with a miniscript one method of approaching a patient with chronic pain.

Present Treatment Strategy in a Positive Fashion Rather Than as a Last Resort. Unfortunately, referral to the clinical health psychologist is sometimes a last resort after traditional medical management has failed. Distressed patients perceive this communication from the physician as "you have failed," and as a rejection. Providing a clear rationale and a more positive explanation of treatment (e.g., the next logical step) can help increase motivation and compliance.

Foster Realistic Expectations About Treatment. Patients generally do not understand the process or time commitment required in psychological treatment. Providing the patient with an outline of how psychological treatment differs from medical treatment is important. Issues of special importance include the absence of a sudden cure, the likelihood that the patient will be a more active participant than in previous medical treatments, and the inevitability of ups and downs in the course of treatment. Such a discussion can prevent premature termination of therapy because of unmet expectations or frustration.

Clarify Other Treatment Roles. The patient will want to know how the psychological treatment will integrate with ongoing medical management. The clinical health psychologist must be familiar with other treatments and be able to provide a clear explanation of how the various treatment procedures could interact and the communication that will be conducted

Exhibit 5.2

Sample Script of Reluctant
Patient Interview

Interviewer: Mr. Jones, what is your understanding about why you are here to see me today?

Patient: Well, my doctor, he told me to come here.

Interviewer: Why do you think he suggested that?

Patient: I don't know. I guess he thinks it would help, but I don't see how, not unless you can give me something that will help with this pain in my back. That's the only thing that's bothering me.

Interviewer: Well, I'm not sure what we have at this point that might be helpful for your pain—that's what we'll try to find out. But I was wondering if you had any thoughts about why you're here to see a psychologist?

Patient: No, my doctor told me to come.

Interviewer: Well, sometimes patients think that they are sent to see me because their doctor doesn't believe that their pain is real. Have you ever felt that way?

Patient: Well, I should know, I feel my pain; I know it's real.

Interviewer: Well, of course it is, and you're right—you are the only one who can feel it. No doctor can. Which I guess might feel a bit lonely sometimes, if it seems no one else can feel what you feel.

Patient: Well, that's true. You know they've done all these tests, and they can't find anything wrong.

Interviewer: What do you mean by "wrong"?

Patient: Well, they can't operate; they say it would just make my back worse.

Interviewer: So maybe what your doctor meant was that he didn't have any medical treatments that might be useful.

(continued)

Exhibit 5.2

**Sample Script of Reluctant
Patient Interview (*Continued*)**

Patient: Yes, that's right. I guess I'm a lost cause. But I think I'm managing as best I can—I mean, I'm not ready for the nuthouse yet.

Interviewer: Well people don't get sent to me because they're ready for the nuthouse. I get to see patients just like you because their doctors understand that there have been developments in the field of psychology that have sometimes been useful to patients with chronic-pain problems.

Patient: Oh, come on, you mean that I could just talk myself out of this pain?

Interviewer: Well, I'm not sure, but it might be possible that you could learn to live with it without suffering so much. Learning is sometimes a big part of pain and coping with pain, you know.

Patient: Now, I didn't learn this pain; I hurt my back at work lifting a sack of cement.

Interviewer: Of course, and you know we can't do anything about that original injury. But you know it's very normal for a pain that has been going on for a while to get affected by other things. You know, bodily processes can be conditioned. Let me give you an example: If I hold up a bright, yellow lemon in front of you—now imagine this in my hand here—and then I cut it with a knife so that you can see the juicy pulp inside. And then I hold it here and begin to squeeze. Now imagine those drops running down and the squishing sound it makes as I squeeze the lemon tight. By the way, do you feel anything in your mouth? Sometimes people do, they actually feel saliva forming under their tongues. And that is

---

(continued)

Exhibit 5.2

Sample Script of Reluctant
Patient Interview (*Continued*)

real, not imaginary, although of course it was a learned response—I mean, you never really felt the lemon itself.

Patient: Yeah, I felt that. So how does this relate to my pain? My pain is caused by that squished disc I have, not some lemon.

Interviewer: Well, I think of pain as a big pie we can divide into pieces. Some of those pieces we might actually be able to take out, like pieces of your pain that could be due to not managing your activity level well, or due to having been conditioned or affected by learning. Some pieces could be affected by your mood. We all know that if we have the flu after a bad day at work, we feel a lot worse than if we have the flu and it's been a good day. You can't have pain without it having affected your life in some way. How has it affected yours?

Patient: Well, I have been more depressed and my family is about fed up with me—you know, they don't understand—I think they think I'm faking this sometimes, but I know I hurt.

Interviewer: Yes, you do, now tell me more about it. . . .

---

among professionals. Be sure the patient understands that this is not an either–or situation.

In general, the psychologist must be vigilant to the overt or covert presentation of concerns by patients and must facilitate open discussion to dispel myths and to reassure them that their concerns are not unusual. The task is not to coerce the patient into obtaining the service but to dispel misconceptions that are barriers to obtaining help. Protection of the patient's right to consent is paramount, except when contraindicated by law. In rare cases, the interview might be terminated and the consultation terminated or deferred until the patient has the opportunity to discuss it in more detail with the referring physician.

New Information

It is often the case that the psychologist is the first professional to listen extensively to what the patient has to report. Hence, he or she might obtain more information than previous health care professionals. The patient might relish the opportunity to tell his or her story by detailing specific events leading up to the referral. Given the chance, patients sometimes tell the psychologist details that had either escaped their memory in the time-pressured discussions with their physicians or were withheld in the absence of sufficient rapport, especially if the information did not appear relevant to the patient. One of our patients revealed for the first time that she had never been adequately treated for a past episode of syphilis because she was afraid her physician would reject her if he knew she had this disease. It is important to document symptoms and history, so that appropriate information becomes available to other health care providers.

Boundary Issues

When working with medical–surgical patients, the clinical health psychologist is likely to encounter special boundary issues that are not as salient in traditional outpatient services. In fact, clinical health psychologists can find themselves involved in a variety of behaviors that are not part of traditional therapeutic practice (e.g., closing a tracheotomy tube so that the patient can speak). As a result, more traditionally trained clinicians might need to make adjustments in their own professional identity, to provide certain services.

Nudity

It is common within inpatient medical settings for the clinician to encounter patients in various states of undress. For example, as part of a heart transplant team, regular attendance on patient rounds might be required. During these rounds, patients are physically examined, which necessitates partial nudity. Not being socialized into the profession with these experiences, psychologists often wrestle with their sense of intrusiveness on patients' rights. Identifying and processing practice issues for different settings, and reframing professional interests as *health care* rather than *psychotherapy*, can help alleviate this initial discomfort. We hope, however, that we will not become insensitive to patients' discomfort with nudity and our potential for intrusiveness.

Touching

In the course of practice of clinical health psychology, therapists might need to touch their patients, a behavior most unusual in traditional practice except for the greeting handshake. As an example, touching occurs in the application of electrodes for biofeedback treatments. Other forms of contact might include gently holding a patient's hand to offer reassurance or a gentle pat on the shoulder. These acts of touching differ dramatically from traditionally established taboos and can cause a certain amount of anxiety for the psychologist.

PITFALLS IN ASSESSMENT

Professional concerns regarding the use of psychometric assessment devices and evaluation procedures include lack of normative data on medical–surgical patients, misuse of psychological data by nonpsychological personnel, and applicability of standard interpretive rules. These are discussed more thoroughly in chapters 6 and 7 of this volume. In addition to those concerns, however, there are other issues and pitfalls in the assessment process.

Dealing With Limitations of Knowledge

Even when good normative data for medical–surgical patients are available, the answers to many diagnostic and treatment questions are not easily answered with available tests. That is, psychological assessment techniques typically do not yield clean interpretations of a patient's problem. Our inability to specifically state that the problem is one thing or another is often quite frustrating to a physician who is hoping to establish a definitive diagnosis. The clinical health psychologist needs to feel comfortable furnishing sometimes-ambiguous results and not succumbing to pressures to go beyond the data to solve a problem.

Failing to Gather Background Information

Sometimes, clinicians accept at face value patient reports that previous treatments have been unsuccessful. For example, patients have reported a lack of success with biofeedback or relaxation, but when questioned in more detail, it became obvious that they lacked understanding of the procedures. We learned that they had not had either an appropriate type or trial of such treatment, had not complied with homework, or had just been told to relax rather than having been provided with systematic training. Failure to gather thorough information on past treatments can lead to erroneous conclusions and recommendations. In another example,

> Dr. Young was a 4th-year psychiatric resident completing his training in a general medical hospital. He received a consultation to assess depression in a patient who had undergone surgery for cancer. When Dr. Young arrived on the ward, the patient's medical records were being used by another service provider. In his rush to complete the consult, Dr. Young interviewed the patient without reviewing the medical record or speaking with nursing staff, making the assumption that the patient was experiencing an adjustment reaction. During the interview, the patient spoke rarely and frequently stared off into space, apparently ignoring the resident's questions. The physician concluded in his report that the patient was severely depressed and was exhibiting signs of catatonia.

Unfortunately for Dr. Young, he later learned that the patient was almost completely deaf and unable to comprehend many of his interview questions. Gathering adequate background information could be the first thing to be ignored by the rushed and time-pressured clinician. However, it is an important aspect of accurate evaluation and treatment, and in fact must be explicitly acknowledged in writing a consultation report according to hospital guidelines. As is reviewed in chapter 7 of this volume, malpractice litigation suggests that one is responsible for being aware of what is in a patient's past records.

Neglecting the Effects of the Environment

Put yourself in the following situation:

> Two days ago, you had a mild heart attack. As a result, you had to
> end all work responsibilities and are now lying in a bed in the car-
> diac care unit. There are no clocks, calendars, or windows in your
> room. You are dressed in a hospital gown, confined to bed, and
> required to use a bedpan. A nurse observes you through a window,
> and another nurse checks your vital signs every hour; you are not
> told the results. You have been given a sedative to help you rest but
> have not been told of potential side effects. There is an intravenous
> tube in your arm, but you are not aware of its purpose. Every once
> in a while a beeper goes off in your room and nurses come in to
> adjust your equipment. You have never been hospitalized before,
> and are unsure as to how to behave. The doctor has not seen you
> today, and you do not know the extent of damage to your heart.
> Your family, also being unfamiliar with the situation, is acting in an
> anxious manner. You hear that faraway relatives are making plans
> to visit you. A clinical health psychologist then enters your room,
> introduces himself, and advises you that your physician has
> requested an evaluation for depressed mood.

In interpreting data obtained from patients, we have repeatedly mentioned the importance of considering the effects of the immediate setting.
In the example just given, the psychologist must take into consideration the
effect of environmental and situational events (e.g., new role as patient,
unfamiliarity with hospitals, intensive care unit stressors) when assessing
potential causes of anxiety and depressed mood. According to attribution
theory, observers (particularly clinicians because of their person-focused
training; Jones & Nisbett, 1971) overestimate the role of dispositional (trait)
factors when inferring causes of behavior. As a safeguard, the clinical
health psychologist should pay particular attention to environmental
cues that could precipitate maladaptive behavior and should be aware
of common environmental stressors in health care. Failure to do so will
result in erroneous conclusions about the causality and permanence of
the patient's condition.

Underestimating Psychopathology

Clinical health psychologists sometimes underestimate the effects of psychopathology and its relationship to the medical–surgical problem. The clinical health psychologist must have as strong a background in psychopathology as any clinical psychologist. For instance, the prevalence of diagnosable psychiatric disorders in a primary care medical patient population is estimated to be between 16% and 43% (Bray, Frank, McDaniel, & Heldring, 2004). When one investigates special medical populations, the incidence is likely to be higher. In a review of the research on psychopathology in chronic pain patients, Weisberg and Keefe (1999) found that the prevalence of diagnosable personality disorders in this patient population ranged between 31% and 59%. Significant rates of diagnosable psychiatric disorders have been found in patients hospitalized in general medical units (Clarke, MacKinnon, Smith, McKenzie, & Herrman, 2000), as well as in surgical patients (Balestrieri et al., 2000). Clinical health psychologists must be especially skilled in the management of depression and anxiety, as well as in how personality disorders and other psychopathologies interrelate with medical–surgical problems and treatment.

Coping With Competing Agendas

In providing clinical services, the psychologist might have to deal with competing agendas with respect to a particular case, and be clear as to who is the client. Consider the following example:

> In one presurgical screening of a kidney donor, we became aware of the referring physician's desire for a "clean bill of psychological health," so that the kidney could be obtained for his own patient. This was his third psychological consultation in an effort to clear the donor for surgery. The potential donor was also eager to undergo the operation, because it gave him the opportunity to atone for perceived sins within the family. The hospital's agenda was for written confirmation of no psychological risk to the donor to avoid malpractice liability. Given the nature of the case, none of these parties was satisfied with the results and recommendations of the psychological evaluation,

which could not provide unqualified clearance. Although the potential donor demonstrated a clear understanding of the procedure, he also had a long history of poor impulse control and instances in which he manifested poor judgment in decisions related to self-care. The organ donation did occur after the patient obtained a court judgment, which satisfied the hospital's malpractice lawyers, that he was not legally incompetent to make this decision. Indeed, the psychologist had insufficient evidence to conclude that the patient was legally incompetent.

Psychologists must be acutely aware of any temptation to please referral sources or employers by modifying interpretations of data obtained.

Coping With the Hostile Physician

As in any profession, there are hostile and arrogant physicians. Strategies for coping include a task-oriented focus on the patient's needs as a mutual goal, consistent assertiveness, confrontation as necessary, and a wealth of good humor. If the goal is to change physician behavior toward the patient, emphasizing benefits that would accrue to the physician is critical to laying the groundwork for change.

SPECIAL ISSUES IN INTERVENTION

Some issues in conducting interventions that can arise include determining an adequate trial, maintaining the therapeutic contract, and interrupting treatment.

Determining an Adequate Trial

It is important for the clinical health psychologist to understand what constitutes an adequate trial of treatment for any given approach because there are significant ethical problems with persisting in an ineffective treatment regimen. In making this decision, the clinician should consider both patient variables (e.g., motivation, attendance, consistency, acceptance of the biopsychosocial model) and treatment variables (e.g., what procedures have been attempted, what revisions in protocol have occurred in response to lack of improvement, what the limitations of the strategy are).

Understanding the nature of previous treatment attempts and reasons for failure can also help the clinician decide when to pursue other forms of intervention or when to cease treatment. We cannot underscore enough the need to obtain numerous details about previous treatments. When closely scrutinized, the relaxation therapy or biofeedback treatment previously obtained may have been inadequate in terms of design and implementation.

In the therapist's zeal to help patients learn to cope with various medical and psychological problems, he or she should not lose sight of the fact that not all problems are treatable, at least by methods currently available. The experienced clinician will accept the limitations of interventions, thereby avoiding a failure experience that could have negative effects on the patient and be unrewarding for the clinician.

Maintaining the Therapeutic Contract

Medical–surgical patients can be in multiple psychological treatments. For example, a patient might be referred by another mental health professional for an adjunctive intervention for tension headache. These patients often begin relating material that is also appropriate to the primary psychotherapy. It is necessary for the clinical health psychologist to deal with this material in the context of the focused treatment, to be aware of potential risks to the primary therapy, and to ensure a collaborative approach to treatment. Alternatively, the therapist might need to renegotiate the existing contract with both patient and referral source.

Interrupting Psychological Treatment

Interruptions can occur because of either planned or unplanned circumstances. It is common for patients to take a hiatus from psychological treatment while attending to acute medical problems. Patients also request interruption of treatment for financial reasons or for personal reasons.

A common reason for treatment interruption has to do with premature discharge, which can occur for a variety of reasons, including insurance coverage. As a result, physicians can discharge their patients as soon as they are medically cleared, not considering psychological intervention a reasonable cause for extending hospitalization. Consequently, the clinician might begin an intervention procedure that he or she is unable to complete. When the clinical health psychologist has had insufficient time to establish adequate rapport with the patient before discharge, it is unlikely that the patient will continue with treatment on an outpatient basis. Furthermore, given that most psychological interventions take time, the patient could be discharged believing that interactions with the psychologist had little or no effect or hope of effect. When this colors the patient's perceptions of the relevance of psychology in the future, the psychological intervention may do more harm than good in the long run.

An additional source of premature termination or separation is created by faculty schedules and student rotations. In large teaching institutions, psychological interns and postdoctoral residents typically rotate through various psychological subspecialties. To help eliminate some of the problems associated with this issue of "temporary therapists," we have found it helpful to clearly state early in the therapy process the time limits imposed by these conditions and to offer the patient reasonable alternatives (e.g., delay onset of treatment, transfer to another trainee, transfer to staff personnel). The potential for interrupted treatment, and the possible consequences, should be considered in treatment planning.

COMMUNICATION OF RESULTS

Within an inpatient setting, the goal of the initial interview is to obtain sufficient information to respond to the consultee's request. This does not mean that the consultation will necessarily be answered in full, but it does mean that the consultee is responded to in a timely fashion. In practicing within an outpatient setting, the consultant is more likely to base case disposition on a number of interviews; thus, the initial communication might reflect a more complete workup of the case.

When physicians consult one another, the consultant typically responds with some objective data and then an opinion. This holds true for lab results, X-ray interpretations, and physical exams. The same expectations are made of psychologists. However, because we often do not have the same type of diagnostic tools available, we find ourselves limited in the type of information we can provide the referral source. Often, our opinion rests on an extensive interview with the patient and a detailed history.

At other times, we base our opinions on psychometric evaluation, data from which is often not appropriate to share with other professionals, as it could be easily misunderstood. When testing is involved, we do not provide the physician with scores, offering, instead, a summary of interpretations. Our statements and opinions need to be presented in a sound manner, reflecting an understanding of the patient and the relevant issues.

Written Reports

In an inpatient setting, whether the initial contact results in a case conceptualization, the clinician must record the contact in the medical chart. Ideally, communication is also done verbally, but given the frequent unavailability of staff because of conflicting schedules and shift changes, it is often impossible to communicate directly. Consequently, the written report becomes paramount to good communication.

Whether the patient is seen in an inpatient or outpatient setting, a note is either placed in the progress notes section of the patient's medical records or written on a separate consultation report and placed in the patient's chart. Although settings can differ, the following are some typical medical record department rules:

- Chart entries must be made only in black ink.
- It is prohibited to leave spaces between entries.
- It is prohibited to black- or white-out errors.
- Errors are marked through with a single line, accompanied by the writer's initials.

- Only approved abbreviations may be used, and then not in discharge summaries.
- Inpatient progress notes require not only date and name of service, but also time and duration.

Although such regulations appear picayune at first, they have developed over time in response to specific needs or problems. They are codified in either Joint Commission on Accreditation of Healthcare Organizations (JCAHO) standards or local rules and regulations; infractions are monitored by special committees and can provide bases for suspension of hospital privileges.

If the clinician attempted to meet with the patient and was unable to complete the assessment, a note so indicating would also be placed in the medical chart. Although this could initially appear to be a trivial exercise, it is important to communicate to the referral source that an attempt was made to respond to the consultation request.

Failure to chart interactions with patients and staff can result in professionally embarrassing situations. Once, we encountered a politically difficult situation in which a mental health professional, who usually did not see medically ill patients, continued to see one of his patients at bedside during a difficult hospitalization. Because the clinician was unfamiliar with protocol, he had not been documenting these contacts in the medical record. The attending physician was unaware of the patient receiving these services and requested psychological evaluation and treatment for depressed mood and anxiety. Although duplication in services was avoided, professional embarrassment was not.

Of course, the content of the report largely depends on the referral question. As previously emphasized, however, "psychobabble" tends only to infuriate medical personnel and fosters the belief that psychology has nothing of practical value to offer. The report should be brief, succinct, relevant, practical, and have explanatory value. It is customary to include an overview of the presenting problem, behavioral observations and mental status information, relevant biopsychosocial interactions, patient strengths and problem areas, impressions, and recommendations. See Exhibit 5.3 for several report formats we have used over the years.

Exhibit 5.3

Sample Report Formats

I. Presurgical evaluation
   Referral information
   Assessment procedures
   Brief background information
      Family of origin
      Education and occupation
      Marital and family history
      Psychological and behavioral health history
      Social support network
      Current issues and stressors
   Findings
      Behavioral observations and mental status
      Test results
      Features specific to the surgical-treatment procedure
      Attitudinal and motivational features
      Informational and cognitive features
      Affective features
      Family issues
      Coping strategies
   Recommendations (with specific references to consultee
      behavior as appropriate)
II. Consultation regarding pain management
   Referral information
   Assessment procedures
   Background information
      Presenting problem
      Other medical history
      Behavioral health history
      Psychosocial factors
      Family history

(*continued*)

Exhibit 5.3

Sample Report Formats (*Continued*)

Occupational history
Marital history
Leisure time
Psychotherapy history
Findings
    Behavioral observations
    Test results
    Factors impacting pain management
        Sensory
        Affective
        Cognitive
        Behavioral
        Compliance issues
        Medication issues
        Recommendations

Recommendations should include a specific treatment or management plan. Even when no treatment is indicated, the clinician should indicate, when appropriate, the implications of the findings for medical management, and for the behavior of health care providers. Psychiatric diagnosis might or might not be included in the written consultation, depending on the nature of the consultation, the rules of the setting, and personal preference. In general, diagnostic labels in and of themselves are of little value to the consultee and are sometimes viewed with disdain by nonpsychiatric physicians. In addition, they can be inadvertently used by other health care professionals in such a manner that the patient becomes defined by his or her diagnosis.

There is always concern as to how much and what type of information to reveal in medical charts, written reports, and through verbal communication. It is common for medical personnel to fix their attention on key words in an assessment summary and miss or deemphasize important subtleties. The following example of a poorly written summary demonstrates this issue:

> The patient was a 49-year-old man with recent onset of cardiac arrhythmias. Psychological testing reveals that this patient does not have limited intellectual abilities. This patient behaves in a manner consistent with type A behavior and is likely to react in a hostile, competitive manner when his goals are thwarted.

First, it is likely that health care professionals reading this will miss the "does not" that precedes the description of intelligence. Consequently, this patient might be perceived to have limited intellectual understanding. Second, it is quite possible that the reader will not focus on the fact that type A behaviors are elicited under certain conditions, and not under all circumstances. As a result, staff could attribute qualities to this man that do not exist or be unduly defensive in response to a perceived risk of general hostile behavior.

ISSUES OF DISPOSITION

Knowing when to refer and follow up are key issues in disposition.

Knowing When to Refer

Being alert to possible changes or oversights in medical conditions is a responsibility of the clinical health psychologist. When the clinician suspects that the patient is behaving in a manner suggestive of organic disease, or symptoms described by the patient point to such a case, it is imperative that the psychologist pursue medical evaluation. Consider the following example:

> The patient was a 34-year-old single woman who sought help from a clinical health psychologist for treatment of her bruxism. She specifically requested hypnosis and biofeedback to stop the clenching and

associated pain. The patient described symptoms of tension and pain in the jaw muscles and of congestion in the nasal passages and stated that her palate felt like a "piece of hard steel." Her dentist had found no abnormality. The psychologist insisted on an examination by an otolaryngologist before beginning treatment. A nasopharyngeal tumor was discovered on this exam and radium implant therapy was begun immediately.

This example illustrates how important assessment of biological targets can be. Patients often do not want to complete medical and dental evaluations because they desire to get on with treatment and are convinced that stress is producing their symptoms. It is imperative that this issue be routinely addressed; as indicated previously, the clinician might need to take on an advocacy role to be sure that this is accomplished.

In other circumstances, the patient might have had a thorough medical workup that yielded negative physical results, yet continued to report symptoms suggestive of an undocumented organic disease. This type of situation requires the clinical health psychologist to carefully document the patient's symptoms while pursuing further medical evaluations. The psychologist should not be intimidated by medical personnel or by hard data attesting to the lack of an organic disease. In more than one case, the insistence on repeated medical evaluations has resulted in the diagnosis of initial stages of disease.

Follow-Up and Follow-Through

Rarely is the single interview or single assessment process sufficient to answer the referral question. As a result, the clinical health psychologist typically allows for follow-up procedures. Usually this contact involves additional assessment procedures, some form of intervention, and evaluation as to the effectiveness of an intervention. Unfortunately, follow-up procedures are not always completed. This happens for a variety of reasons, including premature discharge of the patient, failure of the clinician to recognize the need for follow-up, and reluctance by the patient to provide further information.

In some packaged treatment programs, there is no patient follow up after discharge from the program. Th up is not viewed as necessary, if follow-up procedures ar effective, or if follow-up sessions are not defined as treatme little interest for both patient and clinician. We anticipate that increased demands for patient outcome data will counteract these influences.

Follow-through means ensuring that necessary or recommended procedures have been executed. It is common for the clinical health psychologist to recommend that another service, such as social work or psychiatry, also be consulted on behalf of the patient. Although this information is typically communicated through medical chart progress notes and consultation forms, it is not adequate to assume that the recommended action will automatically occur. Thus, the clinician needs to make direct contact with allied services and continue to follow progress in that department, sometimes coordinating types of services.

ALTERNATIVES

Clinical health psychologists should abide by the following well-known saying: "Stay open-minded, but not so open-minded that your brains fall out." Sometimes rather nontraditional types of assessment and intervention are suggested because highly novel approaches might be required. For example, when attempting to assess a patient for possible self-infection of an open wound (Munchausen's syndrome), one strategy used was to tape the patient's hands (with consent) to determine whether reinfections would decrease. In another case, spot fingernail cultures were ordered to assess more definitively the source and means of infection.

An example of unusual intervention is illustrated by the clinician who suggested to a patient facing laryngectomy (and who had a booming baritone voice, which he used regularly in a barbershop quartet) that he tape various messages to his family as a means of preserving his voice (similar to a family photo album). Thus, his young grandchildren would have a record of what he sounded like before surgery. Guided by the scientific knowledge base of behavior, clinicians are limited only by their creativity in devising innovative solutions to difficult problems.

Obviously, not all special issues and problems have been discussed in this chapter. However, the information presented should alert the reader to common pitfalls in practice, especially with respect to problems with referrals, issues in the conduct of consultations, communication of results, and disposition. In the next chapter, we address ethical issues in the practice of clinical health psychology.

6

Ethical Issues in the Practice of Clinical Health Psychology

Because of the special settings and patient populations encountered, the practice of clinical health psychology brings with it unique ethical issues. This chapter describes some of the special ethical issues encountered, with examples from the authors' own experiences over the years, and addresses the application of the American Psychological Association's (APA) "Ethical Principles of Psychologists and Code of Conduct" (2002b; also available from http://www.apa.org/ethics/code2002.pdf; hereinafter referred to as the Ethics Code) to those situations. It is as important for clinical health psychologists to be knowledgeable of the ethical principles as it is for psychologists in any other area of practice. The Ethics Code (2002; Introduction and Applicability) states the following:

> Membership in the APA commits members and student affiliates to comply with the standards of the APA Ethics Code and to the rules and procedures used to enforce them. Lack of awareness or misunderstanding of an Ethical Standard is not itself a defense to a charge of unethical conduct. (¶ 3)

In addition, it is important for all psychologists, whether APA members or not, to be knowledgeable of the Ethics Code because the ethical standards are one aspect in establishing the professional standard of care in any malpractice or licensing board action.

REVISION OF THE ETHICS CODE

Since our discussion of ethics in the prior edition of this book (Belar & Deardorff, 1995), the APA Ethics Code has been revised. The revision of the previous code (APA, 1992) was started in 1997 to ensure that it continued to be relevant to current issues in professional practice, research, and training. It was completed in 2002, and according to Smith (2003), some of the substantive changes in the revision include eliminating the prohibition that prevents psychologists from releasing raw test data to individuals who are not qualified to use them (Ethical Standards 9.04, 9.11), adding new sections on assessment standards (Ethical Standards 9.02, 9.03), changes to informed consent for "new treatments" (Ethical Standard 10.01b), guidelines for terminating therapy when threatened by a patient (Ethical Standard 10.10b), defining multiple relationships more clearly (Ethical Standard 3.5a), and addressing issues related to use of the Internet and electronic transmission (throughout the Ethics Code).

SPECIAL ETHICAL PROBLEMS IN CLINICAL HEALTH PSYCHOLOGY

The following discussion examines the most current ethical principles relevant to the practice of clinical health psychology.

Competence in Training and Practice

Psychologists planning to provide services, teach, or conduct research involving populations, areas, techniques, or technologies new to them, undertake relevant education, training, supervised experience, consultation, or study (Ethical Standard 2.01c). In those emerging areas in which generally recognized standards for preparatory training do not yet exist, psychologists nevertheless take reasonable steps to ensure the competence of their work and to protect clients/patients, students, supervisees, research participants, organizational clients, and others from harm (Ethical Standard 2.01e). Psychologists' work is based upon established scientific and professional knowledge of the discipline. (Ethical Standard 2.04)

Two types of personal competencies are necessary for high quality practice (Koocher & Keith-Spiegel, 1998; Pope & Brown, 1996). *Intellectual competence* is the acquisition of empirically based knowledge and sound clinical judgment in practice with a particular patient population. Possessing intellectual competence is also being able to recognize what one does and does not know. *Emotional competence* is the clinical health psychologist's ability to emotionally manage clinical material that emerges in treatment. This includes detecting and addressing personal biases, having a capacity for self-care, and accepting that "not all therapists can work with all clients or all kinds of problems" (Koocher & Keith-Spiegel, 1998, p. 55). The concepts of intellectual and emotional competence parallel our discussion of education, training, and personal characteristics necessary for competent and ethical practice in clinical health psychology (see chap. 2, this volume).

Since the 1983 Arden House Conference (G. C. Stone, 1983), there has been further development of the recommendations for training practitioners in health psychology (McDaniel, Belar, Schroeder, Hargrove, & Freeman, 2002). As was the case even in 1983, it is well recognized that weekend workshops do not produce a clinical health psychologist. As discussed in detail in chapter 2 of this volume, core training and preparation for clinical health psychology practice should include specific graduate-level courses in the area as well as supervised practical experience. The APA Division of Health Psychology (Division 38) Web site has extensive information about training for health psychology careers (http://www.health-psych.org). A psychologist should not present him- or herself as a clinical health psychologist unless training has been adequately satisfied. A psychologist is not eligible for a board certification in clinical health psychology from the American Board of Professional Psychology unless certain educational requirements have been met. In addition, Ethical Standard 2.04 suggests that the practitioner should be familiar with evidence-based practice relative to clinical health psychology.

Recognition of One's Boundaries of Competence

Psychologists provide services, teach, and conduct research with populations and in areas only within the boundaries of their competence, based on their education, training, supervised experience, consultation, study, or professional experience. (Ethical Standard 2.01a)

A psychologist must ensure the best interests and welfare of the patient who presents with a problem of psychological factors related to a medical problem. Consider the following example:

> Dr. Smith, a clinical psychologist, works in private practice setting, serving mostly adults. In the course of her work, she began treating a 22-year-old man who was referred by his physician and was experiencing muscle contraction headaches. Dr. Smith had done some reading about the treatment of muscle contraction headaches but had never actually treated a person with this problem. She continued treating the patient but received supervision by a clinical health psychologist experienced in the treatment of chronic headaches.

Dr. Smith acted appropriately and ethically in this example. Had she not received the outside supervision, she could have been acting unethically in providing treatment outside her area of competence (Ethical Standard 2.01a). This is especially true in cases of psychophysiological disorders because there are often clearly specified and empirically validated treatment approaches available for use. Another option might have been for the psychologist to refer the patient to a colleague for concurrent treatment of the headache problem. Although data are not available, in our experience, cross-consultation does not appear to be as frequent in the independent practice of psychology as it does in medicine, other than referrals for neuropsychological and learning disabilities evaluations.

Related to this issue, it is unlikely that a psychologist could be proficient in all areas of practice that fall within the field of clinical health psychology. As indicated in chapter 1 (this volume), clinical health psychology includes such diverse problems as eating disorders and headaches, and such diverse assessments as neuropsychological evaluations and workups of patients with chronic pain. The skills necessary for these different clinical tasks are extremely varied. As in the preceding example, the clinical health psychologist must be aware of his or her limitations even within the field of clinical health psychology and take steps to assure ethical professional behavior. The self-assessment guide described in chapter 2 of this volume can facilitate this process (Belar et al., 2001).

Maintenance of Current Knowledge

Psychologists undertake ongoing efforts to develop and maintain their competence. (Ethical Standard 2.03)

In a field as rapidly changing as clinical health psychology, it is essential to keep abreast of current literature. This is addressed in Ethical Standard 2.03 (Maintaining Competence). Attending continuing education workshops, belonging to professional organizations, completing ongoing Internet research about specific cases, and subscribing to health psychology journals can facilitate this continuing education process. It has been said that the half-life of a PhD in clinical psychology is about 10 years when no further postgraduate education is sought (Dubin, 1972). In the area of clinical health psychology, this estimate may be much lower because of the high level of research and clinical activity as well as changes in medicine and health care.

Working With People of Different Backgrounds

Where scientific or professional knowledge in the discipline of psychology establishes that an understanding of factors associated with age, gender, gender identity, race, ethnicity, culture, national origin, religion, sexual orientation, disability, language, or socioeconomic status is essential for effective implementation of their services or research, psychologists have or obtain the training, experience, consultation, or supervision necessary to ensure the competence of their services, or they make appropriate referrals. (Ethical Standard 2.01b)

Although we know of no research on this, it may be that clinical health psychology patient populations represent more of a cross section of society than the populations presenting to services at mental health clinics. We find that to meet this ethical guideline in the practice of clinical health psychology, an understanding of patients' health belief models is essential. Furthermore, it is important to have an appreciation for cultural and other factors that influence patients' explanatory frameworks for medical problems. The following is an overview of a conceptual model useful in accomplishing these goals.

A conceptual distinction among disease, illness, and sickness is helpful for understanding patients presenting to clinical health psychologists (Engel, 1977; Fabrega, 1974; Hofman, 2002; Kleinman, Eisenberg, & Good, 1978, 2006). *Disease* is an abnormality in physical structure or bodily function; it is the focus of biomedicine. *Illness*, however, is the human experience of sickness and is influenced by interpersonal, social, and cultural variables (Hoffman, 2002; Landrine & Klonoff, 1992; Mechanic, 1972). Illness entails explanation of the disease and how one is supposed to act when ill. It is how we perceive, experience, and cope with disease. In keeping with this model, there is rarely a one-to-one relationship between disease and illness (Beecher, 1956; McMahon & Koltzenberg, 2005; Melzack & Wall, 1983; Zola, 1966). The combined influences of disease and illness yield what we ultimately observe clinically as *sickness*. Patients are generally much more concerned with the treatment of their illness than with simply the cure of the disease.

Ethical Standard 2.01b dictates that the clinical health psychologist have an understanding of the model discussed earlier. The domain of clinical health psychology treatment is often illness behavior, explanatory beliefs, and sickness. When there is a significant discrepancy between the doctor's and patient's explanatory models, problems in treatment can occur.

> Mrs. A. B. was a 56-year-old woman who was recovering from pulmonary edema secondary to atherosclerotic cardiovascular disease and chronic congestive heart failure on a general medical unit. Her physical status was improving, but she was frequently inducing vomiting and urinating in her bed. She became angry when told by the staff to stop these behaviors. Psychological consultation revealed that her physician had told the patient that part of her medical problem

included "water in the lungs." Because of her family's occupation as plumbers, her conception of her anatomy consisted of a pipe connecting her mouth and urethra. She was therefore attempting to remove as much water from her body as possible through vomiting and urinating. She was hesitant to share this belief model with her physician because "he was so rushed" and she felt embarrassed. A sharing of the doctor and patient explanatory models, including a careful didactic session about her anatomy, resulted in a resolution of the problem behaviors and feelings of anger. (Case example adapted from Kleinman et al., 1978, p. 254)

Other common examples of patients' misconceptions about medical treatments include the following: (a) If one pill is good, then two or more must be better; (b) if symptoms are not occurring, then the pills are not necessary (often seen in medication usage for hypertension and diabetes); and (c) continued use of any medication is overdependence. As can be seen, any of these beliefs will have serious consequences for medical treatment.

Kleinman et al. (1978) suggested that in addressing a patient's belief model, one should attempt the following: (a) to elicit the patient's belief model with simple, straightforward questions; (b) to formulate the physician's model in terms the patient can understand and communicate this to the patient; (c) to openly compare models to identify contradictions; and (d) to help the physician and patient engage in a negotiation toward shared models related to treatment and outcome. Awareness of cultural and social issues related to a patient's belief model is crucial in guiding this process. It must also be realized that subgroups other than identified minority cultures may have beliefs about illness that affect behavior (as portrayed in the last example). It may be unethical to fail to address these issues.

Psychological Assessment

Psychologists administer, adapt, score, interpret, or use assessment techniques, interviews, tests, or instruments in a manner and for purposes that are appropriate in light of the research on or evidence of the usefulness and proper application of the techniques. (Ethical Standard 9.02a)

Psychologists use assessment instruments whose validity and reliability have been established for use with members of the population tested. When such validity or reliability has not been established, psychologists describe the strengths and limitations of test results and interpretation. (Ethical Standard 9.02b)

Psychologists do not promote the use of psychological assessment techniques by unqualified persons, except when such use is conducted for training purposes with appropriate supervision. (Ethical Standard 9.07)

Psychologists do not base their assessment or intervention decisions or recommendations on data or test results that are outdated for the current purpose. (Ethical Standard 9.08a)

Psychologists do not base such decisions or recommendations on tests and measures that are obsolete and not useful for the current purpose. (Ethical Standard 9.08b)

Regardless of whether the scoring and interpretation are done by psychologists, by employees or assistants, or by automated or other outside services, psychologists take reasonable steps to ensure that explanations of results are given to the individual or designated representative unless the nature of the relationship precludes provision of an explanation of results (such as in some organizational consulting, preemployment or security screenings, and forensic evaluations), and this fact has been clearly explained to the person being assessed in advance. (Ethical Standard 9.10)

In psychological assessment with medical patients, the clinical health psychologist must be acutely aware of: (a) using the proper standardization data for medical patients when available (Ethical Standard 9.02a), (b) differences in test interpretation with a medical–surgical patient population versus a psychiatric population (Ethical Standard 9.02b), (c) increased risk of inappropriate use of test results by nonpsychologist health care professionals (Ethical Standard 9.07), (d) the language of the test interpretation and risk of misinterpretation (Ethical Standard 9.06), and (e) systemic issues hampering the patient's right to be informed of the test results (Ethical Standard 9.10). Consider the following relatively common example:

The patient was a 34-year-old woman who presented to her primary physician with diffuse and vague somatic complaints, including pain. The patient also revealed that she had been recently experiencing some significant life stressors. The physician hypothesized that these might be contributing to her physical complaints. The initial physical evaluation was negative and, in keeping with the physician's hypothesis, the patient was referred for psychological evaluation, including psychological testing. The consultation request was to "determine if the symptoms might have a functional rather than organic basis." The psychologist preferred using the original Minnesota Multiphasic Personality Inventory (MMPI; Hathaway & McKinley, 1943) because she was more comfortable with it and had her own computer scoring and interpretive software. The MMPI was scored using standard normative data. The patient obtained a classic "conversion V" profile with Scales 1 and 3 primed and all other scales below a t score of 70.

The psychologist gave the following interpretation for the MMPI and sent the recommendations to the physician without discussing them with the patient. (Release of confidentiality had been obtained to release the test results to the physician.)

Patients with similar profiles present themselves as normal, responsible, and without fault. They make extensive use of such defenses as projection, denial, and rationalization and blame others for their troubles. They prefer medical explanations for their symptoms, and lack insight into the psychological basis for their symptoms. These patients are generally considered to be converting personally distressing problems into somatic complaints, which are more socially acceptable. Although these patients are resistant to change, because of firmly entrenched defense systems, a course of psychotherapy targeting the patient's actual source of distress may be useful. (Interpretation on the basis of Graham, 1977; Greene, 1980, 1991, for the original MMPI)

The physician referred the patient for psychological treatment, on the basis of the evaluation described earlier, after explaining to the patient that the psychological testing substantiated that her physical symptoms were "psychosomatic." The psychological treatment was successful in resolving the stressful life circumstances with which the patient was having trouble, but the physical symptoms persisted. The patient was ultimately diagnosed as having multiple sclerosis when further diagnostic work was done.

This example illustrates several major ethical issues related to psychological assessment in clinical health psychology. First, the psychologist used the original version of the MMPI (Hathaway & McKinley, 1943), which was officially withdrawn from use by the test publisher as of September 1999. Even though it is now considered obsolete (Pope, Butcher, & Seelan, 2006), it continues to be used in practice. In addition, the psychologist used standard normative data to derive the patient's profile. Although this can be adequate if the use of such norms is taken into account in the interpretation, a more useful approach would be to use both the standard norms and those for medical patients (either norms generated in one's own clinic or those published in the literature, e.g., Graham, 2005; Greene, 1980, 1991), and compare the difference. Even the MMPI–2 (Butcher, Graham, Ben-Porath, Tellegen, & Dahlstrom, 1989) must be interpreted cautiously when used with medical and presurgery patients and on the basis of research applicable to the patient population being assessed.

Other issues in this example, and more important ones, as they influenced the course of the patient's treatment, were the consultation request itself and the interpretation of the results. First, the physician requested an inappropriate use for psychological testing. Although this type of request is commonly received from medical personnel, reviews of the literature suggest that psychologists who use the MMPI or MMPI–2 to assess pain patients should "not attempt to classify patients as organic, functional, or mixed" (Prokop & Bradley, 1981, p. 96; see also Bradley, McDonald-Haile, & Jaworski, 1992; Graham, 2005). Second, the psychologist used a standard interpretation developed on psychiatric patients. This included conjecture as to the etiology of the physical symptoms as well as several personality labels that might have been cast as pejorative by a non–mental health professional.

Another problem with the response to this referral was that the language of the interpretation might not be in keeping with ethically guarding against the misuse of assessment results and promoting the best interests of the client. Without further explanation, the physician may well have changed his or her opinion of this patient and seen the patient as somehow volitionally controlling the presentation of symptoms or consciously malingering, although there was no evidence of this.

The last ethical issue related to this case is that the psychologist did not "ensure that an explanation of the results [was] provided using language that [was] reasonably understandable to the person assessed" (Ethical Standard 9.10, Explaining Assessment Results). Although Ethical Standard 9.10 does not state that the explanation must be given directly by the psychologist, the psychologist must ensure that an adequate and understandable explanation is provided. We believe that this can be done most effectively if the explanation is given directly by the psychologist. This explanation and feedback process, however it is accomplished, is ethically mandated (Ethical Standard 9.10) unless explicitly waived as part of the informed-consent process.

Sometimes, the consultant will discuss findings with the referring physician and not directly with the patient. However, this can be problematic, and we recommend that, when possible, follow-up with the patient should be provided. It should at least be offered as an option if the patient would like further clarification after feedback from a physician. It is also prudent to inform the referral source of the importance of the feedback process with the patient. Pope (1992) provides guidelines for providing psychological test feedback to patients, including feedback as process, clarification of tasks and roles, informed consent, framing the feedback, documentation, and follow-up.

In summary, in this case, the test results were not used in the best interests of the patient. Even if the patient had not ultimately been found to have multiple sclerosis, psychological evaluation should rarely preclude thorough medical evaluation. Exceptions to this guideline might include extreme cases, such as somatic delusions or factitious disorders, in which there is a documented history of unnecessary extensive medical evaluations and procedures. Even in these cases, it is important to have an open line of communication with the physician. It is important to remember that people with these types of psychological problems (e.g., somatization, symptom amplification) get sick just like everyone else.

Clinical health psychologists must be aware of special psychological assessment issues in working with medical patients, because general practice assessment skills are not always applicable. When the psychologist is not familiar with current literature in the area, he or she is at higher risk for unethical practice. A complete discussion of assessment issues in health psychology can be found in chapter 3 of this volume.

Computerized Psychological Testing

When interpreting assessment results, including automated interpretations, psychologists take into account the purpose of the assessment as well as the various test factors, test-taking abilities, and other characteristics of the person being assessed, such as situational, personal, linguistic, and cultural differences, that might affect psychologists' judgments or reduce the accuracy of their interpretations. They indicate any significant limitations of their interpretations. (Ethical Standard 9.06)

Psychologists who offer assessment or scoring services to other professionals accurately describe the purpose, norms, validity, reliability, and applications of the procedures and any special qualifications applicable to their use. (Ethical Standard 9.09a)

Psychologists select scoring and interpretation services (including automated services) on the basis of evidence of the validity of the program and procedures, as well as on other appropriate considerations. (Ethical Standard 9.09b)

Psychologists retain responsibility for the appropriate application, interpretation, and use of assessment instruments, whether they score and interpret such tests themselves or use automated or other services. (Ethical Standard 9.09c)

The use of computer-based test interpretation (CBTI) has continued to increase over the past several decades (Butcher, Perry, & Atlis, 2000). The ethical principles of assessment listed previously and the *Standards for Educational and Psychological Tests* (American Educational Research Association [AERA], APA, & National Council on Measurement [NCM], 1999) address issues related to computerized testing. The test standards applicable to CBTIs are as follows:

When computer-prepared interpretations of test response protocols are reported, the sources, rationale, and empirical basis for these interpretations should be made available, and their limitations should be described. (Ethical Standard 5.11)

Test users should not rely on computer-generated interpretations of test results unless they have the expertise to consider the appropriateness of these interpretations in individual cases. (Ethical Standard 11.21)

Those who use computer-generated interpretations of test data should evaluate the quality of the interpretations and, when possible, the relevance and appropriateness of the norms upon which the interpretations are based. (Ethical Standard 12.15; AERA, APA, & NCM, 1999)

Specific and practical guidelines for users have also been discussed in various publications (Bersoff & Hofer, 1995; Butcher, 2002; Hofer & Bersoff, 1983). Butcher (2002) has identified nine important issues when evaluating CBTIs. These include validity of the underlying test, expertise of the developers, availability of documentation, availability of updates and revisions, adherence to APA guidelines, detection of response sets, relationship to published test interpretation research, quality of technical support, and inclusion of appropriate interpretative cautions in regard to interpretation.

There are really two major concerns relative to CBTIs: (a) the adequacy of the scoring algorithms and the classification system used to assign statements to particular test scores and (b) the validity of the interpretations inferred from test results. J. E. Williams and Weed (2004) empirically tested these issues by sending the same MMPI–2 raw data to six different interpretative services. The researchers concluded, "Among the CBTI reports, interpretative differences for the sample case were striking" (J. E. Williams & Weed, 2004, p. 80). Findings included the following:

1. "Treatment recommendations also differed among the CBTI reports" (p. 80).
2. "There were also dramatic differences among the diagnostic impressions offered for each report" (p. 80; illustrated in Table 3, p. 82).

3. "The content of the CBTI reports reviewed here varied substantially when reporting on the same MMPI–2 profile" (p. 81).
4. "Most unfortunate, despite the popularity of these programs, CBTI publishers do not provide users with much direct evidence in support of the use of their programs" (p. 81).
5. "The differences suggested by Table 3 (from 23 possible diagnoses to none suggested) imply substantially different parameters underlying test interpretation" (p. 81).

First, the user should be sure that the CBTI scores (raw or scaled) are in keeping with those derived through traditional methods. Although computer hard copy looks accurate, such is not always the case, even after extensive field-testing by the company. Second, the user should have available data on the decision rules used to match test scores with interpretative statements. When this is not possible, the user should be aware of existing research on the computer programs being used. Unfortunately, this is often not available. Third, it is important to know which interpretive statements are linked to which test scores. Many CBTIs do not provide such information, stating that it is proprietary; this makes the guideline difficult to satisfy. Often one can scan the interpretative reports, comparing interpretations with test scores, to help assure validity. Once again, application to clinical health psychology requires use of appropriate norms in interpretation.

Fourth, it must always be kept in mind that computerized interpretive reports are tools of the qualified professional. The clinician is ultimately responsible for the report's validity and use. This means that the clinician might need to edit or amend the computer-generated psychological report to take into account sound clinical judgment. In our experience, we often see the entire computer-generated report simply attached to the end of the evaluation report. This practice is likely to lead to confusion and misuse of the results because these reports often contain every possible interpretive statement. Clinical health psychologists are often involved in computerized psychological testing in the context of a medical center, a comprehensive treatment program (e.g., a chronic-pain program), or on

an individual clinical treatment level. At an early stage of CBTI development, Matarazzo (1986) voiced concern that

> the tremendous advances during the past five years in microcomput-
> erized psychological testing hardware and software have made it pos-
> sible and economically seductive for a psychologist, a physician,
> another health service provider or a hospital administrator to offer
> such testing to unprecedented numbers of patients and clients. (p. 17)

The prediction of Matarazzo (1986) has come true, because major
publishers of CBTIs now market directly to a variety of nonpsychologist
health care providers. Aside from being used by psychologists, computerized interpretive reports are also being used by other health care professionals, who are often accustomed to ordering lab tests from technicians.
It is difficult enough for trained psychologists to force themselves to scru-
tinize the "slick" computer report. Those professionals untrained in psychometric assessment and unaware of the special ethical issues related to
computerized psychological assessment are even less likely to be able to
make adequate judgments. It would be easy for these reports to become
just another piece of data, without interpretation by any psychologist
familiar with the case. This may result in the physician prematurely ascrib-
ing symptoms to emotional distress on the basis of psychological testing
and doing an inadequate diagnostic workup. Cummings (1985) was able
to empirically demonstrate this by showing that the number of diagnoses
missed by physicians increased significantly in proportion to the amount
of psychological assessment information rendered to them.

Recognition of Personal Problems

> Psychologists refrain from initiating an activity when they know or
> should know that there is a substantial likelihood that their per-
> sonal problems will prevent them from performing their work-related
> activities in a competent manner. (Ethical Standard 2.06a)
>
> When psychologists become aware of personal problems that may
> interfere with their performing work-related duties adequately, they
> take appropriate measures, such as obtaining professional consultation

or assistance, and determine whether they should limit, suspend, or terminate their work-related duties. (Ethical Standard 2.06b)

As with any area of professional practice, the clinical health psychologist must be aware of any personal problems that could affect his or her ability to perform duties adequately. This problem is addressed in Ethical Standard 2.06 (Personal Problems and Conflicts).

The unique settings (e.g., the acute-care hospital) and environments (e.g., working with medicine) in which clinical health psychologists find themselves add to the stress of the work and may result in professional burnout. The health psychologist may tend to deny the effects of the work and deal with the stress in a destructive manner, including emotional detachment and substance abuse. As stated by Koocher and Keith-Spiegel (1998), "Burnout has generally been described as a kind of emotional exhaustion resulting from excessive demands on energy, strength, and personal resources in the work setting" (p. 69). They discuss eleven factors that can predispose a person to professional burnout; these include role ambiguity at work, conflict and tension in the workplace, lack of social support at work, chronic helplessness, and overly high expectation of oneself. The clinical health psychologist who works with a variety of medical practices, consults with different hospitals, and is not part of group of practitioners may be at increased risk for burnout.

Research suggests that a practitioner's beliefs about whether it is unethical to practice in a state of burnout will affect whether steps are taken, such as decreasing one's weekly caseload, when impairment is realized (Skorupa & Agresti, 1993). In settings in which clinical health psychologists are more likely to practice (e.g., an acute-care medical hospital), it may be easier to still practice while impaired, thereby providing substandard care, because of diffusion of responsibility issues, which will be discussed shortly.

Imposition of Values Onto the Patient

Psychologists do not knowingly engage in behavior that is harassing or demeaning to persons with whom they interact in their work based on factors such as those persons' age, gender, gender identity, race, ethnicity, culture, national origin, religion, sexual orientation, disability language, or socioeconomic status. (Ethical Standard 3.03)

In keeping with this ethical principle, the clinical health psychologist is not justified in imposing rigid criteria for "healthy behaviors" onto patients. Working within the patient's health belief model and expectations for treatment is necessary to the formulation of treatment goals. Consider, for example, the clinical health psychologist who is a vegan and adamantly opposed to eating meat of any kind. Although the psychologist may be able to cite studies about the health benefits of such a diet, imposing this dietary behavior on a patient who presented for help with weight loss but loves to eat meat would be unethical. Attempting to get this patient to become a vegan would not only risk a treatment failure but might also decrease the probability that a future intervention would be successful.

Advertising for One's Own Services and Endorsements

Psychologists do not make false, deceptive, or fraudulent statements concerning (1) their training, experience, or competence; (2) their academic degrees; (3) their credentials; (4) their institutional or association affiliations; (5) their services; (6) the scientific or clinical basis for, or results or degree of success of, their services; (7) their fees; or (8) their publications or research findings. (Ethical Standard 5.01b)

Psychologists who engage others to create or place public statements that promote their professional practice, products, or activities retain professional responsibility for such statements. (Ethical Standard 5.02a)

Guidelines for advertising by psychologists are addressed in Avoidance of False or Deceptive Statements (Ethical Standard 5.01), Statements by Others (Ethical Standard 5.02), Description of Workshops and Non-Degree-Granting Educational Programs (Ethical Standard 5.03), Media Presentations (Ethical Standard 5.04), Testimonials (Ethical Standard 5.05), and In-Person Solicitation (Ethical Standard 5.06). Advertisements may contain such accurately presented information as name; highest relevant academic degree earned from a regionally accredited institution;

type of certification or licensure; diplomatic status; APA membership status; services offered; fee information; foreign languages spoken; scientific or clinical basis for, or results or degree of success of, their services; and policy with regard to third-party payments.

The clinical health psychologist might include in advertising that he or she specializes in the treatment of psychological issues related to health problems, or in a particular subcategory of practice (e.g., chronic headaches, stress disorders, eating disorders, smoking cessation). Because the Federal Trade Commission has loosened guidelines on professional advertising, most simple information about one's services is probably reasonable (Koocher, 1983, 1994; Koocher & Keith-Spiegel, 1998). What is prohibited in advertising is exaggeration of the uniqueness of services offered. Unwarranted claims such as "hypnotherapy will end smoking and overeating in one day" or "ten sessions of biofeedback will eliminate your headache problem" would be considered unfounded and unethical.

Endorsements

Beyond advertising for one's own services, care must be taken in the endorsement of products or printed materials, and it is generally not recommended (see Koocher & Keith-Spiegel, 1998, for a detailed discussion of this issue). In clinical health psychology, there has been an explosion of technology related to practice (e.g., relaxation tapes, hypnosis tapes, self-help manuals, biofeedback equipment). Unfounded claims related to the efficacy of these procedures might include such statements as the following:

1. In this manual, you will learn to subliminally reprogram yourself to lose weight, eliminate pain, and quit smoking in a short amount of time using these proven audiotapes.
2. These tapes will produce a positive restructuring of self-image, alleviate depression, and increase self-esteem.
3. These relaxation methods are proven to inhibit postoperative swelling, pain, and bleeding and to produce rapid healing. They are also used for all pain management.

4. The real cause of smoking is stress, and you'll learn to control it through this proven and tested home biofeedback system.

These hypothetical statements could be considered unfounded and unethical, because they go beyond what has been validated. Furthermore, they do not specify the context within which these technologies have been tested (e.g., as used in a comprehensive psychological treatment package). The psychologist is ethically bound to protect how his or her name is used, even when production or publication rights have been transferred to a marketing company (Ethical Standard 5.02, Statements by Others).

Improper and Potentially Harmful Dual Relationships

A psychologist refrains from entering into a multiple relationship if the multiple relationship could reasonably be expected to impair the psychologist's objectivity, competence, or effectiveness in performing his or her functions as a psychologist, or otherwise risks exploitation or harm to the person with whom the professional relationship exists. (Ethical Standard 3.05a)

Psychologists do not engage in sexual intimacies with current therapy clients/patients. (Ethical Standard 10.05)

Psychologists do not engage in sexual intimacies with former clients/patients for at least two years after cessation or termination of therapy. (Ethical Standard 10.08a)

Psychologists do not engage in sexual intimacies with former clients/patients even after a 2-year interval except in the most unusual circumstances. (Ethical Standard 10.08b)

Dual relationships have been divided into sexual and nonsexual categories. Sexual relationships with patients are prohibited in the ethical standards and in many laws. This area is relevant to clinical health psychology, as in any other area of practice. One issue that might be unique to the practice of clinical health psychology is the frequent interactions with other professions (e.g., physicians, dentists, attorneys), which have different ethical codes. In some of these other professional ethical codes, there is no prohibition against sexual relationships with patients or former clients. The clinical health psychologist must beware of influences from other professionals, who could be behaving in an ethical manner for their profession, but whose behavior would reflect a clear ethical violation for the psychologist. This issue is discussed in greater detail in the following chapter.

Nonsexual dual relationships can occur in a number of ways. One area of concern that is particularly relevant to clinical health psychology involves the financial incentives provided by a third party for either hospital or outpatient services. This is specifically covered under Ethical Standard 6.07 (Referrals and Fees). There are numerous cases in which for-profit hospital and medical corporations have entered into unethical and illegal "kickback" schemes in which doctors were somehow compensated for placing patients in the hospital, or were billing for services not actually rendered. For instance, one news story described a psychiatrist who did what the nursing staff had termed *wave therapy* on his inpatient cases. He would literally walk through the hospital corridor either waving or saying hello to his patients. These "sessions" were billed as full sessions of psychotherapy treatment. In this same situation, the hospital corporation was paying the doctor's overhead expenses (e.g., rent, secretarial) in exchange for the unwritten understanding that he would keep the census high in the hospital.

Other similar situations have also been common in the workers' compensation area, in which financial arrangements had been developed among doctors, insurance adjusters, and attorneys to form lucrative referral networks. These types of arrangements would be in violation of ethical standards, constitute harmful dual relationships (one with the patient, the other with an institution), and are likely illegal. In these situations, treatment decisions might be based on incentives other than patient needs.

Treating Clinician and Expert Testimony

Another area in which the clinical health psychologist may be more likely to enter a dual relationship is that of being a treating provider who provides expert testimony. An example of how this might occur involves a patient being treated for back pain as a result of a motor vehicle accident.

At some point, the psychologist might be asked by the patient's attorney to provide expert testimony (not just be a factual witness) about the psychological sequelae associated with chronic low-back pain. As discussed by Reid (1998), civil and criminal attorneys will often refer clients for treatment and, subsequently, seek expert testimony from the provider to help with the case. Reid points out that this dual relationship can create conflict in at least four areas:

1. A *treatment* relationship creates an ethical and legal obligation to act in the best interest of the patient, while *forensic* testimony requires objectivity.
2. The clinician may have a personal affinity for the patient's viewpoint, creating a danger of intentional bias.
3. When a treating clinician is aware that reporting to a third party will be required (e.g., the lawyers, the court), this must be disclosed to the patient. This disclosure will likely affect what the patient discusses and impact the validity of any report or testimony.
4. The clinician's role and training are not forensic; therefore, he or she will likely not be aware of the rules of legal proceedings and will be open to manipulation by the attorneys.

An article by Greenburg and Shuman (1997) outlines these issues nicely:

> Engaging in conflicting therapeutic and forensic relationships exacerbates the danger that experts will be more concerned with case outcome than the accuracy of their testimony. Therapists are highly invested in the welfare of their patients and rightfully concerned that publicly offering some candid opinions about their patient's deficits could seriously impair their patient's trust in them. They are often unfamiliar with the relevant law and psycho–legal issues it raises. They are often unaware of much of the factual information in the case, and much of what they know came solely from the patient and is often uncorroborated. What they do know, they know primarily, if not solely, from the patient's point of view. They are usually sympathetic to their patient's plight, and they usually want their patient to prevail. (p. 56)

Not all authors are in agreement that a treating psychologist who offers expert testimony is acting unethically. Although the extensive details of the article are beyond the scope of this discussion, Heltzel (2007) argues that "Although it should be clear that all psychologists must be aware of the ethical challenges associated with expert testimony, it has been demonstrated that the roles of therapist and expert witness are indeed compatible" (p. 128). The Heltzel article was written in response to the State Board of Psychology of Ohio (2003), who issued a warning to psychologists who provide expert testimony about their own patients. The Board cited the article by Greenburg and Shuman (1997) and stated that providing expert testimony about one's own patients involved "inherent dual roles and bias" (p. 2) and concluded, "Prevailing standards essentially demand that you define and remain within one role with a given client" (p. 2).

The conclusions of Heltzel (2007) were addressed by Greenberg and Shuman (2007) who reiterated their original 1997 position and offered further foundation for their assertion that providing expert opinions relative to one's own patients is an ethical dual role violation. The authors cited the work of others (see also Strasberger, Gutheil, & Brodsky, 1997), and also provided evidence that the irreconcilability of therapeutic and forensic roles had gained wide acceptance in ethical guideline interpretations and in the courts.

The details of the arguments for and against this issue are interesting, and any psychologist involved in providing expert testimony should be familiar with these articles. As a general guideline, it appears that functioning in a therapeutic role and an expert witness role for the same patient is in most cases an ethical violation. At the very least, the psychologist must be ready to defend him- or herself and be able to answer the question of why it is not an ethical violation. The psychologist must also keep in mind that this type of dual relationship does not go unnoticed by defense attorneys and almost always is addressed in cross-examination. Campbell and Lorandos (2001) specifically outline how an attorney should cross-examine a clinician who has entered into a dual relationship of being treating therapist and expert witness. Most psychologists would not want to find themselves in the position of having to answer these cross-examination questions.

Providing Mental Health Services to Those Served k

In deciding whether to offer or provide services to those receiving mental health services elsewhere, psychologists carefully consider the treatment issues and the potential client's/patient's welfare. Psychologists discuss these issues with the client/patient or another legally authorized person on behalf of the client/patient in order to minimize the risk of confusion and conflict, consult with the other service providers when appropriate, and proceed with caution and sensitivity to the therapeutic issues. (Ethical Standard 10.04)

In the practice of clinical health psychology, it is not uncommon to be referred a patient who is already in psychotherapy for other issues. It would not be unethical for the clinical health psychologist to proceed with one intervention while a different psychological intervention continues with another mental health professional. However, this can be a potentially confusing and conflictual situation if not handled correctly. Proper management includes clearly informing the patient as to the nature of the intervention and, with appropriate releases, discussing with the other professional how the treatment focuses will be kept distinct and not work at cross-purposes. The guideline of putting the patient's welfare first is of absolute importance in making these types of clinical decisions.

Professional Responsibility

Psychologists establish relationships of trust with those with whom they work. They are aware of their professional and scientific responsibilities to society and to the specific communities in which they work. Psychologists uphold professional standards of conduct, clarify their professional roles and obligations, accept appropriate responsibility for their behavior, and seek to manage conflicts of interest that could lead to exploitation or harm. Psychologists consult with, refer to, or cooperate with other professionals and institutions to the extent needed to serve the best interests of those with whom they work. They are concerned about the ethical compliance of their colleagues' scientific and professional conduct. Psychologists strive to contribute a portion of their professional time for little or no compensation or personal advantage. (Principle B: Fidelity and Responsibility)

The effective and responsible practice of clinical health psychology includes several areas relative to the Fidelity and Responsibility Principle, including: (a) increased responsibility for physical health, (b) necessary interaction with other disciplines, (c) patient-welfare responsibilities when working in institutional systems such as the medical hospital, (d) consultation with other clinical health psychologists regarding ethical issues, and (e) ones' personal behavior. The clinical health psychologist has increased ethical obligations in these all of these areas.

Responsibility for Physical Health

One unique aspect of clinical health psychology is an increased responsibility for physical health. More so than in traditional practice, the clinical health psychologist deals with psychological factors associated with medical conditions. Therefore, such things as concomitant medical evaluation and management must be assured, and this requires consultation and cooperation with one's medical colleagues.

The clinical health psychologist often has to deal with the medical care of patients, both on an individual and an institutional level. This interaction can be intimately tied to patient care (e.g., being sure a particular medical evaluation is completed, helping a patient to confront health care systems problems). To successfully assume this responsibility for patient care, we have found that one must have many of the personal attributes discussed in chapter 2 (this volume).

Interacting With Medical Teams and the Hospital System

The clinical health psychologist must be aware of the risk of diffusion of responsibility when working with patients in a medical facility. Zerubavel (1980) called this risk the "bureaucratization of responsibility." He held that, within the hospital context, there is an ever-increasing segmentation of responsibility for patients. Hospital patients are cared for by a myriad of specialized clinicians. Thus, the responsibility for the patient does not lie with any one clinician but rather with a collective entity such as "the hospital" or "the team." However, as Zerubavel pointed out, the legal responsibility for the patient lies ultimately with the attending physician.

With such a complex organizational structure, the likelihood of diffusion of responsibility or "floating responsibility" becomes great. Under these conditions, passivity on the part of the clinical health psychologist can go unnoticed, because so many aspects of care are occurring simultaneously. For example, such things as treatment planning, record keeping, follow-up, communication with other professionals, and informed consent might not be responsibly completed. The psychologist must take care to provide responsible care to patients even when the structure of the system allows for a diffusion of responsibility or passivity.

Consult, Refer, and Cooperate

Ethical Standard 3.09 states, "When indicated and professionally appropriate, psychologists cooperate with other professionals in order to serve their clients/patients effectively and appropriately" (p. 1065); this is also subsumed under Principle B (Fidelity and Responsibility). As indicated previously, in both inpatient and outpatient settings, multiple clinicians of varying specialties often provide patient care. The psychologist usually provides only one aspect of the complete treatment package. It is imperative that regular communication occurs among professionals. This is often achieved in team meetings, but many times is accomplished chiefly through chart notes. One of the most common complaints we hear from our physician colleagues is that they have referred a patient to a psychologist (or other type of clinician) and have received no feedback on the evaluation or course of treatment. It is helpful to maintain written as well as verbal contact with other professionals to be sure treatments are coordinated in an appropriate manner.

Having a working knowledge of what competencies are encompassed by other professions facilitates enhancement of professional relationships and good patient care. For instance, on one case there could be a surgeon, infectious disease specialist, nutritionist, physical therapist, nursing staff, and clinical health psychologist. Having an understanding of what each profession does will help the psychologist communicate more effectively, gain respect, and be aware of treatment needs of the patient that are not being met adequately. As noted before, it is also important to be aware of varying ethical principles by which different professions abide.

Consult With Colleagues to Avoid Unethical Behavior

It is important to have colleagues with whom to consult regarding ethical dilemmas that occur in daily practice. The type of consulting is dictated by the ethical standards and subsumed under maintaining one's standard of care in practice (see chap. 7, this volume, on malpractice). Although these relationships can be established with those in general practice or in other specialty areas, some of the consultants and colleagues should have competence in clinical health psychology. Documentation of these consultations should be completed to substantiate the decision-making process, if necessary. In addition, one can find assistance from local ethics boards.

Personal Behavior

The clinical health psychologist might be subject to standards of behavior beyond those inherent in general psychological practices. As an extreme example, the clinician who is a heavy smoker, very overweight, drinks an excessive amount of coffee, and consumes more than a moderate amount of alcohol may have special problems in relationships with professional colleagues (i.e., physicians, psychologists) and patients, as well as in representing health psychology to the public. Although this could appear to be an infringement of one's personal freedom of choice, Principle C clearly states that personal behavior can come under ethical scrutiny if it affects professional practice. The clinical health psychologist must be aware of personal health habits, and make decisions about acceptable, ethical public behavior. These behaviors cannot be rigidly defined, nor should they be, but rather, a range of acceptable behaviors must be decided on individually.

Privacy and Confidentiality

Psychologists have a primary obligation and take reasonable precautions to protect confidential information obtained through or stored in any medium, recognizing that the extent and limits of confidentiality may be regulated by law or established by institutional rules or professional or scientific relationship. (Ethical Standard 4.01)

Psychologists discuss with persons (including, to the extent feasible, persons who are legally incapable of giving informed consent and their legal representatives) and organizations with whom they establish a scientific or professional relationship (1) the relevant limits of confidentiality and (2) the foreseeable uses of the information generated through their psychological activities. (Ethical Standard 4.02a)

Unless it is not feasible or is contraindicated, the discussion of confidentiality occurs at the outset of the relationship and thereafter as new circumstances may warrant. (Ethical Standard 4.02b)

Privileged Versus Confidential Information

Privileged communication refers to the legal doctrine that a professional cannot disclosed confidential information without a patient's consent (Reamer, 2003). The limits of this privilege are determined by state statutes and vary from state to state. The privilege of confidentiality lies with the patient, and except in special circumstances, the psychologist must abide by the patient's determination.

Confidentiality is an ethical concept, but it is influenced by legal guidelines (e.g., mandates to breach confidentiality to prevent self-harm or harm to others; see chap. 7, this volume). The psychologist must maintain a confidential relationship with the patient and obtain permission before releasing information.

Special Confidentiality Problems in Clinical Health Psychology

Earlier chapters noted some of the special confidentiality problems in clinical health psychology, including providing information to the referral source, charting treatment notes in a more circulated medical record versus a less available psychological record, and releasing medical records that contain psychological treatment notes to an outside source. Other problems arise in providing services to multiple-bed hospital rooms, case discussion within the context of a multidisciplinary team approach, and discussion of the patient's psychological status with members of the patient's family.

Generally, the clinical health psychologist should strive to maximize confidentiality. One should also inform the patient of the limits to confidentiality set either by law or by institutional organization. For instance, finding a setting to conduct confidential psychological services on a medical-surgical unit can be difficult. Patient consultation rooms are sometimes available, but these are often heavily scheduled. If the patient is nonambulatory and is in a multiple-bed room, it may not be possible to maintain confidentiality, unless services can be scheduled when other patients are out of the room. The patient should be explicitly given the option of declining services if not comfortable with the situation; otherwise, the pressure from an authoritative professional may induce the patient to engage in behavior without true consent. Similarly, when a patient's psychological status is to be discussed in the context of a team-treatment approach, the patient should be informed of what material will be reviewed.

Last, we have found that pressure from family members to discuss the patient's psychological status often arises in the case of brain dysfunction, "conversion" disorders, and compliance problems, which can be closely related to family-systems issues (e.g., eating disorders, compliance with insulin-treatment regimens, chronic-pain management). If the patient is not able to make informed decisions, such as in brain dysfunction cases, legal and ethical guidelines may allow release of confidential information to an appointed person as necessary. Except in these instances, the process of obtaining a written release of confidential information should be followed, as in any traditional psychological case.

Informed Consent

When psychologists conduct research or provide assessment, therapy, counseling, or consulting services in person or via electronic transmission or other forms of communication, they obtain the informed consent of the individual or individuals using language that is reasonably understandable to that person or persons except when conducting such activities without consent is mandated by law or governmental regulation or as otherwise provided in this Ethics Code. (Ethical Standard 3.10a)

Psychologists appropriately document written or oral consent, permission, and assent. (Ethical Standard 3.10d)

The doctrine of informed consent was developed so that patients could weigh the risks and benefits of a treatment and determine for themselves if they wanted to participate (Barton & Sanborn, 1978; Knapp & VandeCreek, 1981; Pizzi, Goldfarb, & Nash, 2001; Simon, 1992). Informed consent was established as a legal standard of care on the basis of the principle that individuals have rights over their own bodies. For surgical and medical procedures, the legal aspects of informed consent were well established by the turn of the century (Beahrs & Gutheil, 2001). However, informed consent for psychological interventions has only just recently been developed. This was likely a result of the fact that psychological interventions are noninvasive, that the psychotherapeutic process was seen as "sacrosanct," that patients are conscious and able to monitor the on-going treatment for themselves, and that it is difficult to demonstrate harm resulting from the treatment (Appelbaum, 1997; Beahrs & Gutheil, 2001, p. 4). However, legal and ethical cases over the past 20 years have increased the focus on informed consent for psychological treatment (see chap. 7, this volume, for a more detailed discussion of these issues).

In the Ethics Code, informed consent is addressed in several places including Third Party Request for Services (Ethical Standard 3.07), Informed Consent (Ethical Standard 3.10), Informed Consent to Research and Recording (Ethical Standards 8.02 and 8.03), Informed Consent in Assessments (Ethical Standard 9.03), and Informed Consent to Therapy (Ethical Standard 10.01). One can conclude, just on the basis of the number of times informed consent is addressed in the ethical code, that it is an important issue. The patient should understand the nature of the proposed treatment, the risks and likelihood of success, and available alternative treatments. Ideally, the procedure of informed consent is meant to force health care professionals to make the patients "active agents" and equal partners in treatment decisions (Beahrs & Gutheil, 2001; A. A. Stone, 1979). Interest in informed consent for medical and psychological treatments has increased with the consumerism movement among patients and judicial involvement in this area (Reamer, 2003; Widiger & Rorer, 1984). Informed consent was not specifically addressed prior to the 1992 Ethics Code, but is addressed in several places in the 2002 revision, as discussed previously.

The legal concept of informed consent includes capacity, information, and voluntariness. *Capacity* means that a patient must have the ability to make rational decisions. This tenet often excludes children and the developmentally disabled from being able to give informed consent and necessitates proxy consent by a guardian. *Information* consists of both the substance of the material presented and the manner in which it is given. It is gauged by demonstrated understanding by the patient. *Voluntariness* means that the patient was able to exercise free choice, without coercion, in making the decision.

Inadequate informed consent is unethical and has been grounds for malpractice in medical and psychiatric–psychological treatments (Beahrs & Gutheil, 2001; R. J. Cohen & Mariano, 1982; Reamer, 2003). A significant problem is how much to actually disclose about treatment (Beahrs & Gutheil, 2001; Halperin, 1980; Schutz, 1982; Simon, 1992). Adequate disclosure is legally determined by the community standard of care (i.e., telling patients what other practitioners in the community would tell their patients under similar circumstances) and "the reasonable person" statute (i.e., telling the patient what a reasonable person would need to know to make an informed decision). However, these guidelines actually offer the practitioner little guidance (A. A. Stone, 1979).

Informed-consent procedures are often inadequate when patient understanding and retention of the material are assessed (Ley, 1982; Pizzi et al., 2001). Problems are sometimes related to readability of consent forms. For example, Christopher, Foti, Roy-Bujnowski, and Appelbaum (2007) completed a review of 154 clinical mental health research studies that used informed-consent forms. All forms were assessed using several standard "readability" formulas. The overall mean readability scores for the informed-consent forms ranged from Grades 12 to 14.5. In addition, the higher the risk of the study, the higher was the mean readability score of the forms.

A review of medical informed-consent studies reached similar conclusions (Pizzi et al., 2001). The results of the National Assessment of Adult Literacy survey most recently completed in 2003 are now being analyzed and published. Part of the 2003 survey included a measure of *health literacy,* defined as, "the ability to use literacy skills to read and understand written health-related information encountered in everyday life" (National Center for Education Statistics, 2003; available from http://nces.ed.gov/NAAL). Although it is beyond the scope of this discussion to define the complex classification system used in the survey, 75 million Americans are estimated to possess Basic and Below Basic health literacy skills, with 114 million at the Intermediate level and only 12 million at the Proficient level. It is unlikely that Americans with Basic or Below Basic health literacy (and probably a vast majority in the Intermediate group) would be able to read and comprehend most informed-consent forms as they are written at a 12- to 15-year-old education readability level (see Pizzi et al., 2001, for a review). Research findings in this area present serious problems for the practitioner in obtaining informed consent. Because of legal pressures, many medical professionals have gone to what might be considered the extreme position of providing all possible risks in graphic detail to ensure completeness. Problems with this approach and suggestions for a process of informed consent are discussed later.

Clinical health psychologists may be involved in several aspects of informed consent in the medical setting. In our work, we are often involved in (a) helping the physician to explore the patient's health belief model about aspects of treatment and determining the extent of the patient's understanding or possible misconceptions; (b) working with patients to encourage behaviors that will increase the likelihood of "true" informed consent (e.g., determining what questions the patient has about the medical treatment, teaching the patient how to obtain the information from the physician); and (c) helping patients deal with the increase in feelings of uncertainty about treatment, which often occur after explicit informed-consent procedures are carried out.

Clinical health psychologists must also deal with the issue of informed consent in the course of service delivery of psychological services. Many practitioners view the informed consent with contempt and rarely provide information about alternate treatments. Several authors have suggested that the informed-consent process is a double-edged sword (Beahrs & Gutheil, 2001; Gutheil, Bursztajn, Hamm, & Brodsky, 1983). The positive aspect is that it clarifies options and stimulates understanding. The negative aspect is that it can increase the patient's uncertainty about treatment and decrease belief in the doctor's ability to cure. We agree with Beahrs and Gutheil (2001) and Gutheil et al. (1983) that the informed-consent procedure should be entered into as a process of mutual discovery rather than as a formality. In the informed-consent process, it is prudent to include the rationale for service, treatment plan, and goals, in an atmosphere of open negotiation. Once a plan is formulated, it is useful to have the patient paraphrase their understanding of the treatment or evaluation, so that misperceptions can be corrected.

We have found that the process of informed consent can often be difficult with patients referred to a clinical health psychologist. Many times, the physician has not given the patient much information about our services, or the physician has given incorrect information. Furthermore, the patient is being expected to shift from a biomedical orientation to a biopsychosocial approach. Overwhelming the patient in the first session with details of a treatment plan and expectations can result in premature termination. The informed-consent procedure can extend over many sessions and, in fact, over the entire course of treatment. Skills in working with people of different backgrounds (and multicultural competence) facilitate the informed-consent process.

The facilitation of the informed-consent process is discussed by Beahrs and Gutheil (2001) and Pizzi et al. (2001); the following summarizes their guidelines:

1. Checking the readability and comprehensibility of informed-consent forms is important for true informed consent. An overly detailed informed-consent form outlining all of the possible risks, benefits, and alternatives to psychological treatment is not necessary and has a great potential to be countertherapeutic. Informed consent (verbal, written) should be conceptualized as an ongoing process throughout treatment, and not simply the signing of an office form after the first session.

2. Using a semistructured discussion of informed-consent issues can help insure that major issues are covered with the first few sessions.

3. Asking the patient to recall his or her understanding of the informed-consent information is an excellent test for comprehension. It also opens the discussion regarding areas of misunderstanding and can begin the treatment process.

4. The use of educational materials relevant to the patient's diagnosis, proposed treatment, and so forth, can be helpful because the patient can review them at a later time and bring questions to the next session.

Clarification of Roles and Third-Party Requests for Services

Clarification of roles is part of informed consent and is addressed in the ethical standards under Multiple Relationships (Ethical Standard 3.05) and Third-Party Requests for Services (Ethical Standard 3.07), which states the following:

> When psychologists agree to provide services to a person or entity at the request of a third party, psychologists attempt to clarify at the outset of the service the nature of the relationship with all individuals or organizations involved. This clarification includes the role of the psychologist (e.g., therapist, consultant, diagnostician, or expert witness), an identification of who is the client, the probable uses of the services provided or the information obtained, and the fact that there may be limits to confidentiality.

The principle of informed consent dictates that psychologists clarify the roles they are performing for all relevant parties and function in accordance with those roles. In clinical health psychology practice, this issue usually arises in clarifying one's role within the context of medical treatment. In the hospital setting, patients are often seen by a variety of providers, and they will often become confused about the type and nature of each service and provider. The patient could mistake the psychologist for a physician, or expect a similar type of care. These roles should be clearly identified for the patient. For the patient who is unfamiliar with psychological interventions, the process of explanation of roles may proceed over several sessions.

The services of a clinical health psychologist are often requested by a physician to provide an evaluation, treatment, or both. The psychologist must always determine the extent of the patient's understanding as to why the consultation was requested and whether services are actually necessary. We find that many times the physician has not told the patient a consultation had been ordered. As with any other case, informed consent must be acquired before proceeding. Furthermore, many consultation requests are found to result from projection on the part of providers, who are experiencing frustration, anger, depression, or some other emotional response to the patient. Intervention is sometimes more appropriately targeted at the staff rather than the patient. A thorny ethical problem that then arises is determining who is going to pay for the staff intervention.

Other areas in which the services of a clinical health psychologist are often requested by a third party include neuropsychological assessment, psychological evaluation for a specific treatment program or procedure, and evaluation as part of filing a workers' compensation or disability claim. Patients are often not aware that in requesting these programs to pay for services, they must agree to release their psychological evaluation as a condition of reimbursement. In any of these situations, the psychologist must fully inform the patient as to the nature of the assessment, the purpose, what the results will be used for, who requested the evaluation, and who will pay for it.

Conflicts of Interest

Psychologists refrain from taking on a professional role when personal, scientific, professional, legal, financial, or other interests or relationships could reasonably be expected to (1) impair their objectivity, competence, or effectiveness in performing their functions as psychologists or (2) expose the person or organization with whom the professional relationship exists to harm or exploitation. (Ethical Standard 3.06)

When one interacts with the health care system, conflicts of interest can arise. There can occur a basic, unacknowledged, antagonistic relationship between patient and hospital or an employee of the institution (Bazelon, 1974; Koocher & Keith-Spiegel, 1998). As Noll (1976) stated, "whenever the mental health professional is employed by an agency or by an institution, the institution needs will almost invariably supersede those of the patient" (p. 1451). Thus, the clinical health psychologist may have a "hidden agenda" when consulting to a medical-surgical unit, depending on the needs of the staff and the reason for the consultation request.

> The patient was a 37-year-old married woman, who had been diag-
> nosed as having lung cancer with multiple metastases. The progno-
> sis was poor. She had been through several courses of chemotherapy
> without significant benefit. A more experimental drug had been
> suggested, but the patient refused, stating that she would rather be
> discharged to home. A referral for psychological evaluation of the
> patient's mental status was made. When the clinical health psychol-
> ogist arrived on the unit, it was verbally communicated to her by the
> staff that "the patient needed to be convinced to stay in the hospital
> for further treatment because it was her only hope of survival." The
> psychological evaluation revealed that the patient had carefully con-
> sidered her options in treatment, was fully informed about risks and
> benefits of each alternative, and had made a decision with a clear sen-
> sorium and intact mental status. The psychologist reported the results
> of her evaluation to the staff and subsequently dealt with the anger
> and frustration staff had toward both her and the patient.

In this example, the psychologist might have easily been influenced by staff issues and have thus seen the patient with a goal of convincing her to have the experimental treatment. Psychologists must remember to be responsible to the patient, to take into account the needs of the patient versus those of the staff, and to clarify the nature of their loyalties and responsibilities.

Patients Who Do Not Benefit From Treatment

> Psychologists terminate therapy when it becomes reasonably clear that
> the client/patient no longer needs the service, is not likely to benefit,
> or is being harmed by continued service. (Ethical Standard 10.10a)

If a patient does not benefit from treatment after a reasonable trial, the psychologist is ethically mandated to terminate the treatment and to help with an appropriate referral. The clinical health psychologist will often receive referrals for "last-option" treatments, in that all previous traditional medical treatments have failed (e.g., chronic-pain syndromes, tinnitus, blepharospasm, atypical facial pain). In these cases, the psychological referral is to "give it a try" because there appear to be no other options. These cases represent clinical challenges in which the therapist must gauge carefully, in realistic negotiation with the patient, when an adequate trial of treatment has been accomplished without significant benefit. The following case illustrates such a decision.

> The patient was a 78-year-old married woman with a postherpetic neuralgia secondary to having herpes zoster several years before. The pain, as well as an excoriated skin surface, was distributed in a dermatomal pattern on the right side of the face and neck. Extensive dermatological treatments had failed to provide relief, and the patient was referred for pain management. Evaluation indicated that the symptoms did fluctuate, with stress and tension being related to an exacerbation of the condition, and relaxed states being associated with symptom relief. A treatment plan was formulated, including relaxation training with suggestions for hypnotic analgesia. After the patient had gained the ability to relax across all settings and had practiced routinely with autohypnosis, no pain relief, as documented by symptom charting, had occurred. It was decided that the patient would not benefit from further treatment with that therapist and that an adequate trial had been given. The patient was referred for evaluation for a trial of an antidepressant and phenothiazine combination (found useful in some cases by Loeser, 1986). She was also given a referral to another psychologist experienced in hypnotic analgesia, to see whether a different approach might be beneficial.

In this example, the psychologist had to make a decision, with the patient's full participation, as to when an adequate trial had been attempted. The psychologist must also provide a referral if other treatments are available. The termination process in these cases must be handled carefully to prevent iatrogenic deterioration effects (e.g., patient being left with a "failure experience") and to capitalize on the positive effects, however small, of the treatment experience.

E-Therapy and Internet Therapy

E-therapy is the provision of mental health treatment through the Internet. In 2004, 23% of Internet users searched for information on mental health issues and 28% for information on a doctor or hospital (Recupero & Rainey, 2005). Those numbers are likely much higher now, with the continued penetration of Internet use into American households. We conducted a simple Google search and obtained 161,000 hits for *online therapy* and 172,000 hits for *e-therapy*. There are now professional organizations for online counselors, including the National Directory of Online Counselors, the American Association of Online Psychotherapists, and the International Society for Mental Health Online. These services offer treatment for virtually every *Diagnostic and Statistical Manual of Mental Disorders, Fourth Edition* (American Psychiatric Association, 1994) diagnosis and, relative to the practice of clinical health psychology, such things as pain management, behavioral management (e.g., smoking, alcohol consumption, weight loss), insomnia, somatization, and eating disorders, just to name a few. These "treatments" are structured in several ways, including private online chat (real time), instant messaging, videoconferencing, e-mail sessions, or a combination thereof. In one of the more interesting arrangements, the "patient" purchases a certain number of words to be placed in a "word bank." With each e-mail, the number of words used by the patient is deducted from the bank.

Although a new area of research, Web-based treatment interventions (WBTIs) are in the initial stages of empirical testing. Ritterband et al. (2003) have reviewed some of these early studies. The studies have been done in such diverse area as smoking cessation, weight loss, headaches, body image, posttraumatic stress and pathological grief, physical activity, panic disorder, tinnitus, diabetes management, and pediatric encopresis. As discussed by Ritterband et al., "These studies all focus on behavioral medicine/health psychology issues, which seem to be more adaptable to Internet interventions because of the highly structured treatment approaches to many problems" (p. 528; see also, Childress & Asamen, 1998). Ritterband et al. presented a detailed model for developing a WBTI, including ascertaining the effectiveness of the traditional face-to-face treatment, considering the legal and ethical issues involved in developing a WBTI, transforming treatment elements into a WBTI, building individualization and feedback components into the WBTI, and then testing the WBTI effectiveness against traditional methods. The WBTI research reviewed by Ritterband et al. generally used the Internet in a more adjunctive fashion (e.g., patients are selected for the approach, the initial session may be face-to-face), rather than a patient simply searching the Internet, finding a therapist who may not be in the same state, paying the money, and starting treatment. As such, the type of rigorous development of an Internet-based treatment approach as reviewed in scientific journals is not what is generally experienced when a patient pursues e-therapy at this time.

As discussed by Recupero and Rainey (2005), e-therapy has provoked controversy in the mental health fields. Proponents argue that e-therapy provides many benefits, such as convenience, a certain level of anonymity preferred by some clients, the ability to reach underserved populations, the ability to do less expensive treatment, and so forth. However, several ethical and liability risks will be discussed subsequently.

E-therapy has not been specifically addressed in the 2002 Ethics Code, but there are plans to address this new intervention approach in future versions. The only guidance at this time is from the APA Ethics Committee (1998):

> Delivery of services by such media as telephone, teleconferencing and Internet is a rapidly evolving area. This will be the subject of APA task forces and will be considered in future revision of the Ethics Code. Until such time as a more definitive judgment is available, the Ethics Committee recommends that psychologists follow Standard 1.04c, Boundaries of Competence, which indicates that "In those emerging areas in which generally recognized standards for preparatory training do not yet exist, psychologists nevertheless take reasonable steps to ensure the competence of their work and to protect patients, clients, students, research participants, and others from harm." Other relevant standards include Assessment (Standards 2.01–2.10), Therapy (4.01–4.09, especially 4.01 Structuring the Relationship and 4.02 Informed Consent to Therapy), and Confidentiality (5.01–5.11). Within the General Standards section, standards with particular relevance are 1.03, Professional and Scientific Relationship; 1.04 (a, b,

and c), Boundaries of Competence; 1.06, Basis for Scientific and Professional Judgments; 1.07a, Describing the Nature and Results of Psychological Services; 1.14, Avoiding Harm; and 1.25, Fees and Financial Arrangements. Standards under Advertising, particularly 3.01–3.03 are also relevant. (pp. 979–980)

There is evidence that many online counseling Web sites are not following accepted ethical guidelines. For instance, Shaw and Shaw (2006) used a 16-item ethical checklist to assess 88 online counseling Web sites. Results demonstrated that less than half of the online counselors were following accepted practice on 8 of 16 items. It is beyond the scope of this chapter to review in detail the ethics, state licensing board, and malpractice risks that are inherent in e-therapy. These have been reviewed elsewhere (Koocher & Morray, 2000; Recupero & Rainey, 2005; Ritterband et al., 2003) and are summarized as follows.

Verifying Patient and Clinician Identity

Aside from videoconferencing or telephone contact, in e-therapy it can be challenging for the patient and therapist to verify each other's identity after a treatment relationship has been established (Recupero & Rainer, 2005). For instance, the therapist must be assured that e-mails, online chat, or instant messaging are not intercepted or responded to by someone else. The clinician must also be sure his or her Internet access is completely secure.

Initial Assessment of Online Patients

When a patient comes strictly from the Internet for e-therapy (without any face-to-face contact or referral from another healthcare provider), the clinician does not have the benefit of an initial evaluation, including a face-to-face interview (with all of the nonverbal data), mental status examination, review of background medical records, discussion with collateral sources if necessary, consultation with other treating doctors, psychological testing, and so forth. Because of the anonymity afforded by e-therapy, the clinician may not know the actual identity of the patient, may be given incorrect contact information, and may be subject to deception. These factors place the clinician at risk for misdiagnosis and various treatment mistakes. If this were to occur, in the event of an emergency such as suicidality or homicidality, the outcome could be disastrous. Attempting a clinical health psychology intervention using e-therapy also does not allow for important interactions with the patient's physician or other health care providers.

Clinician Availability

As discussed by Recupero and Rainey (2005), technical problems may either interrupt the treatment session or cause the clinician to be completely unavailable. This situation might lead to a misattribution on the part of the patient if not anticipated before it occurs (e.g., feeling abandoned). In addition, if the patient needs to reach the clinician in a crisis, having only Internet contact availability may put the client at risk.

Standard of Care

As discussed in chapter 7 (this volume), the community standard of care is what the professional's behavior will be judged against if a question of liability arises. E-therapy is a new, essentially unregulated type of treatment with little empirical support for its effectiveness at this time. As such, the clinician is operating in "uncharted waters" but must always remember that, "One does not cease being a psychiatrist or psychologist when one provides therapy online" (Recupero & Rainey, 2005, p. 407). However, any psychologist doing e-therapy must be aware of the rapid development of online healthcare communication. For instance, The eRisk Working Group for Healthcare is a consortium of liability carriers, medical societies, and state board representatives, established to address online communication issues. They have developed eRisk Guidelines for online doctor–patient communications and these might be held up as a standard of care in the event of an e-therapy liability case. The guidelines are available through http://www.medem.com/phy/phy_eriskguidelines.cfm.

Privacy and Confidentiality

Recupero and Rainey (2005) discuss how the psychologist and patient cannot assume that online interactions are confidential. Online interactions are essentially written transcripts of all treatment sessions. Some guidelines for Internet communication between health care provider and patient recommend a secure network including authentication and encryption in accordance with the Health Insurance Portability and Accountability Act of 1996. Standard e-mail, instant messaging, and online chat do not meet these guidelines. Recupero and Rainey present the hypothetical case of a young woman who has been in online therapy and ultimately reveals that she has been date raped. The psychologist encourages her to report the assault to the police, which she does. The psychologist then receives a subpoena for the records from the prosecuting attorney. The psychologist refuses to release the records, but the attorney asserts that e-therapy is not traditional psychotherapy and may be analogous to self-help, in which case there is no doctor–patient privilege. In addition, the attorney subpoenas the records directly from the Internet service provider.

Informed Consent

As discussed previously (and in chap. 7, this volume), informed consent is an important aspect of health care practice. In e-therapy, informed consent should be explicit, and outline all the potential risks and benefits. In psychological treatment, informed consent also includes reviewing situations under which confidentiality must be breached. All states have mandatory child abuse reporting laws, some states have elder abuse reporting laws, and many states have Tarasoff (duty to warn) laws, but some do not. If a psychologist practices in a non-Tarasoff state (e.g., Virginia) and is providing e-therapy to a patient in a Tarasoff state (e.g., California), what is his or her duty-to-warn obligation if a viable threat is made? These issues are unclear at this time.

Interstate Practice

There may be problems if a psychologist licensed in one particular state provides e-therapy service to a patient in another state. This is because each state has its own set of professional licensing and practice laws to protect their citizens. To assess this issue, Koocher and Morray (2000) conducted a survey of the 50 state attorneys general and asked several questions related to telepsychology. The researchers asked questions about laws regarding telepsychology practice, whether any charges had ever been brought related to this practice, and how the state handles those telepsychology services provided from another state. At that time, 24 states claimed regulatory authority over practitioners residing in other states that provided e-therapy services in their state. Seven states acknowledged receiving complaints about e-therapy services, and charges had been brought in e-therapy cases in at least two states. Given the exceptional advancement and use of the Internet in the 8 years since that publication, things have likely changed. For instance, the California Board of Psychology has a notice to consumers regarding those who choose to seek psychological service over the Internet. The notice provides warning about the practice, the requirement for written informed consent, and the statement, "Individuals who provide psychotherapy or counseling to persons in California are required to be licensed in California" (2008, ¶ 2.) Similar statutes likely exist in other states, and these should be checked carefully by the e-therapy provider.

Malpractice Insurance

Although not specifically related to ethical issues, malpractice coverage may be ambiguous in the practice of e-therapy. The issues include whether a nontraditional treatment such as e-therapy is covered and whether coverage extends from one state (i.e., where the psychologist practices) to another (i.e., where the patient resides).

UNDERSTANDING VERSUS APPLYING THE ETHICAL PRINCIPLES

An important aspect of professional ethics that is just now being researched is the difference between understanding and implementing ethical principles. This is the "should" versus "would" discrepancy. Most research suggests that clinicians generally have high-quality ethical decision-making capacity, but that it is not always put into practice (see T. S. Smith, McGuire, Abbott, & Blau, 1991; Wilkins, McGuire, Abbott & Blau, 1990, for reviews).

For instance, Wilkins et al. (1990) conducted a survey of a random sample of APA members. Research participants were presented with four scenarios that reflected ethical dilemmas in the areas of alcohol-related impairment, dual-role sexual abuse of a client, confidentiality, and need for referral related to competence limits. Participants were asked what they should do according to the APA Ethical Principles and what they would do if actually faced with the situation. These were rated on a scale from *do nothing* (least restrictive) to *report the individual to the ethics board* (most restrictive). Results confirmed that respondents were generally able to recognize ethical conflicts that required action. However, significant differences were found when the "should" ratings were compared with what the respondents "would" do (the "should" results were more restrictive than the "would" results). One important finding was that when the ethical violation was more clear-cut (e.g., misconduct related to sexual abuse, impairment because of substance abuse), and there was a consensus as to what to do vis-à-vis the ethical principles, there was increased congruence between what should and would be done.

These findings are relevant to all areas of psychological practice. All clinicians need to be aware of the likelihood of experiencing the should– would difference. Especially applicable to clinical health psychology is the finding that practitioners will have increased difficulty applying the ethical principles that are defined in a more ambiguous fashion. This might include such principles as those of confidentiality, nonsexual dual relationships, and informed consent. As discussed in previous sections, the clinical health psychologist might be presented with challenges in these areas more frequently than do other areas of practice. Likewise, we anticipate some distinctive issues in liability risks for those practicing in clinical health psychology, the topic of the next chapter.

SUGGESTED READINGS

American Educational Research Association, American Psychological Association, & National Council on Measurement. (1999). *Standards for educational and psychological testing.* Washington, DC: Authors.

American Psychological Association. (2002). Ethical principles of psychologists and code of conduct. *American Psychologist, 57,* 1060–1073.

Belar, C. D. (2000). Ethical issues in managed care: Perspectives in evolution. *The Counseling Psychologist, 28,* 237–241.

Gatchel, R. J., & Blanchard, E. B. (Eds.). (1993). *Psychophysiological disorders: Research and clinical applications.* Washington, DC: American Psychological Association.

Koocher, G. P., & Keith-Spiegel, P. (1998). *Ethics in psychology: Professional standards and cases* (2nd ed.). New York: Oxford University Press.

Pope, K. S. (1990). Ethical and malpractice issues in hospital practice. *American Psychologist, 45,* 1066–1070.

Pope, K. S., & Vasquez, M. J. T. (2007). *Ethics in psychotherapy and counseling: A practical guide* (3rd ed.). San Francisco: Jossey-Bass.

Siegfried, N. J., & Porter, C. A. (2003). Ethical issues for clinicians in behavioral medicine settings. In L. M. Cohen, D. E. McChargue, & F. L. Collins (Eds.), *The health psychology handbook* (pp. 443–455). Thousand Oaks, CA: Sage.

7

Liability Risks in Clinical Health Psychology: Malpractice Claims and Licensing Board Complaints

In this chapter, we discuss some legal issues that may arise in the practice of clinical health psychology. We delineate general concepts of psychological malpractice and focus on those high-risk areas pertinent to clinical health psychology. We also discuss licensing board complaints, which occur much more frequently than malpractice actions and can be as equally devastating professionally, financially, and personally. We discuss ways to minimize risk, but this chapter does not provide legal advice, nor should it substitute for the assistance of legal counsel should a practitioner encounter legal issues in his or her practice. The proper handling of any particular situation depends on the facts unique to that situation and the applicable laws. Those laws may differ from state to state and also may change with some frequency. Psychologists who encounter legal issues in their practices should consult with a competent attorney familiar with laws in their state.

As discussed by Campbell and Lorandos in their classic series *Cross Examining Experts in the Behavioral Sciences* (2001, pp. 10–16),

> It is well stated in law, for example, that patients have (1) the right to psychotherapy treatment in the least restrictive environment, (2) the right to exercise informed consent to treatment alternatives, (3) the right to treatment that satisfies the standard of care, and (4) the right to expect that their therapist will act ethically.

When a psychologist violates any of these rights, he or she is at risk for a liability claim. In the event of a malpractice action or licensing board complaint, the professional behavior of the clinical health psychologist will be judged against the standard of care for the specialty, including such things as the ethical standards, guidelines promulgated by the American Psychological Association (APA), and expert testimony regarding accepted evaluation or treatment procedures. In the previous chapter, we discussed ethical issues in the practice of clinical health psychology. Because transgression of any of these principles may be grounds for a liability action of some type, this chapter presents what might be considered the worst possible outcome to alleged professional misconduct: that of a liability claim. Having an understanding of malpractice and licensing complaint issues can help the psychologist be pro-active by practicing at or above the standard of care and implementing appropriate risk management techniques.

Ideally, malpractice law serves three important social functions (Klein & Glover, 1983; Reamer, 2003). First, it protects the public from professional wrongdoing by providing aversive consequences for misconduct. Second, it transfers the loss from one party to another who is more culpable. Third, it distributes the cost of a professional's negligent conduct across the profession at large through insurance premiums. In these ways, the threat of malpractice provides constant pressure on professional communities to self-regulate and self-scrutinize while giving the public a mechanism for compensation when this does not occur.

As evidenced by spiraling medical costs, partially related to increased malpractice litigation, it appears that the social function of malpractice law has been disrupted by consumers' propensity to initiate litigation. This may either be when negligence has occurred or, increasingly, when no negligence is ultimately determined. We speculate that skepticism about health care treatment and heightened resentment over medical costs, combined with an increase in the number of attorneys per capita, have increased the likelihood of malpractice litigation (VandeCreek & Stout, 1993). Costs are incurred in such legal actions, even if the professional is exonerated. Most cases, the are settled out of court in an effort to avoid higher expenditures, regardless of whether misconduct actually occurred, thus reinforcing litigious behavior independent of the merits of the case (Reamer, 2003; VandeCreek & Stout, 1993). There is a societal cost for such freedom of action, and this is ultimately passed on to consumers.

Mental health professionals have not been threatened by malpractice suits in the same magnitude as physicians (National Practitioner Data Bank, 2007). This is thought to be a result of the nature of the therapist–patient relationship, which inhibits such action (Charles, 1993), and to the difficulty in proving the four malpractice standards that we discuss in this chapter (B. E. Bernstein & Hartsell, 2004). However, along with a greater public awareness of psychologists' professional behavior (Wright, 1981), malpractice claims in psychology are increasing—a trend that is continuing (Montgomery, Cupit, & Wimberly, 1999; National Practitioner Data Bank, 2007; Stromberg & Dellinger, 1993). As concluded by Campbell and Lorandos (2001), "In a very real way, mental health professionals have been 'discovered' by malpractice attorneys in the last 25 years" (pp. 10–80).

Beyond public scrutiny of general psychological practice, psychologists working in the area of clinical health psychology potentially open themselves to a myriad of new malpractice liability risks of which they should be aware (Haley et al., 1998; Hanson, Kerkhoff, & Bush, 2005; Knapp & VandeCreek, 1981; Reamer, 2003). First, because clinical health psychologists practice in close concert with the medical profession and deal more often with physical problems than do psychologists in other areas of practice, liability risks may be heightened. These may include inadvertently practicing medicine without a license, failure to refer or communicate within the health care system, breaching confidentiality of psychological information by placing it within the medical record, not clearing a patient psychologically for an elective medical procedure (e.g., gastric bypass or spine surgery), and being named in a lawsuit that is primarily against a physician associate. Second, the nature of the therapist–patient relationship, often thought to protect the traditional psychotherapist against malpractice, can be different in many clinical health psychology cases. Often, the clinical health psychology intervention may be limited to evaluation or brief treatment. As such, a deep, intimate, long-term psychotherapeutic relationship is not developed, nor is considered necessary for treatment gains. Third, physical harm may be more likely in the practice of clinical health psychology than in more traditional psychological treatment. This is because "many of your patients really are sick" (Haley et al., 1998, p. 238).

HOLOGICAL MALPRACTICE DEFINED

aims fall within two broad categories: a professional error ᴏɪ ᴄᴏᴍᴍ.....-- n (e.g., misfeasance, malfeasance) or omission (e.g., non-feasance). In the first category, claims are made that the practitioner carried out his or her professional duties improperly or in a fashion inconsistent with the profession's standard of care. This might include incorrect or injurious treatment, failure to diagnose, breach of confidentiality, abandonment, and so forth. There is a difference between misfeasance and malfeasance (Reamer, 2003). *Misfeasance* is defined as "the commission of a proper act in a wrongful or injurious manner or the improper performance of an act that might have been performed lawfully" (Reamer, 2003, p. 4). Examples include inadvertently disclosing confidential information or inadequately fulfilling informed consent procedures. *Malfeasance* is defined as "the commission of a wrongful or unlawful act" (Reamer, 2003, p. 4). Examples include sex with a minor, embezzlement, physical assault, wrongful death, and violation of a patient's civil rights.

Malpractice suits have generally been founded in tort or contract law, as opposed to criminal law. The difference is that the former pertains to acts damaging to a person, whereas the latter applies to transgression against society (B. E. Bernstein & Hartsell, 2004; Reamer, 2003; Schutz, 1982). To make a successful civil case of malpractice, the plaintiff must prove, by a preponderance of evidence, the following four elements (Deardorff, Cross, & Hupprich, 1984; Feldman & Ward, 1979; Furrow, 1980; Gifis, 2003; Harris, 1973; Reamer, 2003): (a) that the defendant or practitioner owed a "duty" to the patient, (b) that the defendant or practitioner's behavior fell below the acceptable standard of care or that the "duty" owed to the plaintiff was breached, (c) that an injury was actually sustained by the plaintiff, and (d) that the defendant or practitioner's act or omission was the proximate cause of the plaintiff's injury. Each element is discussed subsequently, along with its implications for clinical health psychology. Each must be demonstrated by a preponderance of evidence. They are summarized by the 4D mnemonic: "Dereliction of—Duty—Directly causing—Damages" (Rachlin, 1984, p. 303).

OWING A DUTY TO THE PATIENT

The first of these allegations, that the practitioner owed a duty to the patient, is usually the easiest to prove (Reamer, 2003; Schutz, 1982). It must be proven that a professional relationship existed between the psychologist and patient; such things as a treatment contract, bill for services, or chart notes, are sufficient evidence. When a professional accepts a case, he or she generally owes a duty to possess a level of skill commensurate with that possessed by the average member of the profession in good standing in the community. This is considered the prevailing standard of care in the profession. Furthermore, this skill must be applied with reasonable care (Deardorff et al., 1984; "Professional Negligence," 1973; Zur, 2005).

PROVING A BREACH OF DUTY

To prove a breach of duty, the plaintiff must show that the practitioner's behavior fell below the acceptable standard of care. This might include not having proper knowledge to treat, or that the knowledge was misapplied. Of course, proving a breach of duty requires that the prevailing standard of care be clearly established. The standard of care is an important concept not only relative to liability claims but also in guiding one's practice. Unfortunately, many therapists do not have an understanding of the concept (C. O. Caudill, 2004). The standard of care is the usual and customary standard of practice in the community for a profession or discipline (C. O. Caudill, 2004; Doverspike, 1999; M. H. Williams, 2003). The standard of care is a complex construct and is not easily set out in any textbooks. Rather, it is derived from six concepts (see C. O. Caudill, 2004; M. H. Williams, 2003; Zur, 2005, for a review):

1. Statutes. Each state has its own statutes (e.g., child abuse reporting laws), and a professional's behavior will be judged against those.
2. Licensing board regulations. Each state has its own set of extensive licensing board regulations, which govern, for example, continuing education, licensing, and supervision.
3. Case law. Case law is one of the most important aspects of standard of care. *Tarasoff v. Regents of the University of California* (1976) is an

example of case law defining a standard of care. It is predicted that the Health Insurance Portability and Accountability Act of 1996 (HIPAA) regulations will become the standard of care through case law (Zur, 2005).

4. Ethical codes. Ethical codes are an important, but controversial, aspect of standard of care. Even though the Ethics Code technically only applies to APA members, in most liability situations, it is also applied to nonmembers. Because professional ethical codes, unlike case law and regulations, may be ambiguous and unclear about what kind of behaviors are mandated or prohibited, they are easily misinterpreted and used against psychologists in legal proceedings. The APA Ethics Code (2002b) specifically states that, "The Ethics Code is not intended to be a basis of civil liability" (Introduction and Applicability, p. 1061) and "Whether a psychologist has violated the Ethics Code standards does not by itself determine whether the psychologist is legally liable in a court action, whether a contract is enforceable, or whether other legal consequences occur" (Introduction and Applicability, p. 1061). However, the Ethics Code is often used as a basis for liability claims (i.e., licensing board complaints, malpractice).

5. Consensus of the professionals. The standard of care is also established by expert witnesses who provide a consensus of other professionals practicing in the same discipline. This can be extremely difficult to establish in a field such as psychotherapy. However, as discussed subsequently, the practice of clinical health psychology is generally based on more well-defined and empirically derived principles than are other areas of clinical psychology, making consensus more likely.

6. Consensus in the community. The standard of care is also derived from community norms. As such, the standard of care might be different across various contexts, such as working with specific religious groups or cultures, practicing in the military environment or Veterans' Affairs facilities, and providing services in a rural area.

Outrageous actions, such as beating a patient (*Hammer v. Rosen*, 1960), engaging in sexual contact with a patient as part of treatment (*Roy v. Hartogs*, 1975; Simon, 1995, 1999), or any nontraditional improper treatment resulting in injury, can provide a prima facie case of malpractice (Cross & Deardorff, 1987; Knapp, 1980; Reamer, 2003). One of the most widely publicized instances of improper and nontraditional treatment was a Colorado case in which a 10-year-old girl died of suffocation as part of "rebirthing" treatment for an attachment disorder. The "treatment" included wrapping the girl in a blanket to provide the rebirthing experience. Unable to breathe, the girl died of asphyxiation. The treating social worker was convicted of death resulting from reckless child abuse and sentenced to 16 years in prison (see Nicholson, 2001; Reamer, 2003, for a review).

Other than cases of this nature, proving a breach of duty has, historically, been difficult in an ambiguous practice such as psychotherapy; however, this situation is clearly changing. With advancements in psychological research, there has been a movement toward identifying empirically supported (evidence-based) treatments and using those criteria to select interventions for particular conditions (Chambless & Ollendick, 2001; Weisz, Hawley, Pilkonis, Woody, & Follette, 2000). Many of these evidence-based guidelines are summarized in such texts as *Handbook of Assessment and Treatment Planning for Psychological Disorders* (Antony & Barlow, 2002) and *A Guide to Treatments That Work* (2nd ed.; Nathan & Gorman, 2002). It is conceivable that future liability actions will rely on published guidelines to help establish the standard of care against which clinical health psychologists' behavior will be judged. However, national organizations such as APA have adopted policies on evidence-based practice that embrace a broader set of constructs than lists of empirically supported treatments. As in medicine, evidence-based psychological practice requires the integration of the best research evidence with the clinical expertise of the practitioner, and the values and perspectives of the patient (APA, 2006).

In the area of clinical health psychology, there has been a focus on empirically based treatment interventions for many years. As discussed by Knapp and VandeCreek as early as 1981, clinical health psychologists may have to adhere to more specifiable standards of care than traditional psychologists because the techniques used can often be more explicitly delineated. This conclusion rings true today. Many treatments used in the practice of health psychology arise from behavioral, cognitive, and social learning frameworks that have a strong empirical base; thus, aspects of evaluation and treatment are often more measurable than in psychodynamically oriented approaches. Examples include neuropsychological assessment, behavioral observation data, and psychophysiological evaluation and treatment.

As reviewed previously, the standard of care against which the practitioner's behavior is judged in malpractice litigation is usually established, in part, by expert testimony (i.e., consensus of the professionals). In the past, it has been difficult to get members of a profession to testify against one another (Markus, 1965), but this is less problematic since the courts abandoned the locality rule, which required the expert witness to be from the same geographical area as the defendant or practitioner. This change in court practice has had two important implications. First, it has successfully diminished the "conspiracy of silence" related to expert witness testimony (Slovenko, 1978). Second, it means that a reasonable standard of care for psychological practice may be set at the national standard instead of a community standard and that the practitioner may have malpractice liability when local standards are below those at the national level (Pope, Simpson, & Myron, 1978; Reamer, 2003).

This may be especially relevant for the practice of clinical health psychology because it is a highly specialized and expanding area. Because there are likely to be fewer clinical health psychologists in a community, the court would be forced to draw expert witnesses from a more national geographical territory. Therefore, the standard of care may be set commensurate with a national, rather than a local, average minimum level of practice expertise. With this in mind, "psychologists who expand their practices into this specialty should obtain appropriate training and expertise before presenting themselves to the public as specialists" (Knapp & VandeCreek, 1981, p. 680). Schutz (1982) and Reamer (2003) contended that if psychologists present themselves as specialists within the practice of psychology they will be held to the highest standard of care of the specialty practice. For those presenting themselves to the public as clinical health psychologists or as specializing in treating disorders primarily within the domain of the specialty, then the higher standard of care will apply.

ESTABLISHMENT OF INJURY

The third element the plaintiff must demonstrate is that he or she suffered harm or injury. When physical harm has been sustained, it is easier to establish injury and specify monetary compensation. When the injury is emotional or psychological, however, it can be difficult to establish compensation amounts (Klein & Glover, 1983; Reamer, 2003). For example, if an injured worker had a dominant arm amputation, it would be relatively easier to estimate compensation on the basis of medical costs, physical disability, lost wages, and pain suffered than it would be in a psychological injury case. Expert witness testimony is often required to help objectify a psychological injury.

PROVING PROXIMATE CAUSE OF PATIENT'S INJURY

The last allegation to prove is that the plaintiff's injury was either directly caused by the practitioner's action or a reasonably foreseeable consequence of such behavior. When the practitioner's behavior is not outrageous, proving this essential causal link between professional conduct and mental injury can be difficult (Reamer, 2003; Slovenko, 1978; Tarshis, 1972). However, if the injury is physical, proof is much easier (Dawidoff, 1966; Reamer, 2003). In the practice of clinical health psychology, the injury is more likely to be physical because the patient is often being treated for psychological factors affecting a physical condition. An example of this might be a psychologist encouraging a cardiac patient to engage in an inappropriate amount of exercise without medical clearance, thus inducing a myocardial infarction.

AREAS OF LIABILITY RISK
IN CLINICAL HEALTH PSYCHOLOGY

Although most articles about psychologists' liability focus on malpractice, a licensing board complaint can be just as devastating to the practitioner and is far more likely to occur. As discussed by Welch (2002), "Most psychologists don't really understand that their vulnerability to an unjustified licensure complaint and resulting investigation is infinitely greater than the risk of a malpractice suit" (p. 3). A malpractice suit is difficult to file and usually requires that the plaintiff or patient convince an attorney that there is enough merit to the case to expect recovery on a contingency basis. However, filing a licensing board complaint requires only filling out a form, which is now usually done online. For instance, in California in 2006, the Board of Psychology received 537 complaints, but this resulted in only 102 investigations being opened. Of those 102 investigations, 23 resulted in some type of penalty decision (e.g., reprimand, revocation) and 36 were sent to the District Attorney for criminal prosecution. It is obvious that only a small percentage of complaints lead to sanctions or prosecution. However, in the 478 cases in which the psychologist was exonerated, the practitioners had to endure the stressful process of defending against a licensing board complaint. Being aware of areas of liability and of risk management strategies can help the psychologist avoid the complaint altogether. Although the following discussion is primarily related to malpractice risk, it also applies to licensing board complaints.

Practicing Medicine Without a License

One of the primary increased malpractice risks one encounters in moving from general clinical work to clinical health psychology is practicing medicine without a license. Several authors (R. J. Cohen, 1979; Furrow, 1980; Knapp & VandeCreek, 1981; Reamer, 2003) addressed this increased malpractice liability, and their discussions are summarized here.

The practice of medicine can be generally defined as "persons who diagnose or treat disease, or who represent themselves as healers of disease" (Knapp & VandeCreek, 1981, p. 678). Although the practice of medicine is clear in such things as surgery or chemotherapy, in other areas it becomes much less definable. These less clear areas relevant to "drugless healers" (e.g., psychologists) include diagnosing and treating patients within the bounds of one's own discipline, and not crossing over into medical practice. Consider the following example:

> A. J. was a 37-year-old woman, who presented with a complaint of headaches that had occurred daily over the past year. The headaches were characterized by a bandlike pain encircling the head. The pain began in the suboccipital region and radiated to posterior cervical

areas. A. J. reported no associated visual or gastrointestinal symptoms. She also stated that the headaches were exacerbated by stress, typically gaining in intensity over the course of the day. A. J. had not had a recent physical exam. The psychologist performing the evaluation diagnosed the case as stress-related muscle-contraction headaches and began treatment.

There are two problems with this case from both liability and ethical standpoints. First, A. J. had not had an appropriate medical workup related to the chief complaint. Within the practice of clinical health psychology, medical evaluation is almost always necessary, and failure to refer or consult can be grounds for malpractice. (This is discussed subsequently.) Second, she had not received a diagnosis of muscle-contraction headaches from a physician. Even though the symptom pattern was certainly suggestive of this disorder, from a legal viewpoint the psychologist could be diagnosing a disease that would be considered within the realm of medical practice. This is because the "practitioner gave an opinion as to the origin or cause of the patient's physical ailments" (Knapp & VandeCreek, 1981, p. 678). However, it would be perfectly appropriate for the health psychologist to make a diagnosis on Axis I of the *Diagnostic and Statistic Manual of Mental Disorders, Fourth Edition* (*DSM–IV*) system (American Psychiatric Association, 1994), such as psychological factors affecting physical condition, because the psychologist would not be diagnosing the physical etiology of the problem.

Another problem is the legal implications of making a diagnosis on Axis III of the *DSM–IV*. The nonphysician, or the psychiatrist who has not done a physical workup, must be careful not to give an Axis III diagnosis that he or she is either unqualified or unprepared to make. When recording an Axis III diagnosis, we find it most prudent to state where the physical diagnosis originated (e.g., "migraine headache per the patient," "per the medical record," "per the referral"). One must also take care in stating the source of the physical diagnosis in the text of the evaluation report. We have often seen statements that suggested that the psychologist was making physical diagnoses.

Beyond diagnosing, clinical health psychologists must take care in treating physical disease. In the practice of clinical health psychology, the practitioner is often involved in the psychological or psychophysiological

treatment of a physical problem. When the psychological treatment inter-
feres or takes the place of appropriate medical treatment (without informed
consent), it could be grounds for malpractice. There is a legal case history
of nonphysician practitioners encouraging their patients to leave standard
medical treatment and being held liable (see R. J. Cohen, 1979; Knapp &
VandeCreek, 1981). Consider the following two examples:

> B. J. was a 45-year-old man referred for adjunctive psychophysiolog-
> ical treatment of his borderline hypertension (HTN). He was taking
> dyazide, which was controlling his HTN adequately, but he was
> excited about learning self-control techniques because of the aversive
> side effects of the medication. As the biofeedback and psychotherapy
> progressed, B. J. was becoming increasingly able to decrease his blood
> pressure while relaxing in the clinic. He incessantly asked his therapist
> about reducing his medication with continued successful training.
> The psychologist suggested this was an appropriate goal, and he was
> encouraged to carefully experiment with lower medication dosages
> while monitoring his HTN with a home-monitoring unit.
>
> The patient was an 82-year-old woman with congestive heart fail-
> ure (CHF), who was referred for treatment of a psychophysiological dis-
> order. The patient was on a complex medication regimen consisting of
> diuretics, potassium, and Valium as needed (prn) for anxiety and sleep.
> The patient was seen for an evaluation and then scheduled for a psy-
> chophysiological baseline assessment. She was instructed not to take
> the Valium before the appointment, so that an accurate baseline assess-
> ment could be done. The patient came in the next week, having not
> taken any of her medications for the day. Her legs were slightly edem-
> atous as a result of water retention. The patient had thought the clin-
> ical health psychologist prescribed that she not take any of her
> medications a day before the evaluation.

These two cases present clear examples of a psychologist practicing
medicine. This is not because reducing medications as the psychological
techniques became more effective was an inappropriate goal but because
these treatment directives must be done by the primary physician on the
basis of mutual consultation. Even more difficult decisions involve patients

who are referred for treatment and are on prn medications. For example, we see many patients referred for psychophysiological treatment of their intractable chronic headaches who are on prn analgesic medication. Although there is no legal case history of whether a nonphysician health care practitioner can be held liable for encouraging a patient to reduce prn medications as treatment proceeds, the most prudent approach is to discuss this strategy with the physician and to document the results of this consultation.

Furthermore, the clinical health psychologist must be careful to ensure that the patient does not mistake him or her for a physician. If this occurs, the practitioner may be held accountable for practicing medicine if a problem arises. In many medical centers, the likelihood of this occurring is increased by the dress code of the institution. Psychologists on both inpatient and outpatient services often wear traditional white lab coats. This can be confusing to patients—a confusion that can often be readily ascertained by the nature of the patient's questions. In keeping with informed-consent procedures, on initial contact, we make a concise statement about the psychologist's realm of expertise, which helps to avoid many problems in this area.

One other area that has emerged over the past 10 years is that of prescription privileges for psychologists. Currently, New Mexico and Louisiana have some type of prescription privileges for psychologists, and legislation is constantly being introduced in other states. The area of psychopharmacology has become of great interest to more and more psychologists as the prescription privilege movement has grown. As such, psychologists have become more knowledgeable, comfortable, and assertive in working with the physicians treating their patients, and making medication recommendations. In fact, in our experience, it is common to see a clinical health psychologist working in close collaboration with a nonpsychiatrist physician and making medication recommendations to the physician for their mutual patient. This might include choosing antidepressant or anxiolytic medications, as well as making recommendations for behavioral techniques related to dosing and tapering of pain medication (e.g., prn vs. time-contingent). However, this must be done in a manner that ensures that the actual medication decisions are made by the physician, and communicated to the patient through him or her. The clinical health psychologist might well be practicing medicine without a license if he or she were to recommend directly to a patient to change the dose of medication, change how the medication is taken, or to stop a medication altogether (National Association of Social Workers, 1990; Reamer, 2003).

On the basis of case law involving other nonphysician health care professionals being sued for practicing medicine without a license, certain recommendations for clinical health psychology practice can be made. First, in providing psychological treatment for medical patients, one must work closely with the medical specialist. A joint treatment plan should be established, preferably in writing, and signed by the patient. Furthermore, this plan should be explicitly stated to the patient, so that he or she understands which aspects of treatment will be handled by each professional. Second, when a self-referred patient seeks treatment for a problem involving a physical complaint, a medical evaluation should be insisted on before treatment ensues. Third, one should communicate and consult, in both verbal and written form, with the primary physician on a periodic basis, so that both medical and psychological treatments can be jointly adjusted as appropriate. These consultations should be documented.

Failure to Refer, Consult, or Communicate

This area of malpractice risk is closely associated with practicing medicine without a license. We address this issue as it relates to working with a physician or providing treatment for a physical disorder. As we discussed in chapter 6 (this volume), the clinical health psychologist is in a position of having increased responsibility for physical health. Malpractice issues can arise when this responsibility is managed in a negligent fashion not in keeping with the prevailing standard of care.

The issue of psychologists being involved with health and medical problems is being vigorously debated in state and federal legislative arenas. The concern, voiced primarily by medicine, is that psychologists are nonmedical providers; therefore, they cannot accurately diagnose mental disorders, will misdiagnose physical conditions as psychological problems, fail to recognize medical problems, and fail to refer to physicians for needed medical care. Some liability cases against nonphysician practitioners suggest that this could be an area of liability risk for the clinical health psychologist. For instance, in one case, a psychologist failed to conduct an adequate mental status examination of the patient and then failed to adequately report any results of the evaluation to the psychiatrist also working on the case. As a result, the psychiatrist prescribed medication that "injured" the patient (*Chambers v. Ingram,* 1988). Stromberg and Dellinger (1993) stated that "this case represents a good lesson in how psychologists, although they cannot usually prescribe medications, may have liability relating to the patient's use of medications" (p. 7). In another case, a psychiatrist failed to rule out a physical cause for the patient's symptoms. The patient received 11 years of psychotherapy before the condition was traced to a brain tumor (*Russo v. Ascher,* 1988; Stromberg & Dellinger, 1993). The psychiatrist was found negligent for not having ruled out a serious physical etiology for the presenting symptoms. In a third case (*Kogensparger v. Athens Mental Health Center,* 1989, as reported in Reamer, 2003), a mental health center had been treating a patient for schizophrenia, even though his complaints included behavioral symptoms and discomfort in his head. After three years of inpatient treatment, the patient had a grand mal seizure and died one week later. An autopsy revealed a slow growing brain tumor, which had likely been developing for years. In the liability case, the mental health center was found negligent for failure to refer for appropriate medical evaluation.

These three examples can easily be extrapolated to the practice of clinical health psychology. As we discussed in the previous section, if the psychologist is treating a physical problem, it is imperative that a physician is also involved, and open communication is important to discuss problems and progress. For instance, the patient may be seeing the psychologist much more frequently than the physician. In this situation, the psychologist may be the first to discover such things as side effects to medications or occurrence of additional physical symptoms. On the basis of the cases mentioned earlier, the psychologist may have a duty to encourage the patient to return for medical evaluation or to communicate these concerns and findings to the physician. These actions must be carefully documented, which is, of course, in keeping with good clinical practice.

Suicide and Malpractice Risk

 uicidal patient presents to a mental health professional, action must be taken to prevent self-harm. If a suicide risk evaluation falls below the standard of care (i.e., failure to diagnose) or if suicidal threats are not taken seriously (i.e., duty to prevent harm) the practitioner may be liable in a malpractice action stemming from the patient's suicide (B. E. Bernstein & Hartsell, 2004; Deardorff et al., 1984; Packman & Smith, 2006a, 2006b; Reamer, 2003). Malpractice cases involving suicides by individuals being treated on an outpatient basis are on the rise (Bongar, Maris, Berman, & Litman, 1998; Jobes & Berman, 1993; Packman & Smith, 2006a). According to Baerger (2001), 20% of psychologists and 50% of psychiatrists will lose a patient to suicide during their careers. The largest number of lawsuits brought against psychiatrists, and the largest monetary settlements, are related to postsuicide claims of negligence (Baerger, 2001). Among psychologists insured by APA's Insurance Trust, patient suicide ranked sixth among claim categories, but second in terms of percentage of total costs (Baerger, 2001).

The suicidal patient may present a special risk for the clinical health psychologist working in a medical setting. Unlike traditional outpatient practice, clinical health psychologists are more likely to evaluate suicidal patients in the emergency room, and as medical inpatients. Thus, the evaluation and diagnosis of suicidality must be done rapidly and, typically, outside the context of a longer-term treatment relationship. The clinical health psychologist must be familiar with the assessment of the suicidal patient and the appropriate precautionary measures (see Bongar, 2002; Simon & Hales, 2006, for review). An excellent resource is the Basic Suicide Assessment Five Step Evaluation (B–SAFE) developed by the Joint Commission of Accreditation of Healthcare Organizations (JCAHO; D. Jacobs & Brewer, 2004; Joint Commission of Accreditation of Healthcare Organizations, 2007). When a therapist follows accepted evaluation and diagnostic procedures, and these do not reveal suicidality in a patient who subsequently commits suicide, there are no grounds for malpractice (Baerger, 2001; *Baker v. United States,* 1964; Hogan, 1979; *Porter v. Maunnangi,* 1988). As concluded by the court,

> a doctor is not a . . . guarantor of the correctness of his diagnosis; the requirement is [merely] that he use proper care and skill. . . . The question is not whether the physician made a mistake in diagnosis,

but rather whether he failed to conform to the accepted standard of care. (*Schuster v. Altenberg,* 1988; Stromberg & Dellinger, 1993)

In addressing the process of evaluating and managing the suicidal patient, the reader is directed to three excellent articles published as a special section in *Professional Psychology: Research and Practice* (Joiner, Walker, Rudd, & Jobes, 1999; Kleespies, Deleppo, Gallagher, & Niles, 1999; Rudd, Joiner, Jobes, & King, 1999). To protect oneself against a malpractice or liability claim, the clinical health psychologist should be familiar with the prevailing standard of care for evaluation and management of these patients.

It is beyond the scope of this chapter to present detailed suicide-risk management strategies as these have been discussed elsewhere, as previously referenced. Packman and Smith (2006b) outline them as follows:

1. Document, document, document. There is a saying in legal circles that "if it isn't written down, it didn't happen." Be sure to document interactions, consultations, professional judgments, and the "whys and why nots" in treatment decision making.
2. Consult. One should consult with colleagues who have experience with suicidal patients.
3. Know legal and ethical responsibilities. Being familiar with legal and ethical responsibilities helps the clinician recognize risk before it becomes liability.
4. Know the risk factors of suicidal patients. Clinicians must know what the literature says about suicidal risk factors to exercise sound clinical judgment. For instance, relative to the clinical health psychologist, patients with physical conditions, such as malignant neoplasms, HIV/AIDS, peptic ulcer disease, kidney failure requiring hemodialysis, pain syndromes, functional impairment including organic brain injuries, diseases of the nervous system (i.e., especially multiple sclerosis, temporal lobe epilepsy), or any chronic medical illness, are at increased risk for suicide (D. Jacobs, 2007).
5. Obtain risk assessment data and adequate history. A thorough clinical assessment of elevated suicidal risk must be completed, consistent with evidence-based research and the standard of care. Guidelines such as those discussed in Joiner et al. (1999) and elsewhere (see previous

references) should be followed. Suicide risk should be reassessed on a regular basis.

6. Determine diagnostic impression. Be sure to provide an accurate diagnosis consistent with the *DSM–IV*. Resist the temptation to "underdiagnose" because this is legally risky and not an advisable risk management procedure.

7. Determine your competence. Be aware of your own proficiency in working with a suicidal patient. Take whatever steps are necessary to ensure adequate evaluation, treatment, and follow through with the patient (e.g., consult, on-going education, refer).

8. Involve the family. It is often important to involve the patient's family in the evaluation and treatment process. If appropriate, family involvement can increase the effectiveness of the intervention and protect the clinician from litigation (Bongar, 2002).

If a practitioner determines that a patient is suicidal, precautionary measures such as involuntary or voluntary commitment for observation may have to be invoked, although, in some cases, using sound clinical judgment, the suicidal patient may be most appropriately managed on an outpatient basis. As long as the standard of care is commensurate with community standards and the treatment decision is in the best interests of the patient, there would be no grounds for negligence (see Bongar, Maris, Berman, & Litman, 1992, 1998, for a review). If a patient is already in the hospital on a medical–surgical unit, other special issues arise. These include determining specific suicide precautions that must be taken and making sure the staff carries them out.

Determination of the suicide precautions that must be taken is guided by a thorough assessment and evaluation of the patient. As discussed in the B–SAFE Guidelines (JCAHO, 2007), the monitoring of a suicidal patient includes a range of frequency of observation, from constant (1:1) to every 30 minutes. In addition, it is important to address safety needs related to the physical environment and access to methods of self-injury. The guidelines specifically state that, "suicidal patients on medical units are in less controlled, therefore, higher-risk physical environments; Safety is increased by providing closer observation, often 1:1 with a sitter" (D. Jacobs, 2007, p. 13). Exhibit 7.1 depicts suicide precautions that can

---

Exhibit 7.1

Examples of Suicide Precaution to Be Used
on an Inpatient Medical Unit

Assessment of medical stability completed

Assessment of the physical environment, focusing on controlling
patient access to methods of self-injury

One-to-one constant staff observation and/or security

Supervised bathroom use, unit restriction, and restriction to
public areas

Elopement precautions

Precautions against common forms of suicide (hanging, suffocation,
jumping)

Search of body and belongings

Administration of psychotropic medications to reduce agitation
and/or application of physical restraints as clinically necessary

---

be used on a medical–surgical unit, listed from most restrictive to least restrictive alternatives. Suicide precautions must be specified precisely in written form, either in the progress notes, or in the doctor's orders section of the chart, depending on hospital guidelines. The psychologist must keep in mind that the staff is a nonpsychiatric one and, hence, they are generally not accustomed to implementing such procedures. The psychologist must also be prepared to deal with the staff's emotional response to the suicidal patient. On medical–surgical units, wherein saving life is the primary goal, the staff will often express anger and frustration toward a suicidal patient in indirect ways (e.g., not administering pain medications on time, not speaking with the patient).

In making sure that the staff carries out the suicide precaution orders, the psychologist would be wise to initiate a staff intervention aimed at education and open communication about exactly what precautions are being taken, who is responsible for carrying them out, and what to do if problems arise. Of course, all information should be documented in the medical or nursing record. One must be particularly careful that adequate communication occurs across different nursing shifts. When this is done inadequately, negligent professional behavior may be found if litigation were to occur.

An excellent method for developing critical thinking relative to practice issues is to be aware of how one's actions, or lack thereof, might stand up to legal cross-examination in the event of a liability claim (i.e., malpractice, licensing board complaint). This approach can be applied to any practice issue or decision that confronts the clinical health psychologist. An example of actual guidelines used by lawyers for cross-examining assessment of suicide risk can be found in Exhibit 7.2 (adapted from Campbell & Lorandos, 2001). It should also be remembered that when a psychologist's behavior is measured against the standard of care, it is primarily the clinical record that will be examined. The psychologist's interview or cross-examination will only carry weight to the degree that the answers are corroborated in the record. As such, one can conceptualize the liability process as weighing the patient's word against the clinical record (Zur, 2005). This underscores the importance of documentation.

Duty to Protect

Increasingly, mental health professionals are being held responsible for protecting the public from the violent acts of their patients. The duty-to-protect doctrine received great publicity in the case of *Tarasoff v. Regents* of the *University* of *California* (1976), a case with which all mental health professionals should be familiar (see DeMatteo, 2005; Gostin, 2002; Kamenar, 1984; VandeCreek & Knapp, 2001).

In *Tarasoff v. Board of Regents of the University of California,* a patient (Prosenjit Podder) told his psychotherapist (Dr. Lawrence Moore) that he intended to kill an unnamed but readily identifiable woman (Tatiana Tarasoff). The treatment session took place at Cowell Memorial Hospital at the University if California in Berkeley. After the session, Dr. Moore immediately contacted the university police and requested they observe Mr. Podder because he might be a danger to himself or others. Dr. Moore followed up the telephone call with a letter requesting the help of the chief of the university police. The campus police took Mr. Podder into custody but released him

Exhibit 7.2

A Cross-Examination of the Assessment of Suicide Risk

The following cross-examination references the article
"Scientizing and Routinizing the Assessment of Suicidality
in Outpatient Practice" (Joiner, Walker, Rudd, & Jobes,
1999) in which seven domains of suicide risk are delineated:
(a) previous suicidal behavior; (b) the nature of current suicidal
symptoms; (c) precipitant stressors; (d) general symptomatic
presentation, including hopelessness; (e) impulsivity and
self-control; (f) other predispositions; and (g) protective factors.
This example cross-examination is adapted from a resource
text for attorneys.

1. Your profession generally subscribes to the premise that
   the best predictor of future behavior is past behavior,
   correct?
2. Suicide "ideators" are identified as individuals who think
   about suicide, but have not overtly attempted it, correct?
3. Accordingly, the literature frequently differentiates between
   those individuals who have who have engaged in multiple
   suicide attempts, those with one attempt, and suicide
   "ideators," correct?
4. Individuals who have attempted suicide on two or more
   occasions present a much greater risk of compared to single
   attempters or ideators, correct?
5. While assessing the patient in this case, did you ascertain how
   many previous times he had attempted suicide?

[Foundational questions are completed here, establishing
that the information in peer-reviewed journals is generally
recognized and accepted by the field, and that the psychologist has a professional obligation to be familiar with such
information.]

(*continued*)

CLINICAL HEALTH PSYCHOLOGY

Exhibit 7.2

A Cross-Examination of the Assessment of Suicide Risk (Continued)

6. The journal *Professional Psychology: Research and Practice* is a generally recognized and accepted, peer-reviewed journal in your field, correct?

7. And a 1999 article by Joiner et al. published in *Professional Psychology: Research and Practice,* titled "Scientizing and Routinizing the Assessment of Suicidality in Outpatient Practice," might be relevant to your opinions in this case, correct?

8. Please consider these comments from the 1999 article by Joiner et al.: "Two main factors summarize the factor space of suicidal symptomatology. The factors were labeled 'resolved plans and preparation' and 'suicidal desire and ideation.' " Now, my question: You accept "resolved plans and preparation," and "suicidal desire and ideation," as factors corresponding to suicidal symptomatology, correct?

9. You have not published anything in a peer-reviewed journal necessitating that we reconsider the position of Joiner et al. in this regard, correct?

10. You cannot cite anything in a peer-reviewed journal necessitating that we reconsider the position of Joiner et al., correct?

11. In accordance with Joiner et al., you agree that "resolved plans and preparation" corresponds to a patient who possesses that courage to make an attempt, correct?

12. And in accordance with Joiner et al., "resolved plans and preparation" indicates that patients feel they can carry through with an attempt, correct?

13. And in accordance with Joiner et al., "resolved plans and preparation" indicates that a patient has the means and opportunity available for an attempt, correct?

(continued)

212

Exhibit 7.2

A Cross-Examination of the Assessment of Suicide Risk (Continued)

14. And in accordance with Joiner et al., "resolved plans and preparation" indicates that a patient has developed a specific plan for an attempt, correct?

15. And in accordance with Joiner et al., "resolved plans and preparation" indicates that a patient has experienced a significant intensity and duration of suicidal ideation, correct?

16. You have not published anything in a peer-reviewed journal necessitating that we reconsider the position of Joiner et al. in this regard, correct?

17. You cannot cite anything in a peer-reviewed journal necessitating that we reconsider the position of Joiner et al., correct?

18. Please consider these comments from the 1999 article by Joiner et al.: "Our view is that the resolved plans and preparation factor is pernicious; accordingly, anyone who displays its symptoms should be designated as at least a moderate risk for suicide." Now, my question: You agree with Joiner et al. indicating that "resolved plans and preparation" factor creates a pernicious risk of suicide, correct?

19. You have not published anything in a peer-reviewed journal necessitating that we reconsider the position of Joiner et al. in this regard, correct?

20. You cannot cite anything in a peer-reviewed journal necessitating that we reconsider the position of Joiner et al., correct?

21. In this case, what did you do to assess the "resolved plans and preparation" factor?

22. Please consider further comment by Joiner et al. in their 1999 article: "Specifically, intensity and duration of ideation load onto the resolved plans and preparation factor." Now my question: You agree that "intensity and duration of ideation" refer to the intensity and duration of suicidal ideation, correct?

(continued)

213

Exhibit 7.2
A Cross-Examination of the Assessment of Suicide Risk (Continued)

23. And if "the intensity and duration" of suicidal ideation load onto the resolved plans and preparation factor, this means that the more intense and the longer the duration of suicidal ideation, the greater the risk of suicide, correct?
24. In this case, what did you do to assess the intensity and duration of the patient's suicidal ideation?
25. And you did not document an assessment of the intensity and duration of the patient's suicidal ideation, correct?

[This structure of questioning is continued for all of the important risk factors for suicide, including stressful life events, diagnostic status, living situation, employment status, health status, presence of hopelessness, chaotic family history, impulsivity, substance use, and so forth.]

Note. From *Cross Examining Experts in the Behavioral Sciences* (pp. 10–91), by T. Campbell and D. Lorandos, 2001, Danvers, MA: Thomson West. Copyright 2001 by Thomson West. Adapted with permission.

after observation and noting that he was rational. Mr. Podder was instructed to stay away from Ms. Tarasoff. Mr. Podder did not return to treatment and subsequently killed Ms. Tarasoff approximately 2 months later. The parents of Ms. Tarasoff sued the psychotherapist, the Board of Regents, and others associated with the case for failing to warn them or their daughter directly.

In the *Tarasoff* (1976) decision, the California Supreme Court stated that

> a therapist determines, or pursuant to the standards of his profession should determine, that his patient presents a serious danger of violence to another, he incurs an obligation to use reasonable care to protect the intended victim against such danger. (p. 347)

The court's ruling means that although there may be no special relationship between a therapist and victim, the relationship between a therapist and patient can be sufficient to impose special legal responsibility on the therapist for the patient's actions if the therapist knows the patient poses a serious threat, or the therapist negligently fails to predict such dangerousness (Southard & Gross, 1982). The court's ruling also stated that when a danger to others exists, the confidential doctor–patient relationship must yield.

The *Tarasoff* ruling was only binding in California, but duty-to-protect doctrine has been adopted by a majority of states (DeMatteo, 2005; Reisner, Slobogin, & Rai, 2004). *Tarasoff* has been modified in subsequent cases. In *Thompson v. County of Alameda* (1980), the California Supreme Court held that *Tarasoff* only applied when there was a specific threat against a clearly identifiable victim. The *Hedland v. Superior Court* (1983) ruling held that a therapist could be liable if the victim was foreseeable, even if not readily identifiable. Most states have followed the ruling regarding a specific threat against a readily identifiable victim, but some states have rejected the *Tarasoff* doctrine altogether (e.g., Virginia, Washington; see DeMatteo, 2005, for a review).

The *Ewing v. Goldstein* (2004) case heard by the California Court of Appeals held that a communication from a patient's family member constitutes "patient communication" that can potentially trigger a therapist's duty to protect (see DeMatteo, 2005, for a review). In *Ewing v. Goldstein* (2004), Dr. David Goldstein provided counseling services to Gene Colello, a former Lost Angeles police officer. During the course of treatment, Mr. Colello became despondent over the breakup of his relationship with Diana Williams. Mr. Colello expressed suicidal ideation and Dr. Goldstein encouraged him to check himself into a psychiatric facility. Also, Dr. Goldstein obtained permission to speak with Mr. Colello's father. Subsequently, Mr. Colello told his father about his desire to harm Ms. William's new boyfriend. Colello's father immediately called Dr. Goldstein and told him of the threats made by his son. Dr. Goldstein arranged for treatment at Northridge Hospital and Colello was admitted under the care of a staff psychiatrist. The staff psychiatrist planned on discharging Colello after just 1 day because there was no evidence of suicidal ideation. Dr. Goldstein contacted the staff psychiatrist and expressed his concern over the release of Colello. Even so, Colello was released. On the following day, Colello murdered Ms. William's new boyfriend, Keith Ewing, and then committed suicide. Ewing's parents sued Dr. Goldstein for wrongful death on the basis of professional negligence. They contended that Colello had communicated a threat against their son to Dr. Goldstein, either directly or indirectly through third persons, and Dr. Goldstein failed to discharge his duty to protect their son from foreseeable danger. Dr. Goldstein contended that Colello had never directly disclosed to him that he intended to harm Ewing; therefore, no duty to protect was triggered. The decision by the Court of Appeals overturned a lower court decision that had concluded that the therapist did not have a duty to warn because there was no direct communication from Dr. Goldstein's patient (rather, it was from the patient's father). The appeals court refused to address the issue of whether communication from another third party could trigger a duty to protect. As discussed by DeMatteo (2005), "therapists must still determine whether a patient's threat is credible, serious, and directed at a reasonably identifiable person, but they may need to make these often difficult determinations based on second-hand information" (p. 20). DeMatteo (2005) states that the *Ewing* decision is only binding in California but may be adopted by courts in other jurisdictions. It should be noted that a California bill (AB 733) went into effect in 2007 and was originally designed to nullify the *Ewing v. Goldstein* effect on *Tarasoff*. However, as discussed by Faltz (2006), the version of AB 733 that was ultimately passed "does not change the effect of the *Ewing* decision" (p. 31). Psychologists should continue to act in accordance with the *Ewing* decision (AB 733 Amends Civil Code § 43.92).

Since *Tarasoff* and *Ewing*, there has been much confusion in the mental health professions as to the specific implications of these rulings. Relative to *Tarasoff*, Schindler (1976) noted that the courts offered no practical guidelines to follow. Southard and Gross (1982) and others (Beigler, 1984; Kamenar, 1984; Monahan, 1993; Quinn, 1984; Reamer, 2003; VandeCreek & Knapp, 2001; Wettstein, 1984) have provided thorough discussions of the misunderstanding surrounding the *Tarasoff* decision while articulating the responsibilities of therapists related to the duty to protect. Briefly, this case is often cited as "duty to warn," but the actual court decision was based on a "duty to care," or to protect. The courts did not rule that warning potential victims was a reasonable course of action in all cases, but rather that the therapist is to take "reasonable care" to protect the potential victim

(Knapp, 1980; Southard & Gross, 1982). Protective action may involve many different possibilities.

Southard and Gross (1982) presented several cases that occurred after *Tarasoff* and that facilitate the understanding of the "duty-to-protect" doctrine. These findings include the following: that *Tarasoff* does not apply to suicide or property damage (Schwitzgebel & Schwitzgebel, 1980), that it does not apply to nonspecific threats against nonspecific persons, and that imminence of danger is necessary for a duty to protect to exist. On the basis of these cases, Southard and Gross (1982, p. 41) provided a "*Tarasoff* Decision Chart" to guide clinical decision making in executing a duty to protect. This chart has been modified to take into account the *Ewing v. Goldstein* ruling and can be seen in Figure 7.1.

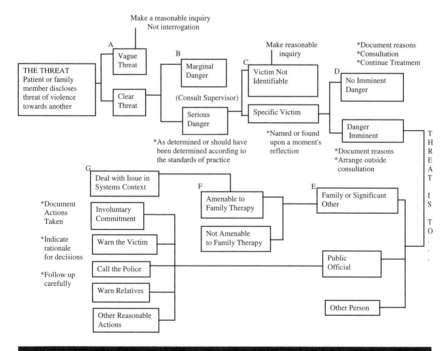

Figure 7.1

Tarasoff decision chart. From *New Directions for Mental Health Services: Vol. 16. The Mental Health Professional and the Legal System* (p. 98), by B. H. Gross and L. E. Weinberger (Eds.), 1982, San Francisco: Jossey-Bass. Copyright 1982 by Jossey-Bass. Adapted with permission.

As can be seen in Figure 7.1, the initial steps (A–B) involve determining whether a "serious" threat exists. Given *Ewing,* the threat can come from the patient or a member of the patient's family. There is no guidance from case law about a threat disclosed by a third party. In these first two phases of assessment, a specific threat is not always the only criterion for invoking *Tarasoff.* If the professional should have known that a patient was dangerous to someone as determined by standards of practice, then there is a *Tarasoff* responsibility (*McIntosh v. Milano,* as cited in Kamenar, 1984; see also Gostin, 2002; VandeCreek & Knapp, 2001). Step C deals with the identifiability of the potential victim. Although there are no clear guidelines regarding identifiability, a discussion by Kamenar (1984) of several cases suggests that even when the potential victim is not identifiable, the professional may have a duty to protect a foreseeable, but unidentifiable, third party. This might include "detaining the patient, inquiring further as to the identity of the possible victim, warning his or her family or law enforcement officials, or taking some other precaution" (Kamenar, 1984, p. 265; Knapp & VandeCreek, 2001). Steps D through E involve determining whether danger is imminent, and within what grouping of people the intended victim falls. Throughout this process of decision making, documentation and consultation are of the utmost importance because the clinician's actions will be judged by the reasonable and prudent practitioner guidelines and community standard of care. Steps F and G are possible actions indicated, on the basis of assessment in the previous steps. Thus, warning the victim is not the sole possibility. In fact, some authors feel that the action taken by the therapists in the *Tarasoff* case was rash because, although threats were made, danger was not imminent, in that Ms. Tarasoff was out of the country. In attempting to have the patient who made threats against Tarasoff committed immediately, the therapists may have destroyed any therapeutic alliance, which might have worked against the violent action that took place (Sadoff, 1979; Southard & Gross, 1982).

Although such decision-making trees are helpful, there is much concern that the courts are extending the duty to protect related to the prediction of dangerousness, beyond what the scientific level of the profession is capable of delivering (DeMatteo, 2005; Goodstein, 1985; Gostin, 2002). A therapist's best defense is careful documentation, clinical reasoning, and consultation. Of course, these behaviors are all consistent with sound clinical practice.

The clinical health psychologist working in a hospital setting has a difficult task related to assessment and management of homicidality. He or she is most likely to be confronted with a *Tarasoff* situation while consulting to the emergency room, or in the assessment of injured patients. Questions regarding perceived causation of the injury and possible motives for revenge are important. However, because the clinical health psychologist will usually not have had a previous relationship with the patient, adequate assessment is often difficult. In these situations, hospitalization may be used more frequently.

Three general principles can be gleaned from *Tarasoff* and subsequent cases (Knapp & VandeCreek, 2001; VandeCreek & Stout, 1993): foreseeability of harm, identifiability of the victim, and the ability of the therapist to protect the potential victim. First, the courts have not found liability when therapists could not have foreseen the danger. Second, the courts have generally found that there is no liability if the potential victim is not identifiable. Third, the courts have generally found that the therapist need only take fairly easy and reasonable steps to warn the potential victim, to fulfill the duty. Thus, the guidelines presented by Southard and Gross (1982; see Fig. 7.1), with the modification taking into account the *Ewing* decision, are still applicable.

Duty to Protect and Patients With HIV

AIDS is caused by HIV. AIDS is an epidemic, and it presents a special issue related to the duty to protect within the context of a psychotherapeutic relationship. Specifically, what is the psychologist to do if a patient discloses that he or she is HIV-positive and also has a sexual or needle-sharing partner who is not aware of the infection? This issue may be more likely to confront clinical health psychologists because of their closer association with the medically ill.

The question is whether the situation entails a necessary invocation of the *Tarasoff* duty to protect. The *Tarasoff* decision was based on long-standing precedents involving physicians' duty to warn third persons about infectious diseases (see Gostin, 2002; Knapp & VandeCreek, 1990, 2001; Totten, Lamb, & Reeder, 1990, for review). As such, legal precedent for a duty to warn in HIV cases antedates the *Tarasoff* decision. Still, one is not expected to invoke the duty to warn in every case of a patient disclosing HIV-positive status who has uninformed persons within his or her psychosocial environment. The breaking of confidentiality in fulfilling the duty to warn must be done with caution after careful consideration of many factors, just as in *Tarasoff* cases.

Legal guidelines for the duty to protect in HIV-positive cases have been developed in many states. It is beyond the scope of this discussion to review each state's guidelines, if they actually exist in a particular state. In addition, these guidelines often change rapidly. Knapp and VandeCreek (1990, 2001) provided a useful presentation of these issues, as well as general guidelines for the duty to protect in HIV-positive cases. They take into account such things as the three general *Tarasoff* guidelines as applied to the HIV-positive case, how to assess the level of risk the patient with HIV is posing, and the clinical management of the patient with HIV who is dangerous. They conclude that psychologists should be aware of state law, consult with colleagues, consult with legal authorities, and document the decision-making process, to deal with these cases in a sound clinical and legal fashion. Other excellent resources include APA Public Interest Directorate, Major HIV/AIDS Topics and Issues (at http://www.apa.org/pi/aids/major.html; see also Dickson,1995; Reamer, 1991; Wood, Marks, & Dilley, 1990).

Confidentiality

Confidentiality is a standard of professional conduct that requires the practitioner not to discuss or disclose information about a patient to anyone. Communication between patient and psychologist within the context of a professional relationship is considered confidential and this has been established in the Ethics Code, legal statutes, and case law (APA, 2002a; Bersoff, 2003; Koocher & Keith-Spiegel, 1998; Reamer, 2003). As with traditional psychological treatment, the clinical health psychologist is mandated to breach confidentiality under special circumstances (e.g., endangerment to others, child abuse, elder abuse, endangerment to self). However, inadvertent breaches of confidentiality can occur (e.g., not securing records, cell phone conversations, Internet communication). When there is an inappropriate breach of confidentiality, it can be grounds for malpractice (*Berry v. Moench,* 1958; *Furniss v. Fitchett,* 1958; see also Koocher & Keith-Spiegel, 1998; Reamer, 2003, for a review). As discussed previously, it is anticipated that case law related to the management of confidential patient information will be shaped by the HIPAA regulations.

The practice of clinical health psychology can present special problems related to confidentiality. One issue has to do with how much information related to the patient's psychological status, history, and condition should be disclosed to the referral source, who is often the primary care physician with whom the clinician is working closely in the management of the patient. In many multidisciplinary practices, release of confidentiality for all treating professionals is required before a patient will be accepted into the treatment. In some cases, if a patient is unwilling to give consent to all practitioners to share and discuss information, he or she may not be accepted into treatment. This is because of the necessity of multidisciplinary communication for the treatment to be effective. Even the sole clinical health psychologist might require a confidentiality release to coordinate care with the patient's physician prior to accepting a case for treatment.

Even with HIPAA, the patient file in large medical centers is relatively open to other professionals on the staff. This, of course, presents problems for confidentiality of psychological services. Many departments of psychiatry and behavioral sciences maintain separate records, a policy that provides more control over access. One procedure we use for responding to a referral involves writing a detailed intake evaluation for our own records, and then excerpting relevant parts to comprise a more general evaluation to be sent back to the referral source. In most cases, this general report is also sent to the medical chart. The evaluation that is sent to the referral source is more symptom focused and treatment plan oriented. It does not include a detailed family history, particularly sensitive information, or a *DSM–IV* diagnosis. This practice is in keeping with Ethical Standard 4.04, which states that, "Psychologists include in written and oral reports and consultation, only information germane to the purpose for which the communication is made" (APA, 2002b). Psychological material even of this general nature should be released only with the patient's knowledge and consent. In many large health care systems, complete confidentiality cannot be promised, and the limits of confidentiality must be outlined to the patient in the informed-consent procedure.

Inpatient psychological treatment of medical patients presents similar problems with confidentiality, as well as others. A major problem is how much information to document in the unit chart, which is perhaps more widely read than clinic charts. It is prudent to follow the recommended guidelines in recording the most general and necessary information in the medical chart. It should be kept in mind that the psychological–behavioral information recorded in the unit chart can often affect how the staff interacts with the patient. When there is information particularly relevant to the treatment of the patient, but not appropriate to put in the medical chart, conveying the information verbally to the necessary health care professionals is indicated. However, the fact that the patient's care was discussed should be documented in the medical chart.

Problems with confidentiality also occur when there is a release for medical information to an outside source, and psychological treatment progress notes or evaluations have been recorded in the medical chart (inpatient or outpatient). General medical release of information forms are not sufficient to release psychological information, even when this information appears in the medical record. This may appear obvious, but in large medical systems, this issue is often overlooked. If the standard medical-information release does not specify the release of psychological information, it is important that the medical records department take appropriate precautions (e.g., deleting psychological progress notes when copying medical records). It may ultimately be the psychologist's responsibility to be sure this is done.

Psychological Evaluation

Psychological evaluation has been an area in which psychologists have been more likely to get sued for malpractice, and this pattern has continued (Montgomery et al., 1999; VandeCreek & Stout, 1993; Wright, 1981). The typical scenario is that the recommendation resulting from the psychological evaluation causes the patient-client to initiate a malpractice complaint concerning misuse of the test or test data. Wright (1981) concluded that in "most instances the filing of the grievance is a retaliatory expression of disappointment because something that the client wanted was denied or the client felt himself or herself to have been presented unfairly" (p. 1490). Stromberg and Dellinger (1993) stated that the courts have generally not been sympathetic to these suits because they understand that they are often of a retaliatory nature. Still, even the prospect of being faced with a malpractice action or licensing board complaint can be traumatic for the psychologist, and everything reasonable should be done to avoid it.

Clinical health psychologists practicing within the limits of their specialty would probably not be involved in areas of psychological evaluation that have more frequently resulted in malpractice litigation. These areas include evaluations for employment decisions (e.g., hiring, firing, promotion), child custody issues, and probation. However, clinical health psychologists are involved in psychological evaluations related to medical treatment or disability decision making that may have increased malpractice risks (e.g., neuropsychological assessment; evaluation for inpatient pain programs; workers' compensation assessments related to occupational injury or evaluation for some type of surgery, such as spine surgery, penile prosthesis, organ transplantation, or gastric bypass). For instance, if a patient is denied access to a treatment program or surgery, or is given the opportunity for an alternative treatment that is more appropriate, but not desired by the patient, a malpractice suit could be precipitated. In initiating the suit, the patient can deny the validity of the findings and express disagreement with the recommendation. Consider the following case example:

> The patient was a 60-year-old married man who was referred for psychological screening in conjunction with evaluation for a penile prosthesis. For the past 5 years, the patient had experienced erectile dysfunction, which had precluded sexual intercourse. Medical evaluation had shown that blood flow and hormonal studies were within normal limits and that no physical etiology could be established. Nocturnal erections during sleep were intact. The patient was not informed about the implications of the psychological evaluation relative to his surgery nor about the feedback process, before being interviewed. The psychological evaluation revealed there were a number of significant marital

problems at the time of the onset of the sexual dysfunction. In addition, the patient had been involved in an extramarital affair about which he felt guilty. Recommendations included a course of behavioral sexual dysfunction therapy and marital counseling. The results of the evaluation were given to the surgeon, who subsequently met with the patient and gave him feedback as to the treatment decision. The patient stated adamantly that he was not interested in psychotherapy, that the problem was physically based, and that he wanted it resolved with the prosthesis. The patient brought a malpractice suit against the surgeon and the psychologist, stating that he was denied the surgical procedure on the basis of unjustifiable reasons.

Of course, clinical health psychologists should not formulate recommendations resulting from evaluations based on attempting to avoid a malpractice suit. However, in the preceding example, the professionals made several errors in handling the informed consent, which may have contributed to the patient's ultimate legal action. In general, the ways to minimize the risk of malpractice stem from what would be considered sound clinical practice, regardless of the malpractice issues. First, the patient should be fully informed about the nature of the evaluation; for instance, who requested it, who will receive copies of the results, where the results will be documented (i.e., psychiatric, medical chart), the ramification of the results, and who will pay for it. After receiving information on the evaluation process, some check of the patient's understanding should be conducted, and then consent for the evaluation should be obtained (see chap. 6, this volume).

Second, after the evaluation, some discussion of the findings should be completed with the patient. This may occur before or after consulting with the referring physician, depending on the case, the psychologist's role as a consultant, and the relationship between the psychologist and the physician. This feedback session with the patient should include an opportunity for the patient to discuss his or her reactions to the results, and to ask any questions about future treatment. Often, when there is a treatment team involved, it is advisable for the team, or various members of the team (e.g., physician, psychologist), to meet with the patient simultaneously for feedback. In doing this, the team can address all questions that the patient may have while reducing the risk of miscommunication or misinformation.

Third, as suggested by Wright (1981) and others (e.g., Rogers, 2003), evaluation instruments should be given in the manner in which they were standardized, and in keeping with the standards for psychological testing. Fourth, careful documentation of informed-consent procedures, findings, the patient's response to the feedback session, consultation to the referral, and so forth, is necessary.

Although the recommendations from psychological evaluations are not always in keeping with patient desires, these guidelines can help reduce the risk of retaliatory or successful malpractice actions without having to equivocate evaluation results to the point of uselessness.

Supervision of Trainees

The clinical health psychologist working in a supervisory capacity must be aware of increased malpractice liability. As the area of clinical health psychology expands, increasing numbers of practitioners will be seeking supervision. In general clinical work, ethical issues related to supervision have been articulated in the literature, as well as in the ethical principles (APA, 2002b; Falender & Shafranske, 2004; Koocher & Keith-Spiegel, 1998). It is essential for supervisors to be aware of ethical and legal aspects of supervision beyond their theoretical orientation and teaching skills (Falender & Shafraske, 2004; Harrar, VandeCreek, & Knapp, 1990). Certainly, one of the most important principles is that the clinical health psychology supervisor be competent to supervise in the specific area of practice. The following discussion assumes such a competence. Also, the supervisor is expected to know the skill level of the supervisee and gauge the assignment of tasks and supervision accordingly (Falender & Shafraske, 2004; VandeCreek & Stout, 1993). Certainly, the supervisee should possess the appropriate educational background and personal characteristics that we discussed in chapter 2 of this volume, prior to being given more responsibility and independence in the practice setting. Harrar et al. (1990) summarized the duties and responsibilities of the supervisor as follows:

1. The supervisor should have sufficient knowledge of each patient to be able to develop and monitor effective treatment plans and countersign written reports.

CLINICAL HEALTH PSYCHOLOGY

2. The supervisor should be available for emergency consultation and direct contact with patients.
3. The supervisor should not supervise more trainees than can be responsibly managed.

Conceptually, the most important thing for the supervisor to bear in mind is that "the relationship of an assistant to a licensed professional is, legally, akin to an 'extension' of the professional himself" (R. J. Cohen, 1979, p. 237). However, both parties must understand that the trainee should not function so that the public would be led to believe that he or she is a fully licensed professional or an expert, if that is not the case. Another issue is that the amount of supervision must be based on the needs of the supervisee and the patient (R. J. Cohen, 1979; Falender & Shafranske, 2004; Pope, 1990). The supervisor is frequently confronted with this issue in training institutions. As Pope (1990) pointed out, it is important that the needs of the institution or the training rotations do not supersede those of the patient. Setting up a structured schedule of supervision is reasonable and commonly practiced, but it should be flexible enough to accommodate clinical issues or problems as they arise. In addition, the needs of the patient and the supervisee must be constantly monitored and addressed.

In relation to schedules of supervision, a record of supervisory activity should be kept. This is most easily recorded in the patient's chart and need not be done at every supervisory session. Rather, the supervisor should periodically document that there is agreement with the supervisee's diagnostic formulation and treatment plan. This guideline should also be followed if the trainee is doing inpatient work and charting in the medical record. In fact, most medical facilities require the supervisor to countersign all charted information.

The recommendations listed here afford increased legal protection for the supervisee as well as the supervisor. Although the supervisory relationship creates supervisor liability for the professional behavior of his or her trainees, the supervisee is not totally absolved of responsibility in malpractice action. Thus, by documenting supervision times and following the previously suggested guidelines, protection is offered to both parties and supervision is of higher quality. It should always be kept in mind that, "courts have generally followed the principle 'What has not been written has not been done'" (Harrar et al., 1990, p. 38).

Sexual Victimization and Malpractice

Although sexual misconduct is not unique to clinical health psychology practice, no discussion of ethical and malpractice issues would be complete without addressing this area. Sexual misconduct always accounts for a high percentage of malpractice claims and licensing board complaints (Pope & Vasquez, 2007). It accounts for the largest costs in malpractice expenses, and is generally excluded from coverage in most malpractice insurance policies. As discussed in the ethics chapter, clinical health psychologists, unlike psychologists in other areas, may be more often associated with disciplines (e.g., medicine) that have different ethical and legal guidelines on sexual relationships with patients and ex-patients. As Stromberg and Dellinger (1993) discussed, "one court explained that therapist–patient sex incurs liability while that sex between lawyer and client, minister and parishioner might not, because only the first professional group offers 'a course of treatment and counseling predicated upon handling the transference phenomenon'" (Stromberg & Dellinger, 1993, p. 8; see *Simmons v. United States*, 1986). This court decision makes it clear that it is important to not be influenced by guidelines for behavior of other disciplines.

Other important court decisions give further instruction in this area (see Reamer, 2003, for a review). First, the initial consent of the patient to a sexual relationship will not be a defense against a later malpractice claim. Second, the courts have generally not accepted the argument that the sexual relationship was consensual. Third, even in the case of sex with a former patient, the courts do not easily accept the view that the therapy relationship has ended. In fact, many malpractice cases involve patients' claims that they were harmed by the sexual relationship that started after treatment termination (Reamer, 2003). The "Ethical Principles of Psychologists and Code of Conduct" (APA, 2002b) provide guidelines in this area that are in keeping with many state laws (e.g., "psychologists do not engage in sexual intimacies with current therapy clients/patients" [Ethical Standard 10.05], "Psychologists do not engage in sexual intimacies with former therapy clients/patients even after a two-year interval except in the most unusual circumstances"

[Ethical Standard 10.08b]). Even so, the most prudent course of action is to avoid sexual intimacies with a patient or ex-patient altogether.

Billing, Collection, and Financial Issues

Countersuits related to fee collection represent an area of increased malpractice risk (Bennett, Bryant, VandenBos, & Greenwood, 1990). Psychologists can avoid many problems in this area by making clear arrangements with patients in advance (B. E. Bernstein & Hartsell, 2004). This should be done in writing as part of the informed-consent process. In their article entitled, "Legal and Ethical Issues in Billing Patients and Collecting Fees," Knapp and VandeCreek (1993) discussed guidelines for effectively managing this aspect of clinical practice. Their guidelines will be summarized here.

First, the clinical health psychologist should keep in mind that he or she is "under no obligation to accept all patients who request service," and that "psychologists may refuse to accept any patient for any reason, including the perception that the patient is unable or unwilling to pay for services" (Knapp & VandeCreek, 1993, p. 25). Ethical Principle B (Fidelity and Responsibility; APA, 2002b) encourages psychologists to "contribute a portion of their professional time for little or no compensation or personal advantage" (p. 1062), which might include seeing patients on a reduced or no-fee basis. This is a choice to be made by the individual psychologist. In certain cases, deciding not to accept a patient into one's practice for the reasons we have discussed may actually avoid antitherapeutic problems, which could occur if treatment were to ensue.

Second, the clinical health psychologist should use a written informed consent procedure that includes financial information, among other things, such as description of treatment, cancellation policy, limits of confidentiality, duty to warn, emergency contact information, consent to treatment, and so forth. This is in keeping with ethical standards (Informed Consent [Ethical Standard 3.10], Informed Consent in Assessments [Ethical Standard 9.03], Informed Consent to Treatment [Ethical Standard 10.01]) and legal suggestions (B. E. Bernstein & Hartsell, 2004; Stromberg & Dellinger, 1993; VandeCreek & Stout, 1993). Financial information to be addressed in the form should include fees, insurance billing, notification that insurance may not cover all of the charges, expected payment schedules, interest charges on balances, and collection procedures. Not allowing the bills to accumulate can help avoid problems at a later date. If an account is turned over to collection, the psychologist must first give the patient notification and opportunity to make restitution (Ethical Standard 6.04, Fees and Financial Arrangements).

Obtaining informed consent related to financial issues can be particularly challenging for the clinical health psychologist who sees a patient in the hospital. Physicians do not commonly address these issues when they do inpatient consultations and treatment. In our experience, it is awkward, and usually countertherapeutic, to walk into a patient's room for a first-time consultation and present a detailed consent form to be signed before beginning. In these cases, the informed-consent procedure may be done over several sessions, and the patient may be asked whether he or she has questions about the financial arrangements. In addition, the psychologist may want to be more understanding in dealing with any subsequent financial issues that arise for patients seen under these circumstances.

Association With Physicians in "Risky" Areas of Practice

Although we are not aware of any case law pertaining to this, clinical health psychologists who are associated with risky areas of medical practice may be vulnerable to being named in a malpractice action if one is initiated against the treating physician. As an example, long-term opioid maintenance is sometimes used to treat appropriate patients with chronic non-cancer pain, but this treatment approach is not without controversy (see Harden, 2002, for a review). According to the medical standard of care, this treatment should be multidisciplinary, and include the services of a clinical health psychologist. The screening criteria for selection and management of patients for this type of treatment is specific; however, in practical settings many patients are receiving long-term opioid treatment who are either not appropriate for the intervention (e.g., history of substance abuse, lack of compliance with non-medicine pain management treatments, getting medications from multiple doctors) or who are being inappropriately medically managed (e.g., lack of frequent consultations, lack of random drug screens, lack of opioid maintenance contract). The literature has demonstrated that patients in this type of treatment are at increased risk for overdose and death (Franklin et al., 2005). As such, the clinical health psychologist might be named in a malpractice lawsuit along with the treating physician if a patient were to die from an overdose, accidental or not, and a wrongful death lawsuit was initiated. We are aware of at least one case in which all the physicians at a multidisciplinary chronic pain program were named in a suit of this nature, although the clinical health psychologist was not sued because she was not involved in that particular case. However, had she been seeing the patient as well, she would have undoubtedly been targeted in the lawsuit. This demonstrates how liability lawsuits will often "cast a broad net" if the patient's attorney believes there may be contributory negligence and that additional damages can be pursued.

This underscores the importance for clinical health psychologists to be aware of the practice style of any physician with whom they associate in a more formal practice setting. We believe other areas of increased risk might include screening for gastric bypass, spine, cosmetic, or other usually elective surgery. This might especially be the case with gastric bypass and plastic surgery, which are now being marketed aggressively to the public as quick and easy means to weight loss and "beautification," respectively. When this type of marketing occurs, one is likely to see a number of cases that are not appropriate for surgery. The clinical health psychologist working in this area might be vulnerable to legal action in cases in which the patient is screened out (sued for not allowing the surgery that the patient desired) or in which the patient is cleared for surgery, undergoes the procedure, and is dissatisfied with the results (sued in conjunction with the physician for damages from the surgery). Any clinical health psychologist who practices in higher risk medical areas should be cognizant of the standard of care (both psychological and medical) and the practice style of the physicians with whom he or she has associated.

Managed Care

Health care reform and managed care are affecting virtually all aspects of psychological practice, including that of clinical health psychology. Managed care relates to malpractice issues in two important ways (Stromberg & Dellinger, 1993). First is whether the standard of care under managed care is measured differently than fee-for-service care that is not subject to limitations dictated by the insurance company (e.g., number of sessions, reimbursement allowance). The argument is that if a patient is enrolled in a health plan that reimburses at a lower rate or has limited psychological treatment benefits, then the therapist should not be liable for providing a lower quality of care or terminating the treatment after the allotted number of sessions. According to Stromberg and Dellinger (1993), the courts have not recognized any lower standard of care based on insurance coverage or managed care guidelines. The same rules (i.e., ethical, legal) apply for all patients, regardless of these issues (Koocher & Keith-Spiegel, 1998). Of course, the psychologist can deal with such things as a limited number of allowed treatment sessions by being aware of such issues for each patient at the beginning of treatment, using informed-consent procedures, and considering other options if necessary.

If the standard of care level being set by the managed care company is unacceptable and results in injury, the company along with the practitioner can be held liable (*Wickline v. State of California*, 1986; see Koocher & Keith-Spiegel, 1998; Newman & Bricklin, 1991, for a review). This issue began in the courts with the *Wickline v. California* (1986) decision, in which the plaintiff suffered the loss of her leg because of the failure of the health plan to provide treatment. Subsequent legal cases (e.g., *Wilson v. Blue Cross of Southern California*, 1990) have reaffirmed that "when a treating physician makes a decision to discharge a patient because an insurance company refuses to pay benefits, either or both may be liable if their conduct was 'a substantial factor in bringing about the harm'" (Stromberg & Dellinger, 1993, p. 13). Stromberg and Dellinger (1993) concluded that the practitioner should at least provide services on an emergency basis regardless of payment, and "energetically seek approval for additional services the patient genuinely needs" (p. 13). Appelbaum (1993) and others (e.g., Koocher & Keith-Spiegel, 1998) provide further guidelines to limit ethical and legal liability within a managed care system. These include a duty to appeal adverse decisions by the insurance company, a duty to disclose to patients the economic implications of their managed care plan and its possible effect on treatment, and a duty to continue treatment under certain circumstances even if benefits have been exhausted. Of course, all actions related to dealing with the managed care system should be documented in writing.

Haas and Cummings (1991) presented considerations to take into account before becoming involved in a particular managed care system. These included consideration of the following questions:

1. How much does the plan intrude into the patient–provider relationship?
2. What provisions exist for exceptions to the rule?
3. Are there referral resources if patient needs should exceed plan benefits?
4. Does the plan provide assistance or training in helping the provider to achieve treatment goals?
5. Are there ways in which the plan is open to provider input?
6. Do plans clearly inform their policyholders of the limits of benefits?

Undoubtedly, malpractice issues related to managed care will continue to arise as these systems become more complex, and patients and clinicians are increasingly influenced by these pressures.

MINIMIZING MALPRACTICE RISKS

Several authors have formulated guidelines for minimizing malpractice risks (Soisson, VandeCreek, & Knapp, 1987; Stromberg & Dellinger, 1993; VandeCreek & Stout, 1993; Welch, 2002). These can be summarized as follows:

1. Maintain accurate records of patient care, and carefully document appropriate information. Remember, in legal action, it is the patient's word against the clinical record.
2. Obtain informed consent in writing of billing procedures, treatment plans, circumstances under which confidentiality must be breached, and so forth.
3. Ensure that all practitioners remain current in knowledge and skills in their areas of practice (commensurate with the standard of care).
4. Coordinate patient treatment with other disciplines involved in the case, with appropriate releases of information (e.g., to physicians).

5. Honor patient rights to confidentiality and privilege.
6. Be thorough in the assessment of patients, especially when suicide and homicide may be potential factors.
7. Avoid dual relationships with patients and ex-patients.
8. Accept only as many patients as can be carefully treated.
9. Terminate treatment carefully and for the proper reasons.
10. Exercise caution with new modalities of treatment and systems of managed care.

Taking these suggestions seriously and implementing them in everyday practice will not only help avoid any malpractice action but also improve the quality of care.

SUMMARY

In this chapter, we outlined general concepts of malpractice law and delineated several areas of increased malpractice risk particularly relevant to the practice of clinical health psychology. We attempted to provide concrete examples of the more common dilemmas that occur in clinical health psychology practice. Even so, the clinical health psychology practitioner may face unique ethical and legal problems on a frequent basis. Because clinical health psychology is a relatively young area, consultation with one's colleagues, ethical panels, and legal counsel is advisable when faced with professional practice issues.

Thus far, we have examined the role of clinical health psychologists, issues in preparation for practice, the conduct of assessment and intervention, and related ethical, legal and professional issues. Our concluding chapter focuses on future issues in clinical health psychology, as we see them.

SUGGESTED READINGS

Bernstein, B. E., & Hartsell, T. L. (2004). *The portable lawyer for mental health professionals* (2nd ed.). Hoboken, NJ: Wiley.

Campbell, T., & Lorandos, D. (2001). *Cross examining experts in the behavioral science.* Danvers, MA: Thomson West.

Knapp, S., & VandeCreek, L. (1993). Legal and ethical issues in billing patients and collecting fees. *Psychotherapy, 30,* 25–31.

Law and Mental Health Professionals series for individual states published by the American Psychological Association.

Lifson, L. E., & Simon, R. I. (1998). *The mental health practitioner and the law: A comprehensive handbook.* Cambridge, MA: Harvard University Press.

Reamer, F. G. (2003). *Social work malpractice and liability: Strategies for prevention* (2nd ed.). New York: Columbia University Press.

Reid, W. H. (2008). *Psychiatry and law updates.* Retrieved March 24, 2008, from http://www.reidpsychiatry.com

VandeCreek, L., & Knapp, S. (2001). *Tarasoff and beyond: Legal and clinical considerations in the treatment of life-endangering patients.* Sarasota, FL: Professional Resource Press.

Ziskin, J. (2000). *Coping with psychiatric and psychological testimony* (Vols. I–III). Los Angeles: Law and Psychology Press.

8

Future Issues for Clinical Health Psychology

The future of clinical health psychology depends on the course of events within the field itself as well as those external to the discipline of psychology. In this chapter, we discuss some of the trends and changes we anticipate, and provide our perceptions of their potential effects. Our purpose is to stimulate thinking, discussion, and research related to these issues rather than to detail in depth particular positions.

SOCIETAL CHANGES

A number of changes in U.S. society affect the future of clinical health psychology. Among these, changes in demographics, globalization, and the use of technology are perhaps the most profound.

Demographic Changes

Our population is increasing in age as well as in ethnic and cultural diversity (see U.S. Census Bureau, 2008). This has significant implications for the types of health problems addressed and the need for culturally and linguistically competent services, as well as a diverse workforce. Moreover, many of the problems conferring risk in later life require a focus on prevention at earlier developmental levels; thus, more population-based health systems, including behavioral interventions, will be required in an expanded model of prevention science (T. W. Smith, Orleans, & Jenkins, 2004).

Globalization

Our interconnectedness in the world has been enhanced at lightning speed by advances in transportation, communication, and industrialization. This also requires "a more 'upstream' focus on economic, social and environmental determinants of health" (Oldenburg, 2002, p. 13) if we are to address the related challenges. Global influences on health, such as war, poverty, migration, and changes in the natural environment, will dramatically affect the kinds of health care prevention and treatment services needed in the future.

Technological Advances

With advances in technology, clinical health psychology will become increasingly technology oriented. More and more assessment tools will be computerized and easily available to nonpsychologist users, sometimes bypassing local psychologists within the health care system. With this change will come the potential for increased abuse of such services, especially given the absence of psychometrically and clinically trained professionals in the interpretation process at the clinical case level. To the extent that diagnostic labels are rendered or treatment decisions are made from such data, there will be increased risk of malpractice suits involving these techniques. Given this, and the fact that many measures have inadequate norms for the relevant medical–surgical population, we could witness in health care the kind of backlash about testing that occurred within the school system surrounding the use of intelligence tests, and within industry with respect to employee selection, honesty, and evaluations for promotion. Psychologists might need to take an increased role in both professional and patient advocacy with respect to this issue.

Another area of technological advance has to do with increased sophistication in psychophysiological measurement. Developments in ambulatory monitoring will permit more accurate psychophysiological profiling and assessment. More in vivo treatment programming will be possible. The potential exists for developing a considerable database for the biopsychosocial model in the real world and for designing protocols that facilitate generalization of treatment efforts.

Advances in technology also permit the creation of virtual environments for treatment planning (e.g., exposure to a virtual public for patients with disfigurements, preparation for surgery, the creation of virtual support groups for patients). Psychologists will continue to be active in the development of psychoeducational materials for patients, many of which will be delivered over the Internet or through computer-assisted group sessions (e.g., Dolezal-Wood, Belar, & Snibbe, 1998). Technology will also provide access to specialized patient services in rural areas, as well as distance education and supervision of psychologists or providers in the field.

As clinical health psychologists contribute their expertise in behavior change to the health care system, there are also more opportunities for coercive control of patients (e.g., to promote compliance with health care providers who reflect the values of the dominant culture). As technology in medicine advances, providers and their patients will experience increased complexity in decision making as well as patient selection and preparation. Although Weiss (1982), in his 1980 presidential address to the Division of Health Psychology, warned about "technology run amok" (p. 89), given technology's inherent amorality, there still remains little focus in the literature on ethical issues in clinical health psychology. We encourage more attention to this area and hope that our chapter on ethical issues will stimulate increased discussion.

DEVELOPMENT OF THE PROFESSION

As clinical health psychology develops, there will be more specialization, a need for education and training, and an increased demand for accountability and knowledge.

More Specialization

As clinical health psychology develops, there will be increased developments related to issues of subspecialization, cross-specialization, and the development of a taxonomy for professional psychology. This is already apparent with respect to pediatric psychology, rehabilitation psychology, geropsychology, and areas such as pain management, psychosocial oncology, and health promotion. It will also become evident within other areas. The concept of subspecialties is one that has been discussed by the American Board of Clinical Health Psychology and the American Board of Professional Psychology, but it is one that is not well-articulated or agreed on in our profession.

With increased specialization comes the risk that patients will be classified by health behavior patterns or problems. Clinicians might take a myopic view in the same manner that physicians have been accused of doing, given medicine's specialization around organ systems. Thus, we could have weight management psychologists, pain management psychologists, organ transplant psychologists, and so forth. We might attempt to simplistically treat smoking behavior without a full appreciation of the context of this behavior within the individual and his or her environment. Such practice would result in a split similar to the mind–body dualism for which we have criticized medicine. This new dualism might be called *behavior–person* dualism. If that occurs, health care will be increasingly fragmented. At best, our treatments will be ineffective; at worst, we will cause damage to our patients. We fully agree that the major focus in clinical health psychology is not on psychopathology, but we are dismayed by comments of health psychologists suggesting that real expertise in this area is not important. The clinical health psychologist must understand behavior and behavior change within both "normal" and "abnormal" domains.

One of the areas that we predict will have the greatest support is that of primary care health psychology—an area of convergence for clinical health psychology, family psychology, and clinical child psychology as well as clinical and counseling psychology. It is noteworthy that since the publication of our last revision of this book, numerous handbooks devoted to primary care psychology have been published and a curriculum for training has been developed (McDaniel, Belar, Schroeder, Hargrove, & Freeman, 2002). Practitioners will need a broad base in mental health and clinical health psychology, and will serve in frontline positions in the health care system of tomorrow. Such systems have been part of integrated-staff model health maintenance organizations (HMOs), such as Kaiser Permanente, for some years. More recently, Veterans Affairs announced a large-scale endeavor to integrate behavioral health services in primary care as well. In these models, we believe the roles of these psychologists will be predominantly consultation to primary care physicians, triage, and program development. Many of the more generic direct-intervention services are likely to be provided by less expensive health personnel.

As our nation's "safety net" for primary care services, community health centers (CHCs) are important for the future of psychology (DeLeon, Kenkel, & Belar, 2007). These centers began as a component of President Lyndon Johnson's War on Poverty, and they continue to receive bipartisan support for expansion across the nation. Receiving grants through the U.S. Health Resources and Services Administration, CHCs serve our nation's most vulnerable. Of the over 15 million patients seen annually, 64% are ethnic minorities and nearly 40% are uninsured (Duke, 2007). For psychologists who want to address health disparities, CHCs provide great opportunities. Perhaps most important, psychology needs to be part of the infrastructure in all CHCs if we are to be recognized as a core component of an integrated health care system of the future.

Education and Training

With respect to education and training, we have repeatedly indicated that it is impossible for the clinical health psychologist to have in-depth knowledge and clinical expertise in the biopsychosocial aspects of such diverse areas as biofeedback for cardiac arrhythmias, treatment of chronic pain, genetic counseling, organ donor evaluations, and death and dying. However, we believe that doctoral training should continue to be generic in both clinical and health psychology, with more focus on problems seen in primary health care settings. Any subspecialization should occur at the postdoctoral level. This will avoid the production of "blacksmiths," who might be quickly outdated without a firm grounding in the discipline of psychology and the breadth of health psychology.

Attention to issues of accreditation in health psychology will continue to increase. At the time of our last revision of this book, American Psychological Association (APA) accreditation of postdoctoral programs in psychology did not exist. By 2008, there were six postdoctoral programs that had received APA accreditation in the specialty of clinical health psychology. At the doctoral level, the scope of accreditation was changed in 2006 to add "other developed practice areas" to the accreditation of programs in clinical, counseling, and school psychology, and combinations thereof. Procedures have now been developed for the addition of new areas, and it will be interesting to see how clinical health psychology evolves in this regard. It has been argued that limiting accreditation to clinical, counseling, and school psychology has actually constricted the growth of clinical health psychology. Clinical health psychology might find a better home for development in academic health centers, but this has not been facilitated because there are existing accredited programs in clinical or counseling psychology on campus and no mechanism has been available for them to create a distinctive identity.

Our own view is that current graduate education needs to increase its emphasis on training in the areas of interdisciplinary functioning, biobehavioral aspects of health and disease, genetics, and health policy. Although these areas have been deemed essential for more than 30 years, students often obtain their first exposure on internship. As promulgated by our earliest model for assessment and intervention (Belar, Deardorff, & Kelly, 1987), the need for what is now referred to as context competence is also critical (Yali & Revenson, 2004). In addition, one needs to be cognizant of the core competencies all health professions will need in the 21st century (Institute of Medicine, 2003): patient-centered care, informatics, interdisciplinary teamwork, evidence-based practice, and quality improvement. With respect to the latter, we need more attention to systematic training in self-assessment and continuous quality improvement methods in psychology. The accreditation criteria for medical residents already include a requirement for a quality improvement project related to their own practice. To "cross the quality chasm" (Institute of Medicine, 2001a), we will need to create a culture supporting the identification of errors and problems in performance, without the shame and blame atmosphere that sometimes exists in highly competitive academic environments and that can serve to censor communications from trainees to supervisors.

Professional Practice

Although the certification of advanced competency in practice is now well established through the board certification process, we anticipate increased attention to the accountability and effectiveness of the provider at the individual practitioner level. These data are already being compiled on physicians, and soon consumer hotlines will be available as health care becomes more consumer oriented in nature. Our earlier predictions that third-party payers will routinely gather measures of patient satisfaction with the psychologist have come to fruition. We also anticipate the development of more systematic recertification programs for assessment of continued competence in our nation's health care workforce. We see the profession increasingly torn between models of excellence and consumerism as core values. There seems little doubt that the individual practitioner will continue to experience a significant loss of perceived autonomy and that this will be a jarring experience.

In practice, we also anticipate an increase in cross-referrals among psychologists and a more prominent focus on training other disciplines in the delivery of specialized services as new information becomes available. Psychology will always give its knowledge away. We believe that psychology has the potential to survive current health care industry crises primarily because of psychologists' expertise in research, program development and evaluation, and the measurement of behavior. Practitioners of other disciplines will assume roles as therapists and do so less expensively. Unfortunately, our own experiences with hiring suggest that many psychologists entering practice see themselves primarily as psychotherapists, with few other skills and training. Because policymakers in large organizations cannot appreciate important distinctions within psychology, our discipline could fail to live up to its potential in the health care system because of our own complacency about the reliability of the product of graduate training (Belar, 1989, 1995).

We believe that areas of future growth in practice include primary care, genetic counseling, reproductive endocrinology, and organ and tissue transplantation. We believe that more nontraditional sites for the delivery of care will be increasingly used, including the Internet, worksites, churches, and school-based health clinics.

Growth of Knowledge

Health care reform is demanding evidence-based health care services (Institute of Medicine, 2001a). There is an increased need for well-controlled clinical trials to assess costs, benefits, and side effects of various psychological interventions. Although we have often complained that our discipline has been held to a higher scientific standard than medical practice itself, the playing field is now more even. We anticipate more interdisciplinary clinical research and more rigorous searches for interactions among biological, psychological, and social interventions. An excellent overview of the ways in which clinical health psychology services can maximize care and economic benefits is provided by Friedman, Sobel, Myers, Caudill, and Benson (1995).

In relation to this, we are concerned about the number of psychologists entering practice from graduate programs without training in the conduct of clinical research and with minimal exposure to research methodology. Not only will these psychologists be unable to contribute to the body of knowledge, but they might also lack the expertise to critically review current findings and make informed decisions about applications. They could therefore unwittingly contribute to a backlash in many areas of clinical health psychology, such as we have experienced to some extent in biofeedback and wellness programs. The focus on self-control and the popularization of related techniques have already produced a new clinical problem: the patient who feels guilty and incompetent that he or she cannot "will" or "visualize" the cancer away, or bring all psychophysiological symptoms under control. We must not promise more than we can deliver, in terms of either quantity of service or power of our techniques.

CHANGES IN PSYCHIATRY

We view psychiatry's "remedicalization" as perhaps a result of economics and the need to realign with medicine as of scientific developments in biological psychiatry. However, the trend toward a reaffirmation of the biological factors in mental illness and a focus on psychopharmacology actually increases opportunities for nonmedical providers of psychological treatment services. In addition, to the extent that psychologists continue to be trained in areas relevant to health care systems in which their psychiatric colleagues are not (e.g., research, program evaluation, measurement of behavior), they will be assured roles on the health care teams.

Psychiatry continues, as does traditional clinical psychology, to be viewed as being preoccupied with mental illness. Thus, the field of clinical health psychology is ripe for continued development. However, our previous prediction that increased competition in the health care industry could result in increased interprofessional conflict appears to have been accurate, a situation we find most unfortunate for psychology, psychiatry, and the general public.

CHANGES IN THE HEALTH CARE SYSTEM

For over 2 decades, a major revolution in the health care system has been predicted for the United States, yet change has been piecemeal. Some precursors were federal programs such as prospective payment systems and fixed-rate reimbursement for diagnostic related groupings, which have already had significant effects on hospital practices. Major themes include universal access, comprehensive mandated health benefits, mental health parity, cost containment, quality, accountability, and safety.

In the private sector, it is clear that service provision as a cottage industry is waning as health care comes increasingly under corporate control. To survive as a practicing clinical health psychologist, sophistication in HMOs, preferred provider organizations, and physician–hospital organizations will be required, because it is estimated that the majority of Americans will obtain their health care through such organizations in the future. Although these issues have not been extensively addressed in graduate education to date, psychologists will need to develop skills in dealing with corporate administrative structures, in providing evidence of accountability, and in using management information systems for cost–benefit analyses. Belar (1989, 1995, 2000) detailed the opportunities for psychologists in HMOs and capitated care, with a focus on implications for graduate education and training.

How will clinical health psychology fare in this new world of health care? As discussed previously, mind–body dualism pervades the insurance industry; different benefit packages are developed for mental health and for physical health. Continued advocacy for coding systems such as the Health and Behavior codes and appropriate reimbursement for psychological services that address medical–surgical problems will be required.

Tovian (2004) provided a concise overview of health psychology market-place issues.

Over 2 decades ago, Cummings (1986) voiced concern that psychologists were "ill prepared for the competitive market for their services that lies ahead" (p. 426). In his treatise, "The Dismantling of Our Health System," he pointed out how psychologists have historically eschewed marketing of their products and have been overly committed to notions of "cure" rather than "brief intermittent psychotherapy throughout the life cycle" (p. 429). In addition, the legislation affecting health care evolves through the political process, about which many psychologists tend to be either naive or uninterested. In our opinion, clinical health psychologists need to become politically involved in health policy at both institutional and legislative levels to ensure our survival. We have many opportunities, but only ourselves to meet the challenges.

SUGGESTED READINGS

Belar, C. D. (1989). Opportunities for psychologists in health maintenance organizations: Implications for graduate education and training. *Professional Psychology: Research and Practice, 20,* 390–394.

Belar, C. D. (1995). Collaboration in capitated care: Challenges for psychology. *Professional Psychology: Research and Practice, 26,* 139–146.

Belar, C. D. (2000). Ethical issues in managed care: Perspectives in evolution. *The Counseling Psychologist, 28,* 237–241.

Belar, C. D. (2004). The future of education and training in academic health centers. *Journal of Clinical Psychology in Medical Settings, 11,* 77–82.

Friedman, R., Sobel, D., Myers, P., Caudill, M., & Benson, H. (1995). Behavioral medicine, clinical health psychology, and cost offset. *Health Psychology, 14,* 509–518.

Institute of Medicine. (2001). *Crossing the quality chasm: A new health system for the 21st century.* Washington, DC: National Academy Press.

Institute of Medicine. (2003). *Health professions education: A bridge to quality.* Washington, DC: National Academy Press.

McDaniel, S. H., Belar, C. D., Schroeder, C., Hargrove, D. S., & Freeman, E. L. (2002). A training curriculum for professional psychologists in primary care. *Professional Psychology: Research and Practice, 33,* 65–72

Smith, T. W., & Suls, J. (Eds.). (2004). Special section on the future of health psychology. *Health Psychology, 23,* 115–157.

Appendix A:
Medical Abbreviations

This is a list of commonly used medical abbreviations. Although abbreviations tend to be standard across settings, when comparing approved lists from different hospitals, we have sometimes noted significant differences. It is imperative that the practitioner obtain the approved list of abbreviations before writing in any hospital's medical records. It is also important to know the conditions under which these abbreviations are used (e.g., usually never in discharge summaries).

A	assessment
$\overline{a}$	before
AAA	abdominal aortic aneurysm
ab	antibody
AB	abortion
abd	abdomen
ABN	abnormal
a.c.	before meals
A.D.	right ear
ad lib	at pleasure
ADL	activities of daily living
AF	atrial fibrillation
AK	above knee
AKA	above knee amputation
A.L.	left ear

ALL	acute lymphocytic leukemia
ALT	alanine aminotransferase (formerly SGPT)
AMA	against medical advice
amb.	ambulatory
ANA	antinuclear antibody
ANS	autonomic nervous system
A/O	alert and oriented
A&P	auscultation and percussion
ARDS	acute respiratory distress syndrome
ASA	aspirin
AU	both ears
A-V	arteriovenous
A&W	alive and well
BAE	barium enema
B/C	birth control
BCP	birth control pills
bid	twice a day
BF	black female
BK	below knee
BM	bowel movement
BMR	basal metabolic rate
BO	bowel obstruction
BOM	bilateral otitis media
BP	blood pressure
BPH	benign prostatic hypertrophy
BrBx	breast biopsy
BRP	bathroom privileges
BS	breath sounds
bs	bowel sounds
BSO	bilateral salpingo-oophorectomy
BTL	bilateral tubal ligation
BUN	blood urea nitrogen
Bx	biopsy
c̄	with
Ca	calcium

CA	carcinoma
CABG	coronary artery bypass graft
CAD	coronary artery disease
CAT	computerized axial tomogram
CBC	complete blood count
CC	chief complaint
CCU	coronary care unit
CF	cystic fibrosis
CHD	coronary heart disease
CHF	congestive heart failure
CNS	central nervous system
C/O	complains of
COPD	chronic obstructive pulmonary disease
CP	cerebral palsy
CPAP	continuous positive airway pressure
CPPB	continuous positive pressure breathing
CPR	cardiopulmonary resuscitation
CRF	chronic renal failure
Cr N	cranial nerve
CS, C/S	cesarean section
CSF	cerebrospinal fluid
C-spine	cervical spine
CVA	cerebrovascular accident
CVD	cardiovascular disease
Cx	cervix
CXR	chest X-ray
d	diastolic
D	dorsal spine
d/c	discontinue
D&C	dilation and curettage
DDx	differential diagnosis
DIFF	differential blood count
DM	diabetes mellitus
DOA	dead on arrival
DOB	date of birth

DOE	dyspnea on exertion
DTRs	deep tendon reflexes
Dx	diagnosis
EA	emergency area
EBV	Epstein–Barr virus
ECG	electrocardiogram
EEG	electroencephalogram
EENT	eyes, ears, nose, throat
EMG	electromyogram
EMS	emergency medical service
ENT	ears, nose, throat
EOM	extraocular movements
ESR	erythrocyte sedimentation rate
ETOH	ethanol
EUA	examination under anesthesia
F	female, Fahrenheit
FB	foreign body
FBS	fasting blood sugar
FEV	forced expiratory volume
FH	family history
FSH	follicle stimulating hormone
F/U	follow-up
FUO	fever of unknown origin
FVC	forced vital capacity
Fx	fracture
G, Gr	gravida
GB	gallbladder
GC	gonococcus
GE	gastroenterology
GG	gammaglobulin
GI	gastrointestinal
gr.	grain
GSW	gunshot wound
gtt	drops
GU	genitourinary

GYN	gynecology
HA	headache
HBP	high blood pressure
HEENT	head, ears, eyes, nose, throat
HIV	human immunodeficiency virus
H&L	heart and lungs
HNP	herniated nucleus pulposus
H&P	history and physical
HPI	history of present illness
hs	at bedtime
htn	hypertension
Hx	history
ICU	intensive care unit
ID	intradermal
I&D	incision and drainage
IDDM	insulin dependent diabetes
IH	infectious hepatitis
IM	intramuscular
imp	improved
IMP	impression
in situ	in normal position
IOP	intraocular pressure
IPPD	intermittent positive pressure breathing
IUP	intrauterine pregnancy
IV	intravenous
IVP	intravenous pyelogram
JRA	juvenile rheumatoid arthritis
KJ	knee jerk
KUB	kidney, ureter, bladder
L&A	light and accommodation
LAB	laboratory results
LAP	laparotomy
LBP	low back pain
LLE	left lower extremity
LLL	left lower lobe

LLQ	left lower quadrant
LMD	local medical doctor
LMP	last menstrual period
LOC	level or loss of consciousness
LOS	length of stay
LP	lumbar puncture
LRQ	lower right quadrant
LS	lumbosacral
LSK	liver, spleen, kidneys
L&W	living and well
Mets.	metastasis
MH	marital history
MI	myocardial infarction
MM	malignant melanoma
MMR	measles, mumps, and rubella
MOD	medical officer of the day
MRI	magnetic resonance imaging
MVA	motor vehicle accident
MVP	mitral valve prolapse
NA	not applicable
NAA	no apparent abnormalities
NAD	no apparent distress
NB	newborn
NC	no change
N/C	no complaints
NG	nasogastric tube
NK	not known
NKA	no known allergies
NL	normal
NPO	nothing by mouth
NR	nonreactive
NSR	normal sinus rhythm
NSSP	normal size, shape, position
NSVD	normal spontaneous vaginal delivery
N&V	nausea and vomiting

O	objective
OB	obstetrics
OBS	organic brain syndrome
Od	overdose
OD	right eye
OM	otitis media
OPC	outpatient clinic
os	mouth
OS	left eye
ot	ear
OU	both eyes
OV	office visit
$\bar{p}$	after
P	plan
P&A	percussion and auscultation
PARA	number of pregnancies
PE	physical examination
PERLA	pupils equal, reactive to light
PERRLA	pupils equal, round, regular, reactive to light and accommodation
PH	past history
PI	present illness
PID	pelvic inflammatory disease
PM	postmortem
PMH	past medical history
PM&R	physical medicine and rehabilitation
PNS	peripheral nervous system
PO	by mouth
POMR	problem oriented medical record
prn	as needed
PTA	prior to admission
PUD	peptic ulcer disease
PVC	premature ventricular contraction
PVD	peripheral vascular disease
Px	physical examination

Q	every
qd	everyday
qh	every hour
qid	four times a day
qm	every morning
qn	every night
QNS	quantity not sufficient
qod	every other day
qs	enough
R	respiration
RA	rheumatoid arthritis
RBC	red blood count
REM	rapid eye movement
R/O	rule out
ROM	range of motion
ROS	review of systems
RR	recovery room
RTC	return to clinic
RTW	return to work
Rx	prescription, treatment
$\overline{s}$	without
S	subjective
SB	stillbirth
SBO	small bowel obstruction
SCC	squamous cell carcinoma
SNS	sympathetic nervous system
S&O	salpingo-oophorectomy
SOB	shortness of breath
S/P	status post
STAT	immediately
SUBQ	subcutaneous
SRG	surgery
Sx	symptoms
T	temperature
T&A	tonsillectomy and adenoidectomy

TAB	therapeutic abortion
TAH	total abdominal hysterectomy
TBLC	term birth, living child
TCDB	turn, cough, deep breath
THR	total hip replacement
TIA	transient ischemic attack
tid	three times a day
TL	tubal ligation
TPR	temperature, pulse, respiration
TSH	thyroid stimulating hormone
TURP	transurethral resection of prostate
TVH	total vaginal hysterectomy
UA	urinalysis
U&C	usual and customary
UCHD	usual childhood diseases
UGI	upper gastrointestinal series
UK	unknown
URI	upper respiratory infection
UTI	urinary tract infection
V	vein
VA	visual acuity
VDRL	Venereal Disease Research Laboratory (syphilis)
VS	vital signs
VSS	vital signs stable
W	widowed
WBC	white blood cells
WDWN	well developed, well nourished
WF	white female
WM	white male
WNL	within normal limits
X	times
XM	cross-match
YO	year old
?	question of

Appendix B:
Journals Relevant
to Clinical Health Psychology

Given the wide range of special interests among health psychologists, specialty journals (e.g., *Pain, Headache, Psychosomatic Obstetrics and Gynecology, Omega*) are not listed. Rather, the following journals reflect general interests in the field.

American Journal of Preventive Medicine. Journal of the American College of Preventive Medicine and the Association for Prevention Teaching and Research. Information and research related to public health and prevention of acute and chronic disease.

American Journal of Public Health. Journal of the American Public Health Association. Focus on risk factors, behavioral health, and risk-factor reduction.

Annals of Behavioral Medicine. Publication of the Society of Behavioral Medicine. Review articles, original research, and comprehensive abstracts of interest to biobehavioral researchers and clinicians.

Anxiety, Stress, and Coping. Official Journal of the Stress and Anxiety Research Society. Research and theoretical articles related to anxiety dimensions, stress, and coping processes.

Applied Psychophysiology and Biofeedback (formerly *Biofeedback and Self-Regulation*). Journal of the Association of Applied Psychophysiology and Biofeedback. An international, interdisciplinary journal devoted to the interrelationship of physiological systems, cognition, social and environmental parameters, and health.

Archives of Physical Medicine and Rehabilitation. Official journal of the American Academy of Physical Medicine and Rehabilitation. Original research and clinical experience in physical medicine and the diagnosis, therapy, and delivery of rehabilitation care.

Behavioral Medicine (formerly the *Journal of Human Stress*). An interdisciplinary journal focusing on behavioral and social influences on mental and physical health.

Biological Psychology. A journal publishing papers on the biological aspects of psychological states and processes.

Brain, Behavior, and Immunity. Journal of the Psychoneuroimmunology Research Society. Devoted to the investigation of neural, endocrine, behavioral, and immune system interactions.

General Hospital Psychiatry: Psychiatry, Medicine, and Primary Care. A journal emphasizing biopsychosocial components in illness and health, and their links to primary care.

Harvard Health Letter. A newsletter of Harvard Medical School. Interprets current medical information for the general reader.

Health Affairs: The Policy Journal of the Health Sphere. Exploration of domestic and international health policy issues.

Health Psychology. Journal of the Division of Health Psychology, American Psychological Association. Broad spectrum of health psychology research.

Health Psychology Review. Journal of the European Health Psychology Society. A new journal designed to provide systematic reviews and integrative analyses of substantive issues in health psychology.

International Journal of Behavioral Medicine. The journal of the International Society of Behavioral Medicine. Focus is on interactions among behavioral, psychosocial, environmental, genetic, and biomedical factors relevant to health and illness, including multicultural and global aspects.

International Journal of Psychiatry in Medicine. Addresses relationships among biological, psychological, social, religious, and cultural systems in patient care, especially primary care.

Journal of Behavioral Medicine. Interdisciplinary journal emphasizing applications of research to prevention, treatment, and rehabilitation.

Journal of Clinical Psychology in Medical Settings. Journal of the Association of Psychologists in Academic Health Centers. Articles on the science and practice of clinical psychology in the medical environment.

Journal of Clinical Psychopharmacology. Intended for practicing clinicians and trainees to maintain current knowledge of clinical psychopharmacology.

Journal of Health Politics, Policy and Law. Publishes articles on the initiation, formulation, and implementation of health policy; analyzes the relations between government and health.

Journal of Health Psychology. An international, interdisciplinary journal that also addresses social contexts for psychological and health processes.

Journal of Health and Social Behavior. Journal of the American Sociological Association. Focus on the health care system, organizations, and occupations; sociological perspectives of health and disease.

Journal of Pediatric Psychology. Journal of the Division of Pediatric Psychology of the American Psychological Association. Focus on theory, research, and practice related to health and illness in children.

Journal of Psychosomatic Research. Journal of the European Association for Consultation–Liaison Psychiatry and Psychosomatics. Covers all aspects of the relationship between medicine and psychology.

Mind/Body Health (formerly *Mental Medicine Update*). A newsletter with updates on mind–body interaction issues with the goal of translating research to practice.

New England Journal of Medicine. Journal of the Massachusetts Medical Society. Some articles relevant to health and behavior. Review articles and commentaries reflect prevailing attitudes in medicine.

Preventive Medicine. Publishes applied research on health promotion and disease prevention.

Psychological Bulletin. Occasional comprehensive and critical reviews of literature relevant to health psychology.

Psychology and Health. Journal of the European Health Psychology Society. Study and application of psychological approaches to health and illness.

Psychoneuroendocrinology. Journal of the International Society of Psychoneuro-endocrinology. Focus on relationships among psychology, neurobiology, endocrinology, immunology, neurology, and psychiatry, with an emphasis on how psychobiological factors interact in the stress response.

Psychophysiology. Journal of the Society for Psychophysiological Research. Oldest journal in its field; publishes basic and applied research in psychophysiology and human neuroscience.

Psychosomatic Medicine. Journal of the American Psychosomatic Society. Wide variety of basic and applied research with a focus on relationships among social, psychological, and behavioral factors and bodily processes in humans and animals.

Psychosomatics. Journal of the Academy of Psychosomatic Medicine. Addresses medical and psychiatric comorbidity, with numerous case reports and a focus on clinical care.

Psychotherapy and Psychosomatics. Articles concerning psychotherapy research related to medical problems. Strong clinical orientation.

Quality of Life Research. Journal of the International Society of Quality of Life Research. Focuses on quality of life research in every aspect of health care.

Social Science and Medicine. An interdisciplinary forum for the social sciences and health, with a focus on implications for practice and health policy.

Appendix C:
Professional and Disease-Specific Organizations

Academy of Behavioral Medicine Research (http://www.academyofbmr.org/)

Academy of Psychosomatic Medicine (http://www.apm.org/)

Alzheimer's Association (http://www.alz.org/)

American Board of Clinical Health Psychology (http://www.abpp.org/brochures/clinical_health_brochure.htm)

American Brain Tumor Association (http://www.abta.org/)

American Burn Association (http://www.ameriburn.org/)

American Cancer Society (http://www.cancer.org/)

American Chronic Pain Association (http://www.theacpa.org/)

American Council of the Blind (http://www.acb.org/)

American Diabetes Association (http://www.diabetes.org/)

American Epilepsy Society (http://www.aesnet.org/)

American Fertility Association (http://www.theafa.org/)

American Geriatrics Society (http://www.americangeriatrics.org/)

American Headache Society (http://www.americanheadachesociety.org/)

American Heart Association (http://www.americanheart.org/)

American Liver Foundation (http://www.liverfoundation.org/)

American Lung Association (http://www.lungusa.org/)

American Pain Society (http://www.ampainsoc.org/)

American Psychological Association (http://www.apa.org/)

    Division 22: Rehabilitation Psychology (http://www.apa.org/about/division/div22.html)

Division 38: Health Psychology (http://www.health-psych.org/)

Division 40: Clinical Neuropsychology (http://www.div40.org/)

Division 54: Society of Pediatric Psychology (http://www.societyof pediatricpsychology.org/)

American Psychosomatic Society (http://www.psychosomatic.org/)

American Public Health Association (http://www.apha.org/)

American Society for Reproductive Medicine (http://www.asrm.org/)

American Tinnitus Association (http://www.ata.org/)

Arthritis Foundation (http://www.arthritis.org/)

Association for Applied Psychophysiology and Biofeedback (http://www.aapb.org/)

Association of Psychologists in Academic Health Centers (http://www.apa.org/divisions/div12/sections/section8/)

Association of Rheumatology Health Professionals (http://www.rheumatology.org/arhp/)

Brain Injury Association (http://www.biausa.org/)

Cystic Fibrosis Foundation (http://www.cff.org/)

Gerontolological Society of America (http://www.geron.org/)

International Academy of Behavioral Medicine, Counselling and Psychotherapy (http://pb.rcpsych.org/cgi/content/full/25/5/200-b)

International Association for the Study of Pain (http://www.iasp-pain.org/)

International Society of Psychoneuroendocrinology (http://www.ispne.org/)

Lupus Foundation of America (http://www.lupus.org/)

Muscular Dystrophy Association (http://www.mdausa.org/)

National Association of the Deaf (http://www.nad.org/)

National Hospice and Palliative Care Organization (http://www.nhpco.org/templates/1/homepage.cfm)

National Kidney Foundation (http://www.kidney.org/)

National Multiple Sclerosis Society (http://www.nationalmssociety.org/)

National Osteoporosis Foundation (http://www.nof.org/)

National Parkinson Foundation (http://www.parkinson.org)

National Rehabilitation Association (http://www.nationalrehab.org/website/index.html)

National Rural Health Association (http://www.nrharural.org/)

National Stroke Association (http://www.stroke.org/)

National Women's Health Network (http://www.nwhn.org/)

Reflex Sympathetic Dystrophy Syndrome Association (http://www.rsds.org/)

Society for Psychophysiological Research (http://www.sprweb.org/)

Society of Behavioral Medicine (http://www.sbm.org/)

Spina Bifida Association (http://www.sbaa.org/)

Appendix D:
Some Medical Problems
That May Present With
Psychological Symptoms

Addison's Disease (Adrenal–Cortical Insufficiency). Depression, negativism, apathy, suspiciousness, thought disorder, confusion, weight loss

Cushing's Disease (Hyperadrenalism). Varied presentation, depression, anxiety, thought disorder, bizarre somatic delusions, weight gain, fatigue tolerance, tremor

Hypercalcemia. Lack of energy, fatigue, irritability, memory deficit, anorexia, nausea, vomiting

Hyperthyroidism. Anxiety, depression, hyperactivity, grandiosity, heat intolerance

Hypocalcemia. Perioral numbness, increased nervousness, irritability, anxiety, increased emotional lability

Hypoglycemia (Islet Cell Adenoma). Anxiety, fear, depression, fatigue, agitation, confusion

Hypothyroidism. Lethargy, anxiety, irritability, thought disorder, somatic delusions, hallucinations, paranoia

Intracranial Tumors. Varied presentation, depression, anxiety, personality changes, headache, loss of memory and judgment

Multiple Sclerosis. Varied presentation, depression, mood swings, sometimes bland euphoria, speech difficulties

Normal Pressure Hydrocephalus. Apathy, psychomotor retardation, forgetfulness, unsteadiness of gait, incontinence

---

Note. See also R. G. Robinson and W. R. Yates (1999). *Psychiatric treatment of the medically ill.* New York: Marcel Dekker.

Pancreatic Carcinoma. Depression, sense of imminent doom, loss of motivation, weight loss

Pernicious Anemia. Depression, guilt feelings, confusion, weight loss

Pheochromocytoma. Anxiety, panic, fear, apprehension, trembling, sweating, headache

Systemic Lupus Erythematosus. Varied presentation, thought disorder, depression, confusion

Vitamin B deficiencies. Clinical evidence of vitamin deficiency occurs only when tissue stores are sharply depleted and these include: sore tongue, weakness, parathesias, lemon-yellow complexion, visual disturbances

Wilson's Disease (Hepatolenticular Degeneration). Can mimic almost any psychiatric disorder; family history may reveal a relative has died at an early age of liver disease, neurological disease, or in a psychiatric hospital

References

Ader, R. (Ed.). (2007). *Psychoneuroimmunology* (4th ed., Vols. 1 & 2). London: Elsevier.

Agency for Healthcare Research and Quality. (2004, February). *National healthcare disparities report: Summary.* Retrieved March 24, 2008, from http://www.ahrq. gov/qual/nhdr03/nhdrsum03.htm

Alexander, F. (1950). *Psychosomatic medicine.* New York: Norton.

American Educational Research Association, American Psychological Association, & National Council on Measurement. (1999). *Standards for educational and psychological testing.* Washington, DC: Author.

American Psychiatric Association. (1994). *Diagnostic and statistical manual of mental disorders* (4th ed.). Washington, DC: Author.

American Psychological Association. (1992). Ethical principles of psychologists and code of conduct. *American Psychologist, 47,* 1597–1611.

American Psychological Association. (1997, November 5). *APA statement on services by telephone, teleconferencing, and Internet: A statement by the Ethics Committee of the American Psychological Association.* Retrieved March 24, 2008, from http://www.apa.org/ethics/stmnt01.html

American Psychological Association. (n. d.). *Archival description of clinical health psychology.* Retrieved March 24, 2008, from http://www.apa.org/crsppp/health.html

American Psychological Association. (2002a). *APA practice directorate announces new health and behavior CPT codes.* Retrieved March 31, 2008, from http://www. apa.org/practice/cpt_2002.html

American Psychological Association. (2002b). Ethical principles of psychologists and code of conduct. *American Psychologist, 57,* 1060–1073.

American Psychological Association. (2005). *Graduate study in psychology 2005.* Washington, DC: Author.

American Psychological Association. (2006). Evidence-based practice in psychology. *American Psychologist, 61,* 271–285.

American Psychological Association Division of Health Psychology. (n. d.). *A summary page of institutions included in the directory.* Retrieved March 24, 2008, from http://www.health-psych.org/educ_trng/directory/ET_directory_Results.php

American Psychological Association Ethics Committee. (1998). Report of the ethics committee: 1997. *American Psychologist, 53,* 969–980.

Anderson, B. J., Svoren, B., & Laffel, L. (2007). Initiatives to promote effective self-care skills in children and adolescents with diabetes mellitus. *Disease Management & Health Outcomes, 15,* 101–108.

Antony, M. M., & Barlow, D. H. (Eds.). (2002). *Handbook of assessment and treatment planning for psychological disorders.* New York: Guilford Press.

Appelbaum, P. S. (1993). Legal liability and managed care. *American Psychologist, 48,* 251–257.

Appelbaum, P. S. (1997). Informed consent to psychotherapy: Recent developments. *Psychiatric Services, 48,* 445–446.

Arena, J. G., & Schwartz, M. S. (2005). Psychophysiological assessment and biofeedback baselines. In M. S. Schwartz & F. Andrasik (Eds.), *Biofeedback: A practitioner's guide* (3rd ed., pp. 128–158). New York: Guilford Press.

Asken, M. J. (1979). Medical psychology: Toward definition, clarification, and organization. *Professional Psychology, 10,* 66–73.

Association of Psychology Postdoctoral and Internship Centers. (2006). *2006 APPIC directory.* Washington, DC: Author.

Austad, C. S., & Berman, W. H. (Eds.). (1991). *Psychotherapy in managed health care: The optimal use of time and resources.* Washington, DC: American Psychological Association.

Ayer, W. A. (2005). *Psychology and dentistry: Mental health aspects of patient care.* Binghamton, NY: Haworth Press.

Baerger, D. R. (2001). Risk management with the suicidal patient: Lessons from case law. *Professional Psychology: Research and Practice, 32,* 359–366.

Bagheri, A. S., Lane, L. S., Kline, F. M., & Araujo, D. M. (1981). Why physicians fail to tell patients a psychiatrist is coming. *Psychosomatics, 22,* 407–419.

Baker v. United States, 226 F. Supp. 129 (S.D. Iowa 1964).

Balestrieri, M., Bisoffi, G., DeFrancesco, M., Eridani, B., Martucci, M., & Tansella, M. (2000). Six-month and 12-month mental health outcome of medical and surgical patients admitted to general hospital. *Psychological Medicine, 30,* 359–367.

Bandura, A. (1969). *Principles of behavior modification.* New York: Holt, Rinehart & Winston.

Bandura, A. (2005). The primacy of self-regulation in health promotion. *Applied Psychology: An International Review, 54,* 245–254.

Barton, W. E., & Sanborn, C. J. (1978). *Law and the mental health professional.* New York: International Universities Press.

Bastien, C., Vallieres, A., & Morin, C. M. (2001). Validation of the Insomnia Severity Index as a clinical outcome measure for insomnia research. *Sleep Medicine, 2,* 297–307.

Baum, A., & Andersen, B. L. (Eds.). (2001). *Psychosocial interventions for cancer.* Washington, DC: American Psychological Association.

Baum, A., Revenson, T. A., & Singer, J. E. (Eds.). (2001). *Handbook of health psychology.* Mahwah, NJ: Erlbaum.

Bazelon, D. L. (1974). Psychiatrists and the adversary process. *Scientific American, 290,* 18–23.

Beahrs, J. O., & Gutheil, T. G. (2001). Informed consent in psychotherapy. *American Journal of Psychiatry, 158,* 4–10.

Beck, A. T. (1972). *Depression: Causes and treatment.* Philadelphia: University of Pennsylvania Press.

Beck, A. T., Rush, A. J., Shaw, B. F., & Emery, G. (1979). *Cognitive therapy of depression.* New York: Guilford Press.

Beck, A. T., Steer, R. A., & Brown, G. K. (1996). *Manual for the Beck Depression Inventory—II.* San Antonio, TX: Psychological Corporation.

Beecher, H. K. (1956). Relationship of the significance of wound to the pain experienced. *Journal of the American Medical Association, 161,* 1609–1613.

Beers, M. H. (2006). *The Merck manual* (18th ed.). Rahway, NJ: Merck Research Laboratories.

Beigler, J. S. (1984). Tarasoff v. confidentiality. *Behavioral Sciences & the Law, 2,* 273–289.

Belar, C. D. (1980). Training the clinical psychology student in behavioral medicine. *Professional Psychology: Research and Practice, 11,* 620–627.

Belar, C. D. (1989). Opportunities for psychologists in health maintenance organizations: Implications for graduate education and training. *Professional Psychology: Research and Practice, 20,* 390–394.

Belar, C. D. (1991). Behavioral medicine. In C. S. Austad & W. H. Berman (Eds.), *Psychotherapy in managed health care: The optimal use of time and resources.* (pp. 65–79). Washington, DC: American Psychological Association.

Belar, C. D. (1995). Collaboration in capitated care: Challenges for psychology. *Professional Psychology: Research and Practice, 26,* 139–146.

Belar, C. D. (1997). Clinical health psychology: A specialty for the 21st century. *Health Psychology, 16,* 411–416.

Belar, C. D. (2000). Ethical issues in managed care: Perspectives in evolution. *The Counseling Psychologist, 28,* 237–241.

Belar, C. D. (2003). Models and concepts. In S. Llewelyn & P. Kennedy (Eds.), *Handbook of clinical health psychology* (pp. 7–19). New York: Wiley.

Belar, C. D. (2004). The future of education and training in academic health centers. *Journal of Clinical Psychology in Medical Settings, 11,* 77–82.

Belar, C. D., Brown, R. A., Hersch, L. E., Hornyak, L. M., Rozensky, R. H., Sheridan, E. P., et al. (2001). Self-assessment in clinical health psychology: A model for ethical expansion of practice. *Professional Psychology: Research and Practice, 32,* 135–141.

Belar, C. D., & Collins, F. L. (2003, March). *Training in evidence-based behavioral medicine: A seminar for teachers and trainers.* Workshop at the annual meeting of the Society of Behavioral Medicine, Salt Lake City, UT.

Belar, C. D., & Deardorff, W. W. (1995). *Clinical health psychology in medical settings: A practitioner's guidebook.* Washington, DC: American Psychological Association.

Belar, C. D., Deardorff, W. W., & Kelly, K. E. (1987). *The practice of clinical health psychology.* New York: Pergamon Press.

Belar, C. D., & Jeffrey, T. B. (1995). Board certification in health psychology. *Journal of Clinical Psychology, 2,* 129–132.

Belar, C. D., & Kibrick, S. (1986). Biofeedback in the treatment of chronic back pain. In A. Holzman & D. Turk (Eds.), *Pain management: A handbook of psychological treatment approaches* (pp. 131–150). New York: Pergamon Press.

Belar, C. D., McIntyre, T. M., & Matarazzo, J. D. (2003). Health psychology. In I. B. Weiner (Ed.-in-Chief) & D. K. Freedheim (Vol. Ed.), *Handbook of psychology: Vol. 1. History of psychology* (pp. 451–464). New York: Wiley.

Belar, C. D., & Perry, N. W. (1992). National conference on scientist–practitioner education and training for the professional practice of psychology. *American Psychologist, 47,* 71–75.

Belar, C. D., & Siegel, L. J. (1983). A survey of postdoctoral training programs in health psychology. *Health Psychology, 2,* 413–425.

Belar, C. D., Wilson, E., & Hughes, H. (1982). Health psychology training in doctoral psychology programs. *Health Psychology, 1,* 289–299.

Beneditti, F., & Amanzio, M. (1997). The neurobiology of placebo analgesia: From endogenous opioids to cholecystokinin. *Progress in Neurobiology, 52,* 109–125.

Bennett, B. E., Bryant, B. K., VandenBos, G. R., & Greenwood, A. (1990). *Professional liability and risk management.* Washington, DC: American Psychological Association.

Bergner, M., Bobbitt, R. A., Carter, W. B., & Gilson, B. S. (1981). The Sickness Impact Profile: Development and final revision of a health status measure. *Medical Care, 19,* 787–806.

Bernstein, D. A., Borkovec, T. D., & Hazlett-Stevens, H. (2000). *New directions in progressive relaxation training: A guidebook for helping professionals.* Westport, CT: Praeger Publishers.

Bernstein, B. E., & Hartsell, T. L. (2004). *The portable lawyer for mental health professionals* (2nd ed.). Hoboken, NJ: Wiley.

Berry v. Moench, 8 Utah 2d 191,331 P.2d 814 (1958).

Bersoff, D. N. (2003). *Ethical conflicts in psychology* (3rd ed.). Washington, DC: American Psychological Association.

Bersoff, D. N., & Hofer, P. J. (1995). Legal issues in computerized psychological testing. In D. N. Bersoff (Ed.), *Ethical conflicts in psychology* (pp. 291–294). Washington, DC: American Psychological Association.

Billowitz, A., & Friedson, W. (1978–1979). Are psychiatric consultants' recommendations followed? *International Journal of Psychiatry in Medicine, 9,* 179–189.

Bjelland, I., Dahl, A. A., Haug, T. T., & Neckelmann, D. (2002). The validity of the Hospital Anxiety and Depression Scale: An updated literature review. *Journal of Psychosomatic Research, 52,* 69–77.

Blake, D. D., Weathers, F. W., Nagy, L. M., Kaloupek, D. G., Gusman, F. D., Charney, D. S., et al. (1995). The development of a clinician-administered PTSD scale. *Journal of Traumatic Stress, 8,* 75–90.

Blanchard, E. B. (2000). *Irritable bowel syndrome: Psychosocial assessment and treatment.* Washington, DC: American Psychological Association.

Blanchard, E. B., & Hickling, E. J. (2004). *After the crash: Psychological assessment and treatment of survivors of motor vehicle accidents* (2nd ed.). Washington, DC: American Psychological Association.

Blechman, E. A., & Brownell, K. D. (Eds.). (1999). *Behavioral medicine and women: A comprehensive handbook.* New York: Guilford Press.

Block, A. R., Gatchel, R. J., Deardorff, W. W., & Guyer, R. D. (2003). *The psychology of spine surgery.* Washington, DC: American Psychological Association.

Boll, T. J., Johnson, S. B., Perry, N. W., & Rozensky, R. H. (Eds.). (2002). *Handbook of clinical health psychology: Vol. 1. Medical disorders and behavioral applications.* Washington, DC: American Psychological Association.

Bongar, B. (2002). *The suicidal patient: Clinical and legal standards of care* (2nd ed.). Washington, DC: American Psychological Association.

Bongar, B., Maris, R. W., Berman, A. L., & Litman, R. E. (1992). Outpatient standards of care and the suicidal patient. *Suicide and Life-Threatening Behavior, 22,* 453–478.

Bongar, B., Maris, R. W., Berman, A. L., & Litman, R. E. (1998). Outpatient standards of care and the suicidal patient. In B. Bongar, A. L. Berman, R. W. Maris, M. M. Silverman, E. A. Harris, & W. L. Packman (Eds.), *Risk management with suicidal patients* (pp. 4–33). New York: Guilford Press.

Boutin-Foster, C., Ferrando, S. J., & Charlson, M. E. (2003). The Cornell Psychiatric Screen: A brief psychiatric scale for hospitalized medical patients. *Psychosomatics, 44,* 382–387.

Bradley, L. A., McDonald-Haile, J., & Jaworski, T. M. (1992). Assessment of psychological status using interviews and self-report instruments. In D. C. Turk & R. Melzack (Eds.), *Handbook of pain assessment* (pp. 193–213). New York: Guilford Press.

Bray, J. H., Frank, R. G., McDaniel, S. H., & Heldring, M. (2004). Education, practice, and research opportunities for psychologists in primary care. In R. G. Frank, S. H. McDaniel, J. H. Bray, & M. Heldring (Eds.), *Primary care psychology* (pp. 3–21). Washington, DC: American Psychological Association.

Bruns, D., & Disorbio, J. M. (2003). *Battery for Health Improvement—2.* Minneapolis, MN: Pearson.

Budman, S. H., & Gurman, A. S. (1988). *Theory and practice of brief therapy.* New York: Guilford Press.

Budman, S. H., Hoyt, M. F., & Friedman, S. (1992). *The first session in brief therapy.* New York: Guilford Press.

Bufka, L. F., Crawford, J. I., & Levitt, J. T. (2002). Brief screening assessments for managed care and primary care. In M. M. Antony & D. H. Barlow (Eds.), *Handbook of assessment and treatment planning for psychological disorders* (pp. 38–63). New York: Guilford Press.

Butcher, J. N. (2002). How to use computer-based reports. In J. N. Butcher (Ed.), *Clinical personality assessment* (2nd ed., pp. 109–125). Oxford, England: Oxford University Press.

Butcher, J. N., Graham, J. R., Ben-Porath, Y. S., Tellegen, Y. S., Dahlstrom, W. G., & Kaemmer, B. (2001). *Minnesota multiphasic personality inventory—2: Manual for administration and scoring* (Rev. ed.). Minneapolis: University of Minnesota Press.

Butcher, J. N., Perry, J. N., & Atlis, M. M. (2000). Validity and utility of computer-based test interpretation. *Psychological Assessment, 12,* 6–18.

Cacioppo, J. T., Petty, R. E., & Marshall-Goodell, B. (1985). Physical, social, and inferential elements of psychophysiological measurement. In P. Karoly (Ed.), *Measurement strategies in health psychology* (pp. 263–300). New York: Wiley.

Cacioppo, J. T., Tassinary, L. G., & Berntson, G. (Eds.). (2007). *Handbook of psychophysiology* (3rd ed.). New York: Cambridge University Press.

California Assembly Bill (AB) 733.

California Board of Psychology. (2008, February 24). *Notice to California consumers regarding the practice of psychology on the Internet.* Retrieved March 24, 2008, from http://www.psychboard.ca.gov/consumers/internet-thrpy.shtml

Camic, P. M., & Knight, S. J. (Eds.). (1998). *Clinical handbook of health psychology: A practical guide to effective interventions.* Toronto, Ontario, Canada: Hogrefe & Huber.

Campbell, T., & Lorandos, D. (2001). *Cross examining experts in the behavioral sciences.* Danvers, MA: Thomson West.

Cattell, R. B., Eber, H. W., & Tatsouka, M. M. (1970). *Handbook for the Sixteen Personality Factor Questionnaire (16PF).* Champaign, IL: Institute for Personality and Ability Testing.

Caudill, C. O. (2004). *Therapists under fire.* Retrieved March 24, 2008, from http://www.cphins.com/riskmanagement/therapists_under_fire.html

Caudill, M. A. (1995). *Managing pain before it manages you.* New York: Guilford Press.

Cautela, J. R. (1967). Covert sensitization. *Psychological Reports, 20,* 459–468.

Chambers v. Ingram, 858 F.2d 351,356 (7th Cir. 1988).

Chambless, D. L., & Ollendick, T. H. (2001). Empirically supported psychological interventions: Controversies and evidence. *Annual Review of Psychology, 52,* 685–716.

Charles, S. C. (1993). The doctor–patient relationship and medical malpractice litigation. *Bulletin of the Menninger Clinic, 57,* 195–207.

Childress, C. A., & Asamen, J. K. (1998). The emerging relationship of psychology and the Internet: Proposed guidelines for conducting Internet intervention research. *Ethics & Behavior, 8,* 19–35.

Chiles, J. A., Lambert, M. J., & Hatch, A. L. (2002). Medical cost offset: A review of the impact of psychological interventions on medical utilization over the past three decades. In N. A. Cummings, W. T. O'Donohue, & K. E. Ferguson (Eds.), *The impact of medical cost offset on practice and research: making it work for you* (pp. 47–56). Reno, NV: Context Press.

Christopher, P. P., Foti, M. E., Roy-Bujnowski, K., & Appelbaum, P. S. (2007). Consent form readability and educational levels of potential participants in mental health research. *Psychiatric Services, 58,* 227–232.

Clarke, D. M., Mackinnon, A. J., Smith, G. C., McKenzie, D. P., & Herrman, H. E. (2000). Dimensions of psychopathology in the medical ill: A latent trait analysis. *Psychosomatics, 41,* 418–425.

Cohen, L. M., McChargue, D. E., & Collins, F. L. (2003). *The health psychology handbook: Practical issues for the behavioral medicine specialist.* Thousand Oaks, CA: Sage.

Cohen, R. J. (1979). *Malpractice: A guide for mental health professionals.* New York: Free Press.

Cohen, R. J., & Mariano, W. E. (1982). *Legal guidebook in mental health.* New York: Free Press.

Coldwell, S. E., Wilhem, F. H., Milgrom, P., Prall, C. W., Getz, T., Spadafora, A., et al. (2007). Combining alprazolam with systematic desensitization therapy for dental injection phobia. *Journal of Anxiety Disorders, 2,* 871–887.

Collins, F. L., Leffingwell, T. R., & Belar, C. D. (2007). Teaching evidence-based practice: Implications for psychology. *Journal of Clinical Psychology, 63,* 607–609.

Contrada, R. J., Leventhal, E. A., & Anderson, J. R. (1994). Psychological preparation for surgery: Marshaling individual and social resources to optimize self-regulation. In S. Maes, H. Leventhal, & M. Johnston (Eds.), *International review of health psychology: Vol. 3* (pp. 219–266). New York: Wiley.

Covino, N. A., & Bottari, M. (2001). Hypnosis, behavioral therapy, and smoking cessation. *Journal of Dental Education, 65,* 340–347.

Cross, H. J., & Deardorff, W. W. (1987). Malpractice in psychotherapy and psychological evaluation. In J. R. McNamara & M. A. Appel (Eds.), *Critical issues, developments, and trends in professional psychology: Vol. 3* (pp. 55–79). New York: Praeger Publishers.

Cummings, N. A. (1985). Assessing the computer's impact: Professional concerns. *Computers in Human Behavior, 1,* 293–300.

Cummings, N. A. (1986). The dismantling of our health care system. *American Psychologist, 41,* 426–431.

Datilio, F. M., & Freeman, A. (Eds.). (2007). *Cognitive-behavioral strategies in crisis intervention* (3rd ed.). New York: Guilford Press.

Davidson, K. W., Trudeau, K. J., Ockene, J. K., Orleans, C. T., & Kaplan, R. M. (2004). A primer on current evidence-based review systems and their implications for behavioral medicine. *Annals of Behavioral Medicine, 28,* 226–238.

Davis, M., McKay, M., & Eshelman, E. R. (2000). *The relaxation and stress reduction workbook* (5th ed.). Oakland, CA: New Harbinger.

Dawidoff, D. (1966). The malpractice of psychiatrists. *Duke Law Journal, 1966,* 696–716.

Deardorff, W. W., Cross, H. J., & Hupprich, W. (1984). Malpractice liability in psychotherapy: Client and practitioner perspectives. *Professional Psychology: Research and Practice, 15,* 590–600.

Deardorff, W. W., & Reeves, J. L. (1997). *Preparing for surgery: A mind–body approach to enhance healing and recovery.* Oakland, CA: New Harbinger.

DeGood, D. E. (1983). Reducing medical patients' reluctance to participate in psychotherapies: The initial session. *Professional Psychology: Research and Practice, 14,* 570–579.

DeLeon, P. H., Kenkel, M. B., & Belar, C. D. (2007). A window of opportunity. *Monitor on Psychology, 38,* 24.

DeMatteo, D. (2005). Legal update: An expansion of Tarasoff's duty to protect. *American Psychology Law Society, 25,* 2–20.

de Ridder, D., & de Wit, J. (Eds.). (2006). *Self-regulation in health behavior.* New York: Wiley.

Derogatis, L. R. (1983). *SCL–90–R: Administration, scoring and procedures manual— II.* Towson, MD: Clinical Psychometric Research.

Derogatis, L. R. (1986). The Psychosocial Adjustment to Illness Scale (PAIS). *Journal of Psychosomatic Research, 30,* 77–91.

Derogatis, L. R., & Lopez, M. C. (1983). *The Psychosocial Adjustment to Illness Scale (PAIS + PAIS–SR): Administration, scoring and procedures manual.* Baltimore: Johns Hopkins University Press.

Dickson, D. T. (1995). *Law in the health and human services.* New York: Free Press.

Dodgen, C. E. (2006). *Nicotine dependence: Understanding and applying the most effective treatment interventions.* Washington, DC: American Psychological Association.

Dolezal-Wood, S., Belar, C. D., & Snibbe, J. (1998). A comparison of computer-assisted psychotherapy and cognitive–behavioral therapy in groups. *Journal of Clinical Psychology in Medical Settings, 5,* 103–114.

Doverspike, W. (1999). *Ethical risk management: Guidelines for practice, a practical ethics handbook.* Sarasota, FL: Professional Resource Press.

Drotar, D. (2006). *Psychological interventions in childhood chronic illness.* Washington, DC: American Psychological Association.

Dubin, S. S. (1972). Obsolescence or lifelong education: A choice for the professional. *American Psychologist, 27,* 486–496.

Duke, E. M. (2007, August). *Remarks to the National Association of Community Health Centers, Dallas, TX.* Retrieved March 24, 2008, from http://newsroom. hrsa.gov/speeches/2007/NACHCaugust.htm

Eifert, G. H., Thompson, R. N., Zvolensky, M. J., Edwards, K., Frazer, N. L., Haddad, J. W., et al. (2000). The Cardiac Anxiety Questionnaire: Development and preliminary validity. *Behavior Research and Therapy, 38,* 1039–1053.

Elfant, A. B. (1985). Psychotherapy and assessment in hospital settings: Ideological and professional conflicts. *Professional Psychology: Research and Practice, 16,* 55–63.

Ellis, A. (1962). *Reason and emotion in psychotherapy.* New York: Lyle Stuart.

Engel, G. L. (1977, April 8). The need for a new medical model: A challenge for biomedicine. *Science, 196,* 129–136.

Evans, D. (2004). *Placebo: Mind over matter in modern medicine.* New York: Oxford University Press.

Ewing v. Goldstein, 15 Cal. Rptr. 3d 864 (Cal. Ct. App. 2004).

Fabrega, H. (1974). *Disease and social behavior.* Cambridge, MA: MIT Press.

Falender, C. A., & Shafranske, E. P. (2004). *Clinical supervision: A competency-based approach.* Washington, DC: American Psychological Association.

Faltz, C. (2006, November/December). Nation bill (AB 733) passes: Psychologists advised to continue following Ewing v. Goldstein. *The California Psychologist,* p. 31.

Feldman, S. R., & Ward, T. M. (1979). Psychotherapeutic injury: Reshaping the implied contract as an alternative to malpractice. *North Carolina Law Review, 58,* 63–96.

Folstein, M. F., Folstein, S. E., & McHugh, P. R. (1975). "Mini-mental state": A practical method for grading the cognitive state of patients for the clinician. *Journal of Psychiatric Research, 12,* 189–198.

Fordyce, W. E. (1976). *Behavioral methods for chronic pain and illness.* St. Louis, MO: Mosby, Inc.

Fordyce, W. E. (1995). *Back pain in the workplace: Management of disability in nonspecific conditions.* Seattle, WA: IASP Press.

France, C. R., Masters, K. S., Belar, C. D., Kerns, R. D., Klonoff, E. A., Larkin, K. T., et al. (in press). Application of the competency model to clinical health psychology. *Professional Psychology: Research and Practice.*

Frank, R. G., Baum, A., & Wallander, J. L. (Eds.). (2004). *Handbook of clinical health psychology: Vol. 3. Models and perspectives in health psychology.* Washington, DC: American Psychological Association.

Frank, R. G., McDaniel, S. H., Bray, J. H., & Heldring, M. (2004). *Primary care psychology.* Washington, DC: American Psychological Association.

Franklin, G. M., Mai, J., Wickizer, T., Turner, J. A., Fulton-Kehoe, D., & Grant, L. (2005). Opioid dosing trends and mortality in Washington State's workers' compensation. *American Journal of Industrial Medicine, 48,* 91–99.

Fried, R. (1993). *The psychology and physiology of breathing.* New York: Plenum Press.

Friedberg, F., & Jason, L. A. (1998). *Understanding chronic fatigue syndrome: An empirical guide to assessment and treatment.* Washington, DC: American Psychological Association.

Friedman, R., Sobel, D., Myers, P., Caudill, M., & Benson, H. (1995). Behavioral medicine, clinical health psychology, and cost offset. *Health Psychology, 14,* 509–518.

Furniss v. Fitchett, NZLR 396 (1958).

Furrow, B. (1980). *Malpractice in psychotherapy.* Lexington, MA: Heath.

Garfield, S. L. (1998). *The practice of brief psychotherapy* (2nd ed.). New York: Wiley.

Garner, D. M. (2004). *Eating Disorder Inventory* (3rd ed.). Los Angeles: Western Psychological Association.

Garner, D. M., & Olmsted, M. P. (1984). *The eating disorder inventory manual.* Odessa, FL: Psychological Assessment Resources.

Gatchel, R. J. (2005). *Clinical essentials of pain management.* Washington, DC: American Psychological Association.

Gatchel, R. J., & Blanchard, E. B. (Eds.). (1993). *Psychophysiological disorders: Research and clinical applications.* Washington, DC: American Psychological Association.

Gatchel, R. J., & Oordt, M. S. (2003). *Clinical health psychology and primary care: Practical advice and clinical guidance for successful collaboration.* Washington, DC: American Psychological Association.

Gentry, W. D. (Ed.). (1984). *Handbook of behavioral medicine.* New York: Guilford Press.

Gentry, W. D., & Matarazzo, J. D. (1981). Medical psychology: Three decades of growth and development. In C. K. Prokop & L. A. Bradley (Eds.), *Medical psychology: Contributions to behavioral medicine* (pp. 5–15). New York: Academic Press.

Gentry, W. D., & Owens, D. (1986). Pain groups. In A. D. Holzman & D. C. Turk (Eds.), *Pain management: A handbook of psychological treatment approaches* (pp. 100–112). New York: Pergamon Press.

Gifis, S. H. (2003). *Law dictionary* (5th ed.). Hauppauge, NY: Barron's.

Golden, W. L., Dowd, E. T., & Friedberg, F. (1987). *Hypnotherapy: A modern approach.* New York: Pergamon Press.

Goldfried, M. R., & Davison, G. (1976). *Clinical behavioral therapy.* New York: Holt, Rinehart & Winston.

Goodstein, L. D. (1985). *White paper on duty to protect.* Washington, DC: American Psychological Association Committee on Legal Issues.

Goreczny, A. J., & Hersen, M. (1998). *Handbook of pediatric and adolescent health psychology.* Boston: Allyn & Bacon.

Gostin, L. O. (2002). Tarasoff v. Regents of the University of California. In *Public health law and ethics: A reader* (pp. 1–30). Retrieved March 24, 2008, from http://www.publichealthlaw.net/Reader/docs/Tarasoff.pdf

Graham, J. R. (1977). *The MMPI: A practical guide.* New York: Oxford University Press.

Graham, J. R. (2005). *MMPI–2: Assessing personality and psychopathology.* New York: Oxford University Press.

Greenburg, S. A., & Shuman, D. W. (1997). Irreconcilable conflict between therapeutic and forensic roles. *Professional Psychology: Research and Practice, 28,* 50–57.

Greenburg, S. A., & Shuman, D. W. (2007). When worlds collide: Therapeutic and forensic roles. *Professional Psychology: Research and Practice, 38,* 129–132.

Greene, R. L. (1980). *The MMPI: An interpretive manual.* New York: Grune & Stratton.

Greene, R. L. (1991). *The MMPI–2/MMPI: An interpretive manual.* Boston: Allyn & Bacon.

Grimaldi, K. E., & Lichtenstein, E. (1969). Hot, smoky air as an aversive stimulus in the treatment of smoking. *Behaviour Research and Therapy, 7,* 275–282.

Gross, B. H., & Weinberger, L. E. (Eds.). (1982). *New directions for mental health services: Vol. 16. The mental health professional and the legal system.* San Francisco: Jossey-Bass.

Guess, H. A., Kleinman, A., Kusek, J. W., & Engel, L. W. (Eds.). (2002). *The science of the placebo.* London: BMJ Books.

Gutheil, T. G., Bursztajn, H. J., Hamm, R. M., & Brodsky, A. (1983). Subjective data and suicide assessment in the light of recent legal developments. Part I: Malpractice prevention and the use of subjective data. *International Journal of Law and Psychiatry, 6,* 317–329.

Gylys, B. A., & Wedding, M. E. (2004). *Medical terminology systems: A body systems approach* (5th ed.). Philadelphia: Davis.

Haas, L. J. (Ed.). (2004). *Handbook of primary care psychology.* New York: Oxford University Press.

Haas, L. J., & Cummings, N. A. (1991). Managed outpatient mental health plans: Clinical, ethical, and practical guidelines for participation. *Professional Psychology: Research and Practice, 22,* 45–51.

Haley, W. E., McDaniel, S. H., Bray, J. H., Frank, R. G., Heldring, J., Johnson, S. B., et al. (1998). Psychological practice in primary care settings: Practical tips for clinicians. *Professional Psychology: Research and Practice, 29,* 237–244.

Halperin, D. A. (1980). Misinformed consent. *Bulletin of the American Academy of Psychiatry and Law, 8,* 175–178.

Hamilton, M. (1959). The assessment of anxiety status by rating. *British Journal of Medical Psychology, 32,* 50–55.

Hammer v. Rosen, 7 NY 2d 376, 165 NE 2d 756, 198 NYS 2d (1960).

Hanson, S. L., Kerkhoff, T. R., & Bush, S. S. (2005). *Health care ethics for psychologists: A casebook.* Washington, DC: American Psychological Association.

Harden, R. N. (2002). Chronic opioid therapy: Another appraisal. *American Pain Society Bulletin, 12,* 1–12.

Harrar, W. R., VandeCreek, L., & Knapp, S. (1990). Ethical and legal aspects of clinical supervision. *Professional Psychology: Research and Practice, 21,* 37–41.

Harrington, A. (Ed.). (1999). *The placebo effect: An interdisciplinary exploration.* London: Harvard University Press.

Harris, M. (1973). Tort liability of the psychotherapist. *University of San Francisco Law Review, 8,* 405–436.

Hathaway, S. R., & McKinley, J. C. (1943). *The Minnesota multiphasic personality inventory.* Minneapolis: University of Minnesota Press.

Health Insurance and Portability and Accountability Act of 1996, Pub. L. No. 104–191.

Heap, M., & Aravind, K. K. (2002). *Hartland's medical and dental hypnosis* (4th ed.). London: Churchill Livingstone.

Hedland v. Superior Court, 669 P.2d 41 (Cal. 1983).

Heide, F. J., & Borkovec, T. D. (1984). Relaxation-induced anxiety: Mechanisms and theoretical implications. *Behavior Research and Therapy, 22,* 1–12.

Hellinger, F. J., & Encinosa, W. E. (2003). *Impact of state laws limiting malpractice awards on geographic distribution of physicians.* Retrieved May 1, 2007, from U.S. Department of Health and Human Services, Agency of Healthcare Research and Quality, Center for Organization and Delivery Studies: http://www.ahrq.gov/research/tortcaps/tortcaps.htm

Heltzel, T. (2007). Compatibility of therapeutic and forensic roles. *Professional Psychology: Research and Practice, 38,* 122–128.

Hersen, M., & Biaggio, M. (Eds.). (2000). *Effective brief therapies: A clinician's guide.* San Diego, CA: Academic Press.

Hilgard, E. R., & Hilgard, J. R. (1994). *Hypnosis in the relief of pain.* New York: Brunner/Mazel.

Hoch, T. A., Babbitt, R. L., Coe, D. A., Krell, D. M., & Hackbert, L. (1994). Contingency contracting: Combining positive reinforcement and escape extinction procedures to treat persistent food refusal. *Behavior Modification, 18,* 106–128.

Hofer, P. J., & Bersoff, D. N. (1983). *Standards for the administration and interpretation of computerized psychological testing.* (Available from D. N. Bersoff, Suite 511, 1200 Seventeenth Street, NW, Washington, DC 20036)

Hofman, B. (2002). On the triad of disease, illness and sickness. *Journal of Medicine and Philosophy, 27,* 651–673.

Hogan, D. (1979). *The regulation of psychotherapists: Vol. 3. A review of malpractice suits in the United States.* Cambridge, MA: Ballinger.

Holmes, T. H., & Rahe, R. H. (1967). A Social Readjustment Rating Scale. *Journal of Psychosomatic Research, 11,* 213–218.

House, J. S., Landis, K. R., & Umberson, D. (1988, July 29). Social relationships and health. *Science, 241,* 540–545.

Institute of Medicine. (2001a). *Crossing the quality chasm: A new health system for the 21st century.* Washington, DC: National Academy Press

Institute of Medicine. (2001b). *Health and behavior: The interplay of biological, behavioral, and societal influences.* Washington, DC: National Academy Press.

Institute of Medicine (2003). *Health professions education: A bridge to quality.* Washington, DC: National Academy Press.

Jacob, R. G., & Moore, D. J. (1984). Paradoxical interventions in behavioral medicine. *Journal of Behavior Therapy and Experimental Psychiatry, 15,* 205–213.

Jacobs, D. (2007). *A resource guide for implementing the Joint Commission on Accreditation of Healthcare Organizations (JCAHO) 2007 patient safety goals on suicide.* Retrieved April 14, 2008, from http://www.naphs.org/Teleconference/documents/ResourceGuide_JCAHOSafetyGoals2007_final.pdf

Jacobs, D., & Brewer, M. (2004). American Psychiatric Association practice guideline provides recommendations for assessing and treating patients with suicidal behaviors. *Psychiatric Annals, 34,* 373–380.

Jacobs, J., Bernhard, R., Delgado, A., & Strain, J. J. (1977). Screening for organic mental syndromes in the medically ill. *Annals of Internal Medicine, 86,* 40.

Jacobson, E. (1939). *Progressive relaxation.* Chicago: University of Chicago Press.

James, L. C., & Folen, R. A. (Eds.). (2005). *The primary care consultant: The next frontier for psychologists in hospitals and clinics.* Washington, DC: American Psychological Association.

James, T. (2000). *Hypnosis: A comprehensive guide.* London: Crown House Publishing.

Janis, I. L. (1958). *Psychological stress: Psychoanalytic and behavioral studies of surgical patients.* New York: Wiley.

Jenkins, C. D., Zyzanski, S. J., & Rosenman, R. H. (1979). *Jenkins Activity Survey manual.* New York: Psychological Corporation.

Jensen, M., & Patterson, D. R. (2006). Hypnotic treatment of chronic pain. *Journal of Behavioral Medicine, 29,* 95–124.

Jensen, M. P., Turner, J. A., Romano, J. M., & Lawler, B. (1994). Relationship of pain-specific beliefs to chronic pain adjustment. *Pain, 57,* 301–309.

Jobes, D. A., & Berman, A. L. (1993). Suicide and malpractice liability: Assessing and reusing policies, procedures, and practice in outpatient settings. *Professional Psychology: Research and Practice, 24,* 91–99.

Johnson, M. R., & Kreimer, J. L. (2005). Guided fantasy play for chronically ill children: A critical review. In L. A. Reddy, T. M. Files-Hall, & C. E. Schaefer (Eds.), *Empirically based play interventions for children* (pp. 105–122). Washington, DC: American Psychological Association.

Johnston, M., & Vogele, C. (1993). Benefits of psychological preparation for surgery: A meta-analysis. *Annals of Behavioral Medicine, 15,* 245–256.

Joiner, T. E., Walker, R. L., Rudd, M. D., & Jobes, D. A. (1999). Scientizing and routinizing the assessment of suicidality in outpatient practice. *Professional Psychology: Research and Practice, 30,* 447–453.

Joint Commission on Accreditation of Healthcare Organizations. (2007). *2007 patient safety goals on suicide featuring the Basic Suicide Assessment Five-Step Eval-*

uation (B–SAFE). Retrieved April 1, 2008, from http://www.jointcommission. org/PatientSafety/NationalPatientSafetyGoals/07_bhc_npsgs.htm

Jones, E., & Nisbett, R. (1971). The actor and observer: Divergent perceptions of the causes of behavior. In E. E. Jones, D. E. Kanouse, H. H. Kelly, R. E. Nisbett, S. Valins, & B. Weiner (Eds.), *Attribution: Perceiving the causes of behavior* (pp. 79–94). Morristown, NJ: General Learning Press.

Jordan, J., Barde, B., & Zeiher, A. M. (2007). *Contributions toward evidence-based psychocardiology: A systematic review of the literature.* Washington, DC: American Psychological Association.

Kamenar, P. D. (1984). Psychiatrists' duty to warn of a dangerous patient: A survey of the law. *Behavioral Sciences and the Law, 2,* 259–272.

Kanner, A. D., Coyne, J. C., Schaefer, C., & Lazarus, R. S. (1981). Comparison of two modes of stress measurement: Daily hassles and uplifts versus major life events. *Journal of Behavioral Medicine, 4,* 1–39.

Kaplan, R. M. (2000). Two pathways to prevention. *American Psychologist, 55,* 382–396.

Kasper, D. L., Braunwald, E., Fauci, A., Hauser, S., Longo, D., & Jameson, J. L. (2005). *Harrison's principles of internal medicine* (16th ed.). New York: McGraw-Hill.

Katz, S. T., Downs, H., Cash, H., & Grotz, R. (1970). Progress in the development of the index of ADL. *The Gerontologist, 10,* 20–30.

Kazarian, S. S., & Evans, D. R. (Eds.). (2001). *Handbook of cultural health psychology.* San Diego, CA: Academic Press.

Kellogg, S. H., Burns, M., Coleman, P., Stitzer, M., Wale, J. B., & Kreek, M. J. (2005). Something of value: The introduction of contingency management interventions into the New York City Health and Hospital Addiction Treatment Service. *Journal of Substance Abuse Treatment, 28,* 57–65.

Kerns, R. D., Turk, D. C., & Rudy, T. E. (1985). The West Haven–Yale Multi-dimensional Pain Inventory. *Pain, 23,* 345–356.

Kleespies, P. M., Deleppo, J. D., Gallagher, P. L., & Niles, B. L. (1999). Managing suicidal emergencies: Recommendations for the practitioner. *Professional Psychology: Research and Practice, 30,* 454–463.

Klein, J. I., & Glover, S. I. (1983). Psychiatric malpractice. *International Journal of Law and Psychiatry, 6,* 131–157.

Kleinman, A., Eisenberg, L., & Good, B. (1978). Culture, illness, and care: Clinical lessons from anthropological and cross-cultural research. *Annals of Internal Medicine, 88,* 251–258.

Kleinman, A., Eisenberg, L., & Good, B. (2006). Culture, illness, and care: Clinical lessons from anthropological and cross-cultural research. *Focus, 4,* 140–147.

Knapp, S. (1980). A primer on malpractice for psychologists. *Professional Psychology, 11*, 606–612.

Knapp, S., & VandeCreek, L. (1981). Behavioral medicine: Its malpractice risks for psychologists. *Professional Psychology, 12*, 677–683.

Knapp, S., & VandeCreek, L. (1990). Application of the duty to protect to HIV-positive patients. *Professional Psychology: Research and Practice, 21*, 161–166.

Knapp, S., & VandeCreek, L. (1993). Legal and ethical issues in billing patients and collecting fees. *Psychotherapy, 30*, 25–31.

Knapp, S., & VandeCreek, L. (2001). Ethical issues in personality assessment in forensic psychology. *Journal of Personality Assessment, 77*, 242–254.

Koocher, G. P. (1983). Ethical and professional standards in psychology. In B. D. Sales (Ed.), *The professional psychologist's handbook* (pp. 77–109). New York: Plenum Press.

Koocher, G. P. (1994). APA and the FTC New adventures in consumer protection. *American Psychologist, 49*, 322–328.

Koocher, G. P., & Keith-Spiegel, P. (1998). *Ethics in psychology: Professional standards and cases* (2nd ed.). New York: Oxford University Press.

Koocher, G. P., & Morray, E. (2000). Regulation of telepsychology: A survey of state attorneys general. *Professional Psychology: Research and Practice, 31*, 503–508.

Kop, W. J. (2005). Psychological interventions in patients with coronary heart disease. In L. C. James & R. A. Folen (Eds.), *The primary care consultant: The next frontier for psychologists in hospitals and clinics.* (pp. 61–81). Washington, DC: American Psychological Association.

Korchin, S. J. (1976). *Modern clinical psychology.* New York: Basic Books.

Kovner, A. R., & Knickman, J. R. (Eds.). (2008). *Jonas and Kovner's health care delivery system in the United States* (9th ed.). New York: Springer Publishing Company.

Landrine, H., & Klonoff, E. (1992). Culture and health-related schemas: A review and proposal for interdisciplinary integration. *Health Psychology, 11*, 267–276.

Landrine, H., & Klonoff, E. A. (2001). Cultural diversity and health psychology. In A. Baum, T. A. Revenson, & J. E. Singer (Eds.), *Handbook of health psychology* (pp. 851–891). Mahwah, NJ: Erlbaum.

Lang, P. J., & Melamed, B. G. (1969). Avoidance conditioning therapy of an infant with chronic ruminative vomiting. *Journal of Abnormal Psychology, 74*, 139–142.

LeCron, L. (1970). *Self-hypnosis.* New York: New American Library.

Leigh, H., & Reiser, M. F. (1980). *Biological, psychological, and social dimensions of medical practice.* New York: Plenum Press.

Leigh, H., & Streltzer, J. (Eds.). (2007). *Handbook of consultation-liaison psychiatry.* New York: Springer Publishing Company.

Ley, P. (1982). Studies of recall in medical settings. *Human Learning, 1*, 223–233.

Lifson, L. E., & Simon, R. I. (1998). *The mental health practitioner and the law: A comprehensive handbook.* Cambridge, MA: Harvard University Press.

Linden, W. (1991). *Autogenic training: A clinical guide.* New York: Guilford Press.

Linton, J. C. (2004). Psychological assessment in primary care. In L. J. Haas (Ed.), *Handbook of primary care psychology* (pp. 35–45). New York: Oxford University Press.

Linton, S. J. (2005). *Understanding pain for better clinical practice.* Edinburgh, Scotland: Elsevier.

Lipowski, Z. J. (1967). Review of consultation psychiatry and psychosomatic medicine: I. General principles. *Psychosomatic Medicine, 29,* 153–171.

Lipowski, Z. J. (1977). Psychosomatic medicine in the seventies: An overview. *American Journal of Psychiatry, 134,* 233–243.

Llewelyn, S., & Kennedy, P. (Eds.). (2003). *Handbook of clinical health psychology.* New York: Wiley.

Lorig, K., Chastain, R. L., Ung, E., Shoor, S., & Holman, H. R. (1989). Development and evaluation of a scale to measure perceived self-efficacy in people with arthritis. *Arthritis and Rheumatism, 32,* 37–44.

Lucente, F. E., & Fleck, S. (1972). A study of hospitalization anxiety in 408 medical and surgical patients. *Psychosomatic Medicine, 34,* 304–312.

MacLachlan, M. (2006). *Culture and health: A critical perspective towards global health* (2nd ed.). New York: Wiley.

Magrab, P. R., & Papadopoulou, Z. L. (1977). The effect of a token economy on dietary compliance for children on hemodialysis. *Journal of Applied Behavior Analysis, 10,* 573–578.

Malament, I. B., Dunn, M. E., & Davis, R. (1975). Pressure sores: An operant conditioning approach to prevention. *Archives of Physical Medicine and Rehabilitation, 56,* 161–165.

Markus, R. M. (1965). Conspiracy of silence. *Cleveland Law Review, 14,* 520–533.

Matarazzo, J. D. (1980). Behavioral health and behavioral medicine. *American Psychologist, 35,* 807–817.

Matarazzo, J. D. (1986). Computerized clinical psychological test interpretation: Unvalidated plus all mean and no sigma. *American Psychologist, 41,* 14–21.

Mayberry, R. M., Mili, F., & Ofili, E. (2000). Racial and ethnic differences in access to medical care. *Medical Care and Research and Review, 57,* 108–145.

McDaniel, S. H., Belar, C. D., Schroeder, C., Hargrove, D. S., & Freeman, E. L. (2002). A training curriculum for professional psychologists in primary care. *Professional Psychology: Research and Practice, 33,* 65–72.

McDaniel, S. H., & Hepworth, J. (2004). Family psychology in primary care: Managing issues of power and dependency through collaboration. In R. G.

Frank, S. H. McDaniel, J. H. Bray, & M. Heldring (Eds.), *Primary care psychology* (pp. 113–132). Washington, DC: American Psychological Association.

McKay, M., Davis, M., & Fanning, P. (2007). *Thoughts and feelings* (3rd ed.). Oakland, CA: New Harbinger.

Mechanic, D. (1972). Social psychological factors affecting the presentation of bodily complaints. *New England Journal of Medicine, 286,* 1132–1139.

Meichenbaum, D. (1977). *Cognitive behavior modification: An integrative approach.* New York: Plenum Press.

Melamed, B. G., & Siegel, L. J. (1980). *Behavioral medicine: Practical applications in health care.* New York: Springer Publishing Company.

Melzack, R. (1975). The McGill Pain Questionnaire: Major properties and scoring methods. *Pain, 1,* 277–299.

Melzack, R., & Wall, P. D. (1983). *The challenge of pain.* New York: Basic Books.

Miller, G. E., & Cohen, S. (2001). Psychological interventions and the immune system: A meta-analytic review and critique. *Health Psychology, 20,* 47–63.

Miller, S. M. (1992). Individual differences in the coping process: What to know and when to know it. In B. Carpenter (Ed.), *Personal coping: Theory, research and application* (pp. 77–91). Mahwah, NJ: Erlbaum.

Millon, T. (1982). On the nature of clinical health psychology. In T. Millon, C. J. Green, & R. B. Meagher (Eds.), *Handbook of clinical health psychology* (pp. 1–27). New York: Plenum Press.

Millon, T., Antoni, M., Millon, C., Meagher, S., & Grossman, S. (2001). *Millon Behavioral Medicine Diagnostic.* Bloomington, MN: Pearson Assessments.

Millon, T., Davis, R. D., & Millon, C. (1997). *MCMI–III manual* (2nd ed.). Minneapolis, MN: National Computer Systems.

Moerman, D. E., & Jonas, W. B. (2002). Deconstructing the placebo effect and finding the meaning response. *Annals of Internal Medicine, 136,* 471–476.

Monahan, J. (1993). Limiting therapist exposure to Tarasoff liability: Guidelines for risk containment. *American Psychologist, 48,* 242–250.

Montgomery, L. M., Cupit, B. E., & Wimberly, T. K. (1999). Complaints, malpractice, and risk management: Professional issues and personal experiences. *Professional Psychology: Research and Practice, 30,* 402–410.

Mookadam, F., & Arthur, H. M. (2004). Social support and its relationship to morbidity and mortality after acute myocardial infarction. *Archives of Internal Medicine, 164,* 1514–1518.

Moos, R. H. (Ed.). (1977). *Coping with physical illness.* New York: Plenum Press.

Moos, R. H. (1981). *Work Environment Scale manual.* Palo Alto, CA: Consulting Psychologists Press.

Moos, R. H., & Moos, B. (1981). *Family Environment Scale manual.* Palo Alto, CA: Consulting Psychologists Press.

Morey, L. C. (1991). *Personality Assessment Inventory: Professional manual.* Tampa, FL: Psychological Assessment Resources.

Morrow, G., & Clayman, D. (1982). *A membership survey of the Division of Health Psychology, American Psychological Association.* Unpublished manuscript.

Nader, R., Petkas, P., & Blackwell, K. (Eds.). (1972). *Whistle blowing.* New York: Bantam Books.

Nathan, P. E., & Gorman, J. M. (Eds.). (2002). *A guide to treatments that work* (2nd ed.). New York: Oxford University Press.

National Association of Social Workers. (1990, June). Member blows whistle on Rx refills. *NASW News,* p. 11.

National Center for Education Statistics. (2003). *National assessment of adult literacy (NAAL).* Retrieved April 13, 2007, from http://nces.ed.gov/NAAL/

National Practitioner Data Bank. (2007). *NPDB summary report.* Retrieved April 20, 2007, from http://www.npdb-hipdb.hrsa.gov/publicdata.html

Newman, R., & Bricklin, P. M. (1991). Parameters of managed mental health care: Legal, ethical, and professional guidelines. *Professional Psychology: Research and Practice, 22,* 26–35.

Nicholson, K. (2001, June 19). "Rebirth" therapists get 16 years. *Denver Post.* Retrieved from http://www.denverpost.com

Noll, J. D. (1976). The psychotherapist and informed consent. *American Journal of Psychiatry, 133,* 1451–1453.

Oldenburg, B. (2002). Preventing chronic disease and improving health: Broadening the scope of behavioral medicine research and practice. *International Journal of Behavioral Medicine, 9,* 1–16.

Olson, R. A., Mullins, L. L., Gillman, J. B., & Chaney, J. M. (Eds.). (1994). *The sourcebook of pediatric psychology.* Des Moines, IA: Allyn & Bacon.

Osler, W. (1971). The principles and practice of medicine. In W. P. D. Wrightsman (Ed.), *The emergence of scientific medicine.* Edinburgh, Scotland: Oliver & Boyd.

Packman, W., & Smith, G. (2006a, May/June). Suicide and malpractice risk: Part I. Legal basics. *The California Psychologist,* p. 23–24.

Packman, W., & Smith, G. (2006b, July/August). Suicide and malpractice risk: Part II. Risk management strategies. *The California Psychologist,* pp. 29–30.

Park, D. C., & Liu, L. L. (Eds.). (2007). *Medical adherence and aging: Social and cognitive perspectives.* Washington, DC: American Psychological Association.

Patenaude, A. F. (2005). *Genetic testing for cancer.* Washington, DC: American Psychological Association.

Phelps, L. (Ed.). (2006). *Chronic health-related disorders in children: Collaborative medical and psychoeducational interventions.* Washington, DC: American Psychological Association.

Physicians' desk reference (61st ed.). (2007). Boston: Thomson PDR.

Pilisuk, M., Boylan, R., & Acredolo, C. (1987). Social support, life stress, and subsequent medical care utilization. *Health Psychology, 6,* 273–288.

Pizzi, L. T., Goldfarb, N. I., & Nash, D. B. (July, 2001). Procedures for obtaining informed consent. In K. G. Shojania, B. M. Duncan, K. M. McDonald, & R. M. Wachter (Eds.), *Making health care safer: A critical analysis of patient safety practices.* Retrieved March 25, 2008, from http://www.ahrq.gov/clinic/ptsafety/chap48.htm

Poole, H., Bramwell, R., & Murphy, P. (2006). Factor structure of the Beck Depression Inventory—II in patients with chronic pain. *Clinical Journal of Pain, 22,* 790–798.

Pope, K. S. (1990). Ethical and malpractice issues in hospital practice. *American Psychologist, 45,* 1066–1070.

Pope, K. S. (1992). Responsibilities in providing psychological test feedback to clients. *Psychological Assessment, 4,* 268–271.

Pope, K. S., & Brown, L. S. (1996). *Recovered memories of abuse: Assessment, therapy, forensics.* Washington, DC: American Psychological Association.

Pope, K. S., Butcher, J. N., & Seelen, J. (2006). *The MMPI, MMPI–2, and MMPI–A in court* (3rd ed.). Washington, DC: American Psychological Association.

Pope, K. S., Simpson, H. J., & Myron, M. F. (1978). Malpractice in outpatient psychotherapy. *American Journal of Psychotherapy, 32,* 593–600.

Pope, K. S., & Vasquez, M. J. T. (2007). *Ethics in psychotherapy and counseling: A practical guide* (3rd ed.). San Francisco: Jossey-Bass.

Poppen, R. (1998). *Behavioral relaxation training and assessment* (2nd ed.). Thousand Oaks, CA: Sage.

Porter v. Maunnangi, 764 S.W.2d 699 (Mo. App. E.D. 1988).

Pressman, M., & Orr, W. C. (Eds.). (2000). *Understanding sleep: The evaluation and treatment of sleep disorders.* Washington, DC: American Psychological Association.

Professional negligence. (1973, January). *University of Pennsylvania Law Review, 121,* 627–690.

Prokop, C. K., & Bradley, L. A. (Eds.). (1981). *Medical psychology: Contributions to behavioral medicine.* New York: Academic Press.

Puckhaber, H. L. (2006). *New research in biofeedback.* Hauppauge, NY: NOVA Science Publishers.

Qualls, S. H., & Benight, C. C. (2007). The role of clinical health geropsychology in the health care of older adults. In C. M. Aldwin, C. L. Park, & A. Spiro III (Eds.), *Handbook of health psychology and aging* (pp. 367–389). New York: Guilford Press.

Quinn, K. M. (1984). The impact of Tarasoff on clinical practice. *Behavioral Sciences and the Law, 2,* 319–329.

Rachlin, S. (1984). Double jeopardy: Suicide and malpractice. *General Hospital Psychiatry, 6,* 302–307.

Raczynski, J. M., & Leviton, L. C. (Eds.). (2004). *Handbook of clinical health psychology: Vol. 2. Disorders of behavior and health.* Washington, DC: American Psychological Association.

Radloff, L. S. (1977). The CES–D scale: A self-report depression scale for research in the general population. *Journal of Applied Psychological Measurement, 1,* 385–401.

Reamer, F. (Ed.). (1991). *AIDS and ethics.* New York: Columbia University Press.

Reamer, F. G. (2003). *Social work malpractice and liability: Strategies for prevention* (2nd ed.). New York: Columbia University Press.

Recupero, P., & Rainey, S. E. (2005). Forensic aspects of e-therapy. *Journal of Psychiatric Practice, 11,* 405–410.

Reid, W. H. (1998). Treating clinicians and expert testimony. *Journal of Practical Psychiatry and Behavioral Health, 4,* 121–123.

Reid, W. H. (2008). *Psychiatry and law updates.* Retrieved March 24, 2008, from http://www.reidpsychiatry.com

Reisner, R., Slobogin, C., & Rai, A. (2004). *Law and the mental health system: Civil and criminal aspects* (4th ed.). St. Paul, MN: West.

Ritterband, L. M., Gonder-Frederick, L. A., Cox, D. J., Clifton, A. D., West, R. W., & Borowitz, S. M. (2003). Internet interventions: In review, in use, and into the future. *Professional Psychology: Research and Practice, 34,* 527–534.

Robinson, R. G., & Yates, W. R. (1999). *Psychiatric treatment of the medically ill.* New York: Marcel Dekker.

Rogers, R. (2003). Forensic use and abuse of psychological tests: Multiscale inventories. *Journal of Psychiatric Practice, 9,* 316–320.

Rosenman, R. (1978). The interview method of assessment of the coronary-prone behavior pattern. In T. M. Dembroski, S. M. Weiss, J. L. Shields, S. G. Haynes, & M. Feinleib (Eds.), *Coronary-prone behavior* (pp. 95–106). New York: Springer-Verlag.

Roy v. Hartogs, 85 Misc.2d 891, 381 N.Y.S.2d 587 (1975).

Rozensky, R. H., Sweet, J. J., & Tovian, S. M. (1997). *Psychological assessment in medical settings.* New York: Plenum Press.

Rudd, M. D., Joiner, T. E., Jobes, D. A., & King, C. A. (1999). The outpatient treatment of suicidality: An integration of science and recognition of its limitations. *Professional Psychology: Research and Practice, 30,* 437–446.

Russo v. Ascher, 545 A.2d 714 (Md. App. 1988).

Russo, D. C., Bird, P. O., & Masek, B. J. (1980). Assessment issues in behavioral medicine. *Behavioral Assessment, 2,* 1–18.

Sackett, D. L., Straus, S. E., Richardson, W. S., Rosenberg, W., & Haynes, R. G. (2000). *Evidence-based medicine: How to practice and teach EMB* (2nd ed.). Edinburgh, Scotland: Churchill Livingstone.

Sadoff, R. L. (1979). Changes in mental health law: Progress for patients—problems for psychiatrists. In S. Halleck (Ed.), *New directions for mental health services: Coping with the legal onslaught* (No. 4). San Francisco: Jossey-Bass.

Sajwaj, T., Libet, J., & Agras, W. S. (1974). Lemon-juice therapy: The control of life-threatening rumination in a six-month-old infant. *Journal of Applied Behavior Analysis, 7,* 557–566.

Sakairi, Y. (2004). Autogenic training as a training of self-regulation skills: Beneficial use and prevention of unpleasant experiences during practice. *Japanese Journal of Autogenic Therapy, 23,* 12–19.

Samuels, M., & Samuels, N. (1975). *Seeing with the mind's eye: History, techniques and usages of visualization.* New York: Random House.

Sanders, S. H. (2002). Operant conditioning with chronic pain: Back to basics. In D. C. Turk & R. J. Gatchel (Eds.), *Psychological approaches to pain management* (2nd ed., pp. 128–137). New York: Guilford Press.

Sarafino, E. P. (2005). *Health psychology: Biopsychosocial interactions* (5th ed.). New York: Wiley.

Sarason, I. G., Johnson, J. H., & Siegel, J. M. (1978). Assessing the impact of life changes: Development of the Life Experiences Survey. *Journal of Consulting and Clinical Psychology, 46,* 932–946.

Satcher, D., & Pamies, R. J. (Eds.). (2006). *Multicultural medicine and health disparities.* New York: McGraw-Hill.

Sayette, M. A., & Mayne, T. J. (1990). Survey of current clinical research trends in clinical psychology. *American Psychologist, 45,* 1263–1266.

Schag, C. A., Heinrich, R. L., Aadland, R. L., & Ganz, P. A. (1990). Assessing problems of cancer patients: Psychometric properties of the Cancer Inventory of Problem Situations. *Health Psychology, 9,* 83–102.

Schenkenberg, T., Peterson, L., Wood, D., & DaBell, R. (1981). Psychological consultation/liaison in a medical and neurological setting: Physicians' appraisal. *Professional Psychology, 12,* 309–317.

Schindler, R. J. (1976). Malpractice—another new dimension of liability: A critical analysis. *Trial Lawyer's Guide,* 129–151.

Schnurr, P. P., & Green, B. L. (Eds.). (2003). *Trauma and health: Physical health consequences of exposure to extreme stress.* Washington, DC: American Psychological Association.

Schofield, W. (1969). The role of psychology in the delivery of health services. *American Psychologist, 24,* 565–584.

Schultz, J. H., & Luthe, W. (1969). *Autogenic therapy.* New York: Grune & Stratton.

Schuster v. Altenberg, 424 N.W.2d 159 (Wis. 1988).

Schutz, B. M. (1982). *Legal liability in psychotherapy: A practitioner's guide to risk management.* San Francisco: Jossey-Bass.

Schwartz, G. E., & Weiss, S. M. (1978). Behavioral medicine revisited: An amended definition. *Journal of Behavioral Medicine, 1,* 249–251.

Schwartz, M. S., & Andrasik, F. (Eds.). (2005). *Biofeedback: A practitioner's guide* (3rd ed.). New York: Guilford Press.

Schwitzgebel, R. L., & Schwitzgebel, R. K. (1980). *Law and psychological practice.* New York: Wiley.

Seeburg, K. N., & DeBoer, K. F. (1980). Effects of EMG biofeedback on diabetes. *Applied Psychophysiology and Biofeedback, 5,* 289–293.

Shaw, H. E., & Shaw, S. F. (2006). Critical ethical issues in online counseling: Assessing current practices with an ethical intent checklist. *Journal of Counseling and Development, 84,* 41–53.

Shelley, M., & Pakenham, K. (2007). The effects of preoperative preparation on postoperative outcomes: The moderating role of control appraisals. *Health Psychology, 26,* 183–191.

Sheridan, E. P., Matarazzo, J. D., Boll, T. J., Perry, N. W., Weiss, S. M., & Belar, C. D. (1988). Postdoctoral education training for clinical service providers in health psychology. *Health Psychology, 7,* 1–17.

Shevitz, S. A., Silberfarb, P. M., & Lipowski, Z. J. (1976). Psychiatric consultations in a general hospital: A report on 1,000 referrals. *Diseases of the Nervous System, 37,* 295–300.

Shorter, E. (1992). *From paralysis to fatigue: A history of psychosomatic illness in the modern era.* New York: Free Press.

Shows, W. D. (1976). Problem of training psychology interns in medical schools: A case of trying to change the leopard's spots. *Professional Psychology, 7,* 393–395.

Siegfried, N. J., & Porter, C. A. (2003). Ethical issues for clinicians in behavioral health settings. In L. M. Cohen, D. E. McChargue, & F. L. Collins (Eds.), *The health psychology handbook* (pp. 443–455). Thousand Oaks, CA: Sage.

Simmons v. United States, 805 F.2d 1363 at 1366 (9th Cir. 1986).

Simon, R. I. (1992). *Clinical psychiatry and the law* (2nd ed.). Washington, DC: American Psychiatric Publishing.

Simon, R. I. (1995). The natural history of therapist misconduct: Identification and prevention. *Psychiatric Annals, 25,* 90–94.

Simon, R. I. (1999). Therapist–patient sex: From boundary violations to sexual misconduct. *Forensic Psychiatry, 22,* 31–47.

Simon, R. I., & Hales, R. E. (2006). *Textbook of suicide assessment and management.* Washington, DC: American Psychiatric Publishing.

Singer, J. L. (2006). *Imagery in psychotherapy*. Washington, DC: American Psychological Association.

Skorupa, J., & Agresti, A. A. (1993). Ethical beliefs about burnout and continued professional practice. *Professional Psychology: Research and Practice, 24*, 281–285.

Slovenko, R. (1978). Psychotherapy and informed consent: A search in judicial regulation. In W. E. Barton & C. J. Sanborn (Eds.), *Law and the mental health professions: Friction at the interface* (pp. 51–70). New York: International Universities Press.

Smith, D. (2003). What you need to know about the new code. *Monitor on Psychology, 34*, 62.

Smith, J. C. (1999). *ABC relaxation training: A practical guide for health professionals*. New York: Springer Publishing Company

Smith, T. S., McGuire, J. M., Abbott, D. W., & Blau, B. I. (1991). Clinical ethical decision making: An investigation of the rationales used to justify doing less than one believes one should. *Professional Psychology: Research and Practice, 22*, 235–239.

Smith, T. W., Orleans, C. T., & Jenkins, C. D. (2004). Prevention and health promotion: Decades of progress, new challenges and an emerging agenda. *Health Psychology, 23*, 126–131.

Smith, T. W., & Suls, J. (Eds.). (2004). Special section on the future of health psychology. *Health Psychology, 23*, 115–157.

Soisson, E. L., VandeCreek, L., & Knapp, S. (1987). Thorough record keeping: A good defense in a litigious era. *Professional Psychology: Research and Practice, 18*, 498–502.

Southard, M. J., & Gross, B. H. (1982). Making clinical decisions after Tarasoff. In B. H. Gross & L. E. Weinberger (Eds.), *New directions for mental health services: Vol. 16. The mental health professional and the legal system* (pp. 93–101). San Francisco: Jossey-Bass.

Spielberger, C. D. (1988). *State–Trait Anger Expression Inventory*. Odessa, FL: Psychological Assessment Resources.

Spielberger, C. D., Gorsuch, R. L., & Lushene, R. (1970). *The State–Trait Anxiety Inventory manual*. Palo Alto, CA: Consulting Psychologists Press.

Stabler, B., & Mesibov, G. B. (1984). Role functions of pediatric and health psychologists in health-care settings. *Professional Psychology: Research and Practice, 15*, 142–151.

Starr, P. (1982). *The social transformation of American medicine*. New York: Basic Books.

State Board of Psychology of Ohio. (2003, Fall). *Alert!* Retrieved March 24, 2008, from http://psychology.ohio.gov/pdfs/ALERT2003revised.pdf

Stedman's medical dictionary (28th ed.). (2006). Baltimore: Lippincott, Williams & Wilkins.

Stetter, F., & Kupper, S. (2002). Autogenic training: A meta-analysis of clinical outcome studies. *Applied Psychophysiology and Biofeedback, 27,* 45–98.

Stone, A. A. (1979). Informed consent: Special problems for psychiatry. *Hospital and Community Psychiatry, 30,* 321–327.

Stone, G. C. (Ed.). (1983). National Working Conference on Education and Training in Health Psychology. *Health Psychology, 2*(Suppl. 5), 1–153.

Stone, G. C., Weiss, S. M., Matarazzo, J. D., Miller, N. E., Rodin, J., Belar, et al. (Eds.). (1987). *Health psychology: A discipline and a profession.* Chicago: University of Chicago Press.

Strasberger, L., Gutheil, T., & Brodsky, A. (1997). On wearing two hats: Role conflict in serving as both psychotherapist and expert witness. *American Journal of Psychiatry, 154,* 448–456.

Stroebe, M. S., Hansson, R. O., Stroebe, W., & Schut, H. (Eds.). (2001). *Handbook of bereavement research: Consequences, coping, and care.* Washington, DC: American Psychological Association.

Stromberg, C. D., & Dellinger, A. (1993, December). Malpractice and other professional liability. In *The psychologist's legal update* (pp. 1–15). Washington, DC: National Register of Health Service Providers in Psychology.

Suinn, R., & VandenBos, G. R. (Eds.). (1999). *Cancer patients and their families: Readings on disease course, coping, and psychological interventions.* Washington, DC: American Psychological Association.

Tarasoff v. Regents of the University of California, 131 Cal. Rptr. 14551 P.2d 334 (1976).

Tarshis, C. B. (1972). Liability for psychotherapy. *University of Toronto Faculty Law Review, 30,* 75–96.

Thompson v. County of Alameda, 614 P.2d 728 (Cal. 1980).

Thorn, B. E. (2004). *Cognitive therapy for chronic pain.* New York: Guilford Press.

Tibbs, T. L., & Tarr, K. L. (2004). Cancer. In L. J. Haas (Ed.), *Handbook of primary care psychology* (pp. 249–262). New York: Oxford University Press.

Totten, G., Lamb, D. H., & Reeder, G. D. (1990). Tarasoff and confidentiality in AIDS-related psychotherapy. *Professional Psychology: Research and Practice, 21,* 155–160.

Tovian, S. M. (2004). Health services and health care economics: The health psychology marketplace. *Health Psychology, 23,* 138–141.

Trzepacz, P. T., & Baker, R. W. (1993). *The Psychiatric Mental Status Examination.* New York: Oxford University Press.

Turk, D. C., & Gatchel, R. J. (2002). *Psychological approaches to pain management.* New York: Guilford Press.

Turk, D. C., Meichenbaum, D., & Genest, M. (1983). *Pain and behavioral medicine: A cognitive–behavioral perspective.* New York: Guilford Press.

Turk, D. C., & Melzack, R. (2001). *Handbook of pain assessment* (2nd ed.). New York: Guilford Press.

Ulrich, R. S. (1984, April 27). View through a window may influence recovery from surgery. *Science, 224,* 420–421.

U.S. Census Bureau. (2008, May 1). U.S. Census Bureau news [Press release]. Retrieved from http://www.census.gov/Press-Release/www/releases/archives/population/011910.html

VandeCreek, L., & Knapp, S. (2001). *Tarasoff and beyond: Legal and clinical considerations in the treatment of life-endangering patients.* Sarasota, FL: Professional Resource Press.

VandeCreek, L., & Stout, C. E. (1993). Risk management in inpatient psychiatric care. In D. Ruben, C. Stout, & M. Squire (Eds.), *Current advances in inpatient psychiatric care: A handbook* (pp. 53–67). New York: Greenwood Press.

Vingerhoets, A. (Ed.). (2001). *Assessment in behavioral medicine.* New York: Taylor & Francis.

Wallston, K. A., Wallston, B. S., & DeVellis, R. (1978). Development of the Multidimensional Health Locus of Control (MHLC) scales. *Health Education Monographs, 6,* 160–170.

Wedding, D., & Mengel, M. (2004). Models of integrated care in primary settings. In L. J. Haas (Ed.), *Handbook of primary care psychology* (pp. 47–60). New York: Oxford University Press.

Weeks, G. R. (Ed.). (1991). *Promoting change through paradoxical therapy.* New York: Brunner/Mazel.

Weisberg, J. N., & Keefe, F. J. (1999). Personality, individual differences, and psychopathology in chronic pain. In R. J. Gatchel & D. C. Turk (Eds.), *Psychosocial factors in pain* (pp. 56–73). New York: Guilford Press.

Weisman, A. D. (1978). Coping with illness. In T. P. Hackett & N. H. Cassem (Eds.), *Massachusetts general hospital handbook of general hospital psychiatry* (pp. 264– 275). St. Louis, MO: Mosby.

Weiss, S. M. (1982). Health psychology: The time is now. *Health Psychology, 1,* 81–91.

Weisz, J. R., Hawley, K. M., Pilkonis, P. A., Woody, S. R., & Follette, W. C. (2000). Stressing the (other) three R's in the search for empirically supported treatments: Review procedures, research quality, relevance to practice and the public interest. *Clinical Psychology: Science and Practice, 7,* 243–258.

Welch, B. (2002). Defending a licensing board complaint: Financial devastation? *Insight, 1,* 1–6.

Werth, J. L., & Blevins, D. (Eds.). (2006). *Psychosocial issues near the end of life: A resource for professional care providers.* Washington, DC: American Psychological Association.

Wettstein, R. M. (1984). The prediction of violent behavior and the duty to protect third parties. *Behavioral Sciences and the Law, 2,* 291–317.

Wickline v. California, 228 Cal. Rptr. 661,670 (Cal. App. 2d Dist. 1986).

Widiger, T. A., & Rorer, L. G. (1984). The responsible psychotherapist. *American Psychologist, 39,* 503–515.

Wilkins, M. A., McGuire, J. M., Abbott, D. W., & Blau, B. I. (1990). Willingness to apply understood ethical principles. *Journal of Clinical Psychology, 46,* 539–547.

Williams, J. E., & Weed, N. C. (2004). Review of computer-based test interpretation software for the MMPI–2. *Journal of Personality Assessment, 83,* 78–83.

Williams, M. H. (2003). The curse of risk management. *Independent Practitioner, 23,* 202–205.

Wilson v. Blue Cross of Southern California, 271 Cal. Rptr. 276 (Cal. App. 2d Dist. 1990).

Wolff, H. G. (1953). *Stress and disease.* Springfield, IL: Charles C Thomas.

Wolff, H. G., & Wolf, S. (1951). The management of hypertensive patients. In E. T. Bell (Ed.), *Hypertension.* Minneapolis: University of Minnesota Press.

Wolpe, J. (1958). *Psychotherapy by reciprocal inhibition.* Stanford, CA: Stanford University Press.

Wood, G. J., Marks, R., & Dilley, J. W. (1990). *AIDS law for mental health professionals.* San Francisco: University of California AIDS Health Project.

World Health Organization. (1992). *International statistical classification of diseases and related health problems* (10th rev., ICD-10). Geneva, Switzerland: Author.

Wright, R. H. (1981). Psychologists and professional liability (malpractice) insurance. *American Psychologist, 36,* 1484–1493.

Yali, A. M., & Revenson, T. A. (2004). How changes in population demographics will impact health psychology: Incorporating a broader notion of cultural competence into the field. *Health Psychology, 23,* 147–155.

Zerubavel, E. (1980). The bureaucratization of responsibility: The case of informed consent. *Bulletin of the American Academy of Psychiatry and Law, 8,* 161–167.

Ziskin, J. (2000). *Coping with psychiatric and psychological testimony* (Suppl.; Vols. I–III). Los Angeles: Law and Psychology Press.

Zola, I. K. (1966). Culture and symptoms: An analysis of patients presenting complaints. *American Sociological Review, 3,* 615–630.

Zur, O. (2005). *The standard of care in psychotherapy and counseling: Bringing clarity to an illusive standard.* Retrieved March 24, 2008, from http://www.drzur.com/standardofcaretherapy.html

Author Index

Derogatis, L. R., 64, 71, 75
DeVellis, R., 75
Dickson, D. T., 220
Dilley, J. W., 220
Disorbio, J. M., 69
Dolezal-Wood, S., 237
Doverspike, W., 195
Dowd, E. T., 100
Downs, H., 74
Dubin, S. S., 151
Duke, E. M., 239
Dunn, M. R., 105

Eifert, G. H., 76
Eisenberg, L., 152
Elfant, A. B., 36
Ellis, A., 108
Emery, G., 108
Engel, G. L., 50, 152
Engel, L. W., 91
Eshelman, E. R., 96
Evans, D. R., 60, 91

Fabrega, H., 152
Falender, C. A., 225, 226
Faltz, C., 216
Fanning, P., 99
Feldman, S. R., 194
Ferrando, S. J., 48
Fleck, S., 60
Folen, R. A., 44
Follette, W. C., 197
Folstein, M. F., 65, 74
Folstein, S. E., 65
Fordyce, W. E., 106
Foti, M. E., 176
France, C. R., 9, 23
Frank, R. G., 92, 135
Franklin, G. M., 230
Freeman, A., 95
Freeman, E. L., 149, 238
Fried, R., 96
Friedberg, F., 100

Friedman, R., 242
Friedman, S., 94
Friedson, W., 40
Furrow, B., 194, 200

Gallagher, P. L., 207
Ganz, P. A., 75
Garfield, S. L., 94
Garner, D. M., 75
Gatchel, R. J., 64, 106
Genest, M., 96
Gentry, W. D., 6, 8, 94
Gifis, S. H., 194
Gilson, B. S., 75
Glover, S. I., 192, 199
Golden, W. L., 100
Goldfarb, N. I., 175
Goldfried, M. R., 108
Good, B., 152
Goodstein, L. D., 218
Goreczny, A. J., 105
Gorman, J. M., 94, 197
Gorsuch, R. L., 74
Gostin, L. O., 210, 218, 220
Graham, J. R., 67, 155, 156
Greenburg, S. A., 167, 168
Greene, R. L., 155, 156
Greenwood, A., 228
Grimaldi, K. E., 105
Gross, B. H., 216, 217, 218, 219
Grossman, S., 70
Grotz, R., 74
Guess, H. A., 91
Gurman, A. S., 94
Gutheil, T., 168, 175, 176, 177, 178
Guyer, R. D., 64
Gylys, B. A., 20

Haas, L. J., 232
Hackbert, L., 105
Hailey, W. E., 193
Hales, R. E., 206
Halperin, D. A., 176

Subject Index

About the Authors

Cynthia D. Belar received her doctorate in clinical psychology from Ohio University in Athens in 1974 after an internship at Duke University Medical Center in Durham, North Carolina. From 1974 to 1984, she was on the faculty of the Department of Clinical and Health Psychology at the University of Florida Health Science Center in Gainesville, where she developed the Pain and Stress Management Laboratory as well as the medical psychology service and training components of the doctoral and internship programs. From 1983 to 1990, she served as chief psychologist and clinical director of behavioral medicine for the Kaiser Permanente Medical Care Program, Los Angeles, California. From 1990 to 2000, she served as director of the doctoral program in clinical psychology at the University of Florida in Gainesville. She has served as chair of the Association of Postdoctoral and Psychology Internship Programs, chair of the Council of University Directors of Clinical Psychology, president of the American Board of Clinical Health Psychology, and president of the American Psychological Association's (APA) Division 38 (Health Psychology). Her research has been in the areas of pain, stress management, biofeedback, and reproductive endocrinology. Dr. Belar is currently the executive director of the APA Education Directorate and professor emerita at the University of Florida.

William W. Deardorff received his doctorate in clinical psychology from Washington State University in Pullman in 1985 after an internship at the

University of Washington Medical School in Seattle. He then completed a postdoctoral fellowship in clinical health psychology at the Kaiser Permanente Medical Care Program, Los Angeles, California. He is board certified in clinical health psychology by the American Board of Professional Psychology, is a fellow of the American Psychological Association's (APA) Division 38 (Health Psychology) and Division 42 (Independent Practice), and is on the clinical faculty of the University of California, Los Angeles, School of Medicine. He is the coauthor of several books, including *Preparing for Surgery* (1997), *Win the Battle Against Back Pain* (1996), *Back Pain Remedies for Dummies* (1999), and *The Psychology of Spine Surgery* (2003). He is one of the few psychologist–members of the North American Spine Society (NASS) and the National Association of Spine Specialists. As part of NASS, he is a member of the Outcome Measures task force, the Research Project Management committee, and the Scientific Review committee for the national professional meeting. He also serves on the medical advisory board for http://www.Spine-Health. com. Dr. Deardorff is in private practice in Beverly Hills, California, with a multidisciplinary group specializing in disorders of the spine.